Winner - Next Genei
Shortlist - Independent Literary Awards
Four "Best Books of the Year" Lists

Kergan Edwards-Stout's
Songs for the New Depression

"Kergan Edwards-Stout has crafted a work of fiction reminiscent of some classic tales in *Songs for the New Depression*. Even better, Edwards-Stout's debut boasts the kind of dark humor that made Augusten Burroughs (*Running with Scissors*) a household name." Advocate.com

"Simply stunning..." Dana Miller, Frontiers Magazine

"Compelling, beautifully written debut novel... The author's darkly comic, brutally honest prose reads like poetry and has a melodic flow that is equally funny and heartbreaking. A quintessential page-turner and the product of a truly gifted author." Edge on the Net

"The characters are dynamic, interesting, and real, and the relationships are painful and funny and romantic and sexy and sad all at once." Q Magazine

"Engaging debut. Edwards-Stout infuses reality and hopefulness into a bittersweet story about compassion and personal growth. A distinctively entertaining novel written with moxie and bolstered by pitch-perfect perspectives." Kirkus Reviews

"The laughs make the book deceptively breezy. *Songs* shines with psychological truth and historical accuracy." A&U Magazine

"Brilliantly conceived and masterfully written... You'll read this once for its emotional impact and again to see how the author achieves it. But no matter how many times you dive in, you'll be impressed." Out in Print Reviews

"If a roller-coaster ride of sadness and humor sounds right up your alley, then look for *Songs for the New Depression.* I won't tell you the end. Read the book."
Terri Schlichenmeyer, *The Bookworm Sez* syndicated column

"*Songs for the New Depression* is an enjoyable and addictive read. In fact, don't be surprised if you find yourself not answering texts and neglecting your Facebook updates as you finish the book in one read. I did." Q Vegas Magazine

"Many tout this book as an important piece of fiction that should be read by all because of its portrayal of AIDS. I would add that it's not only an important piece of fiction because of the message, but it's a great piece of fiction writing regardless of the message." LGBT Book Review Blog

"An affecting novel, written with great literary flair. I recommend it." Michael Nava, five-time Lambda Literary award-winning author, honored with the Bill Whitehead Lifetime Achievement Award for Gay and Lesbian Literature

Praise for

Kergan Edwards-Stout's
Gifts Not Yet Given

"In 14 stories, Edwards-Stout assumes an impressive range of voices... This willingness to step inside the minds of such disparate, often nonmainstream characters hints at Edwards-Stout's confidence as a writer and his broad life experiences. Edwards-Stout's stories are original and important... Provocative stories with a clear, vital message." Kirkus Reviews

"The stories in *Gifts Not Yet Given* are vital, essential and remind us that much of human life is gained or lost through family. Edwards-Stout shines a light on contemporary life with skill and wit. A dynamic and engaging read." – Trebor Healey, two-time Ferro-Grumley Fiction Award winner

"Kergan Edwards-Stout's stories are muscular, funny, sad and an antidote to holiday treacle, no matter the holiday. You will want to give his book as a gift." – Richard Kramer, novelist, *These Things Happen*

"Check this one out — the stories are original and intriguing, and the characters are strong and flawed, loving and broken." – Alfred Lives Here (Top 5 Books of the Year)

"Edwards-Stout writes beautifully, and the stories are charming and uplifting." Queer Books with Julie (Top Books of the Year)

NEVER TURN YOUR BACK ON THE TIDE

(Or, How I Married a Lying, Psychopathic
Wannabe-Murderer and Kinda Lived to Tell)

NEVER TURN YOUR BACK ON THE TIDE

(Or, How I Married a Lying, Psychopathic
Wannabe-Murderer and Kinda Lived to Tell)

A *Fictional* Memoir

Kergan Edwards-Stout

C

circumspect press

Never Turn Your Back on the Tide (Or, How I Married a Lying, Psychopathic Wannabe-Murderer and Kinda Lived to Tell). A Fictional Memoir.

Copyright © 2020 Kergan Edwards-Stout

C

circumspect press

Library of Congress Control Number: 2020902819
ISBN: 978-0-9839837-5-0 (pbk)
ISBN: 978-0-9839837-6-7 (ebk)
ISBN: 978-0-9839837-7-4 (audio)
10 9 8 7 6 5 4 3 2 1

Book Jacket Design by Russell Noe
Author Photograph by Sara + Ryan Photography

Printed in the United States of America, LaVergne, Tennessee.

For
Mason Edwards,
who accompanied me,

and for
Russ Noe and Marcus Edwards,
who saved me.

FOREWORD

I have thought long and hard about how to best tell this story and, indeed, whether it should ever be told at all. Some who know my journey have urged that I let sleeping dogs lie, and I acknowledge the wisdom therein. But I learned long ago that the best way to move forward is with a clear understanding of the role our past plays in determining our future. There is nothing to be gained by sweeping things under the rug, save an uncomfortable carpet on which to tread. Life is about acknowledging our foibles, making peace, and taking steps forward, as best we can.

I am also aware that some of the truths within might, in fact, cause some embarrassment or discomfort. That is not my intent.

While I've written this primarily for myself, to help in healing, it is also for my eldest son, Mason. We have a special bond, of being survivors, and I want him to have record, for what it's worth, of all that we have journeyed together.

Lastly, while this book has been vetted by those who were present when the events occurred, and buttressed by my years of notes and journal entries, this is a memoir, as opposed to an autobiography. Memories, while in essence true, have a way of shifting over time. I've done my best to create a factual record of the events as they occurred, however, I fully acknowledge that there may be other versions of the truth.

In the end, however, memories are what remain, and seem a fitting way to tell this story.

NEVER TURN YOUR BACK ON THE TIDE

(Or, How I Married a Lying, Psychopathic
Wannabe-Murderer and Kinda Lived to Tell)

PROLOGUE

If truth be told, and it *always* should, I was taken in by the view, as countless others, before and since. The rhythmic, perennial shift of the waves makes it easy to be lulled into seeing only what we choose. We take in the vast expanse the big blue offers, transfixed by its beauty, unpredictability, and the pleasures found within. Its rocking cadence immerses us into contentedness, allowing us to forget that beneath the brilliant sheen, reflecting our every desire, there are not only unexplored depths, but danger, darkness, and even death. And yet, knowing this, we continue to dive in, time and again, believing that its pleasures outweigh any personal risk.

It wasn't the sea itself that proved my downfall, but a pair of eyes. Eyes made to drown in.

I have a photograph of my then-husband taken in a train in Portugal, on our return from Cascais to Lisbon, just hours after he asked me to marry him. When people see it, they gasp. Not because of his considerable beauty, which was easily apparent, but because of his eyes. The warm, sparkling pools peer directly into the camera, and at me, who holds it. They speak to the viewer, telling those who gaze into them that safety and comfort lie within.

I made a mistake, however, in believing that such messages were reserved solely for me. Indeed, whomever opted to gaze into those eyes would find their every desire reflected and confirmed as well. Have you long searched for someone who shares your varied interests and tastes? Rest easy; you have found him. Do you want to be held, kissed, loved forever? So it is. Or maybe you're only after a quick, anonymous fuck in the middle of the afternoon? Eyes is yours, any place, any time. Whoever you are, whatever your wish, desire, or peccadillo, those eyes can fulfill. Just say "yes," and your dreams will come true.

Equally, though, while you may say "yes" to those eyes, those eyes rarely say "no" to others.

And eventually you might find yourself waking up to discover that the little house you'd set up, that cozy cottage and picture-perfect life, complete with baby, is being shared with any number of others who have also dipped their toes into the waters.

Like all oceans, with Eyes there was an undertow lurking, just out of view. But my child—our child—proved to be my life raft, and in the end just barely managed to save me from drowning.

LIFE LESSON #1

If you should ever find yourself in Segovia, Spain, lingering in the trees beneath the famous castle silhouetted above, rehearsing the words to the proposal you are about to offer your beloved, only to find yourself hit with an unexpected, irrepressible case of diarrhea, heed that as the warning sign that it is. I didn't.

(Also, a mini-life lesson: utilizing leaves as toilet paper is not the most romantic way to launch your engagement.)

LIFE LESSON #2

Should you ever open an email not intended for you, please understand that you may not like the path onto which it propels you.

My path spectacularly derailed in October 2001, prompted by one line in this innocuous email exchange from my civil-union husband, Eyes, who had checked his email on my laptop, with a friend I didn't know, who asked, "How are the wedding plans coming?"

To which Eyes replied, "My relationship is growing stronger and stronger and I should be moving in about two weeks. I already spend every night there. He really is a great guy, and is SO good with Mason."

Now, what's so bad about that, you might ask?

Eyes and I were already as married as two gay men could legally be in California at that time. Mason was our one and a half-year-old adopted son. I was a stay-at-home dad, and Eyes and I had planned to adopt more kids. Thus, I quickly learned that Eyes was in a relationship with someone other than me—someone to whom he'd introduced our son.

With just that one sentence, I entered my own personal Lifetime TV movie, in which I was played by Valerie Bertinelli, discovering that my handsome airline pilot husband had multiple families in other states, with none knowing about the other. My world was quickly turned upside down and I found myself in the depths of hell... A place I'd be for many years.

LIFE LESSON #3

Should you date someone who cavalierly mentions that, if you ever want to knock anyone off, they have a friend who has in the past hired actual hit men, make note of that person's name. I did. And all these years later, I still have it, tucked away among my important papers, should the police ever need it.

PATIENCE, PLEASE

I know what you want, but you're not going to get it. Not yet, at least.

You're intrigued and want to know more about Eyes. What he looks like. His power. His sexual proclivities. You really could care less about me. You just want me to spill his dirty deeds. There are many, and they are very dirty, and we'll get to each and every one of them, in due time. My time.

Because, you see, for every lollipop, there is a sucker. And to understand Eyes, and his success in my deception, you need to understand me. The ultimate sucker.

THERE'S A SUCKER BORN EVERY MINUTE

This particular sucker plopped out of the womb of one Dottie Kergan on March 5, 1965, at 7:00 a.m., at Long Beach Memorial Hospital in Long Beach, California.

Correction: I didn't "plop," as I'm certain nothing ever actually plopped out of my mother until her later years, over which she had no control. In her prime, Miss Dorothy May Aycock was more tightly wound than a Swiss clock, made by Germans.

I would like to say that Dottie was a good mother. She turned out to be a great grandmother. But as a mother, there was much to be desired. Never a nurturing figure, growing up, our household always felt on edge. My dad, sister and I stepped gingerly around the beast, not wanting to upset it. We plied it with treats, trying to gain favor. We complimented and acquiesced, but nothing we ever did or said was good enough or turn out exactly as the beast desired. And when favor was not granted, the crying and wailing and gnashing of teeth would echo throughout the house.

Of course, Dottie wasn't an actual beast. She was in fact a Southern belle, a genuine Georgia peach, burst forth from the red dirt of Waycross. Prim and proper, her foremost concern was always about appearances, rather than reality. She alternated between fragile and steely, and when I saw the movie *Ordinary People,* I instantly perceived my mother in Mary Tyler Moore's disquieting performance.

The baby of four children, Dottie grew to become a woman who expected life to be handed to her on her own terms, and any deviation resulted in displeasure, endured by the entire family. Life was all about making Dottie happy. My dad, Fred, tried his best, but his best was never good enough. Her call to him, *"Freeeeeeeeeeeed..."*, would echo endlessly through the house, like nails on chalkboard—her screech filling me with dread. We wouldn't at that moment know exactly what my dad had done, but clearly it wasn't good. It rarely was, in her eyes. And that screech of my dad's name, and the emotional reaction I had to it, is the main reason I eventually changed my own name, leaving "Frederick Edward Kergan III" far behind.

On occasions when my sister or I had severely misbehaved, Dottie would request that we go into the yard and find a sufficient switch—a stick—with which to spank us. Years later, in therapy with Dottie, she denied ever doing that, but then added that choosing her own switch was exactly the punishment her mother had bestowed upon her.

Each special family occasion, my stomach would tie itself into knots, wanting desperately to make Dottie happy. One winter, as she was preparing a holiday luncheon for her lady friends, she asked if I would create an invitation for her, which my dad would later copy on the Xerox at his work. I loved to draw and, wanting to impress her, spent quite a bit of time crafting an exquisite invitation, designing an ornate holly berry and leaves border around the party details. Upon presentation, she glared at me: "It should have been 'Dottie', not Dorothy. Do it over." I sunk inside.

To me, 'Dottie' sounded—well, loony and backwoods.

At least 'Dorothy' sounded elegant and refined. Plus, she had "Fred and Dorothy Kergan" as the return label for her stationary—shouldn't they be in sync? But mindful of her scowl, I crumpled up my work and started over—but careful to not do quite as well on this newly requested version as I had on the first. Not that she would notice the difference.

On another Christmas, my hopes were raised when Dottie said to me, "You know what I'd like most from you? I'd like to have your old plastic rocking horse, Neigh, turned into a planter."

Given this specific directive, I set out in advance to assure I'd curry favor. I spent countless hours sawing and painting my old weathered brown pony, turning it into a colorful horse, as if from a carousel, complete with chains for hanging and a hole for a pot. Upon its unwrapping, Dottie simply grimaced. There was no "thank you" or pretense of pleasure. There would be no polite acknowledgement of the time and effort put forth. There were simply Dottie's pursed lips, which told me all I needed to know. Never was a potted plant to be placed into the slot, and the old rocking horse was soon relegated to the side yard, next to the trash bins, where it eventually withered away under the hot Orange County sun.

On one of her birthdays, we planned a surprise party. It was our tradition that on the morning of one's birthday, coming into the dining room you'd be met with balloons and streamers, which we dutifully placed that particular year, as always. But I guess the balloons and streamers on this occasion weren't special enough to please Dottie. Thus, I came home from elementary school to find her crying uncontrollably in the backyard. Worried, I called my dad, who immediately came home from work and, to quiet her tears, was forced to reveal our actual plans for her celebration, ruining our attempts for a pleasant surprise.

In my late teens, one night I was getting dressed to go out. Clashing patterns were all the rage in the club scene of the 80s, so I'd spent quite a bit of time selecting the perfect combination of blue plaid pants and white shirt with small blue dots. After a long time in the bathroom, flawlessly spiking my hair, I emerged, feeling good about myself. Mom took one unsettling look at me. "Looks like you're off to join the circus."

Even in her later years, when she had vastly improved and wasn't nearly as judgmental, Mom could still be a handful. In her 80s, as our family gathered to celebrate her birthday and open presents, she reached out to take the card my father had prepared for her. Knowing how difficult it was to please her, he had decided that he would make life easy on himself and give her a check, so that she could buy whatever she desired. Upon opening the card, she squinted at the check to make sure she was reading it correctly. "Four hundred dollars—Is that *it?*" The crestfallen look in my dad's eyes said it all.

I do have one memory, however, of an absolutely delightful experience involving my mother. Each year growing up, the entire extended family would gather on Christmas Eve at my Aunt Jewel's. There was always a potluck, during which someone would inevitably exclaim, "Boy, it's gotten so quiet in here," and someone else would dutifully reply, "It's because we're all eating such good food!"

After the meal, the family gathered in a large circle for

the gift exchange. In those days, we bought gifts for each and every person, cost be damned. This particular Christmas Eve, as we went around the room, taking turns, the women each opened up their gifts to find that one of my cousins had given each ugly floral pajamas. As my mom looked down at her box, shaped differently than the others, she assumed her gift was different and, thinking she was safe, exclaimed, "Boy, I sure hope no one gave *me* floral pajamas."

To this day, I smile, just thinking about that box opening, her horrified face, and the triumphant, sly glances exchanged between relatives, pleased to see the high-and-mighty Dottie Kergan taken down, even if just one notch.

BACKWOODS BARBIE

To be fair, there are reasons why my mother was as she was, just as there are defining factors in my own make-up. I'm sure some of it had to do with growing up in Waycross, a small town in Southern Georgia, not far from the Florida border. Whenever we flew in to visit, for summer vacations, weddings or funerals, we'd fly into Jacksonville airport, rent a car, and drive the hour and a half into Waycross.

When my mom was born, her family lived at 501 Lee Avenue, not far from where my grandmother used to run a drug store, complete with soda fountain, on Reynolds Street. 501 Lee was a typical old southern-style two-story, complete with front porch. Years later, my mom drove me to the deteriorating building, its white paint flaking and stripped, with weeds growing up around it, two feet tall. We stopped, and she told me about growing up in the house. The stories didn't involve any of her own family members, however, but rather the black women—the servants—who raised her. She might have had a mother, a few stepfathers, and three other siblings, but it was the servants she remembered most fondly. Yet, when driving me through another part of Waycross, she noted that it was the "colored part" of town and quickly reached over to lock her car door.

A few doors down Lee Avenue was the palatial home of the ghostly Mrs. Beech, the closest I've ever come to a living version of Charles Dickens' Miss Havisham. Mrs. Beech had taken a liking to my mom as a child, and later, our family would make a point to visit her, each trip to Waycross. She lived alone in an old creaky house, which had been beautifully decorated in the late 1800's and untouched since. A huge magnolia tree was centered in her yard and her central chimney offered each room its own fireplace, which seemed to me quite grand. Mrs. Beech treated my sister and me gently, with kindness, prompting me to wonder why my own mother couldn't have turned out the same.

Today, that old family house at 501 Lee is an abandoned lot, and Mrs. Beech's magnificent house gone, razed to build the local library.

I don't have to tell you that summers in Georgia are hot. And I mean *hot*, as in, hot and fucking miserable. As kids, we'd relish the afternoons, as it meant a thunderstorm, which would do little to lift the heat, and a trip to either 7/11 or Dairy Queen to cool off. One summer, 7/11 was offering souvenir cups emblazoned with DC Comics superhero characters on them. As a huge fan of Saturday morning's *Super Friends* cartoon, each day I'd beg and plead until an adult would take me over for a half cherry/half Coca Cola flavored Slurpee. That summer, I got the whole DC set.

At Dairy Queen, as a kid, it was all about the dipped cone. (Now, as an adult, I fully realize that it is all about the Blizzards and apologize for my past DQ indiscretions.) However, anything ice cold was truly a treat, offering a brief respite from the heat you could swallow with each breath.

But when my mom was a kid, there were no 7/11's or DQ's. There was no quick fix for easing summer's malaise, except my grandmother's drug store, where my mom was often allowed to make her own shakes and malts.

Granny was, back in the day, quite a beauty. Even in my memory, her dark hair, dark lashes, and pointed smile always held a joke or a knowing comment. She could be quite sassy, but also stern.

Upon moving from 501 Lee, Granny's new place was a red brick ranch-style home, set back on a large grass field, which demanded continual mowing. Whenever we visited, I would relish the opportunity to hop on the mower and take a spin. If only mowing grass back at home had been as much fun.

Granny's living room was the kind into which no one actually stepped foot. I remember her carpet as being white, which would explain why the room's doors were always shut, but why anyone would one select white carpet with rich, red Georgia dirt just outside is beyond me. Whatever the case, we were discouraged from entering the room, which proved impossible, given the room's many glass and porcelain trinkets, demanding exploration. It was the kind of room you held your breath in, careful not to alter its fragile beauty.

I'm not sure in which home my mother, as a child, was sexually abused. Or even if she was abused at all. But her claims rocked the family, turning side against side, and it would not be the last time she'd make such unverifiable accusations.

VICTIM

In the 1980s, you couldn't get away from the McMartin Preschool scandal, as its initial sexual abuse allegations morphed into all manner of horrors, including flying people, secret tunnels, children being flushed down toilets, a child identifying the actor Chuck Norris as his abuser, and—of course—Satanism.

The lurid allegations and subsequent trial were omnipresent, on TV almost daily, and it was during this era that my mother began seeing a Christian therapist. In addition to wanting to deal with her own psychological issues, which were plentiful, Dottie had an interest in the field of therapy, and I recall one instance—likely after a McMartin Preschool mention on the news—in which my mother explained to me that occasionally therapists could inadvertently conjure within a patient "memories" which had not actually occurred, called False Memory Syndrome. Given all of this, it was not entirely surprising to discover just a few years later that my mom had sent out a mass letter to all female relatives, detailing her own recently-discovered abuse. She reported being sexually abused at the hands of a deceased stepfather and physically abused at the hands of her brother.

My mom's brother was a sweet, caring, and sensitive man. He had a great love for aviation and soloed a plane at age 16. A true Southern gentleman, emphasis on the "gentle," it was hard for anyone to envision him being physically abusive, especially to my mom, the baby of the family, and his favorite sibling.

When I was old enough to understand all that she had claimed, I asked what her brother had done. She replied, "One day he rolled me up in a rug and sat on me. He said he was going to kill me. I felt like I was suffocating."

"But he let you out, right?"

"Yes."

"Isn't that just playing around—? I mean, I understand you were scared—"

"He tried to kill me."

"But all kids—"

"He really was trying to kill me!"

To that, I had no response. Needless to say, her brother was shattered by her accusations. She had always been his favorite, and her allegations would drive a wedge between them that was never fully repaired.

I AM A SURVIVOR OF SEXUAL ABUSE

You'd think, being so close with my dad throughout the years, I would've realized sooner. I would have had some knowledge or lingering resentment toward him, for what he had done... sexually abusing me.

I mean, if it had happened, I should remember something, right...? *Anything?*

I only found out about this abuse from my mom. Correct that: although she couldn't be bothered to share this life-altering news directly with me—that I had been sexually abused by my own father—she felt totally comfortable sharing such information with my sister.

Sis had just had her first son. After he was six months old, she'd hoped to return to work two days a week and had asked my dad and I to take turns babysitting. The idea that my abuser dad would be alone with Sis' helpless infant prompted Mom to warn my sister about my abuse, so that nothing sinister might happen to her innocent babe. My sister called me, incredulous that I had held something so emotionally troubling inside myself all the preceding years, but this was truly the first I'd heard about it. And nothing about it felt right.

My dad had always been my most cherished of parents. He showed up for every play I was in, long after my mom had decided that my acting and directing efforts were sacrilegious. He was the one I felt most comfortable in confiding or asking questions. He was always the one to shield us from my mercurial mother, whenever possible. How could I have been so wrong about him???

Family therapy quickly ensued.

It turns out that my mother had witnessed one single, solitary incident when I was an infant, and my dad was changing my diaper. Without going into specifics, my dad essentially made a joke about my penis. That was it. Nothing pervy. Nothing remotely sexual. A stupid joke, told to my mother.

Was it abuse? No. Simply a bad attempt at humor.

However, this raised the thought that if my mom had viewed that single interaction 30 years prior as having been abuse, what were the "facts" of her own "abuse"? In my case, and hers, she felt it was of primary importance to alert surrounding others about the incidents, rather than facing those directly involved...

This is all to say that while I'm not saying my mother's abuse didn't occur, I do have substantial doubt.

THE OTHER GRANDMOTHER

I used to be quite fond of my dad's mom, Grandma Lucy. As kids, my sister and I would occasionally stay with her if our folks were out of town. She was incredibly old, but alert and lively, and we always enjoyed visiting.

I remember a sweet powdered scent in her home, as if talcum were everywhere. I remember laying on her sofa in the living room, watching movies on TV like *Willie Wonka and the Chocolate Factory* and *Godspell* before falling asleep. Her huge bushes of beautifully-hued hydrangeas. I remember an amazing white angel food cake, with delicious strawberry frosting, all homemade from scratch. No box cakes for Lucy! I recall her overgrown backyard, bursting with wildflowers in the spring. Her card shuffler, where you'd insert a deck of playing cards and crank the handle until the deck was sufficiently rearranged. I still have that card shuffler to this day, even if it goes unused.

But as I grow older, what I remember most was a game she liked to play. She asked to play it repeatedly, even though it always ended the same.

"Repeat after me..." she'd encourage.

I'd shake my head, but she'd insist, "Repeat, please."

Although I knew how this would play out, obedient child that I was, I would do as instructed. It always occurred in three's:

First time. "Grandmother, Grandmother, thee, thee, thee..."

"Again."

With a deep breath, I'd repeat as requested, "Grandmother, Grandmother, thee, thee, thee..."

"Again, please."

I knew what was coming. It was always on the third repetition. I should've stopped, but I never did. I continued, "Grandmother, Grandmother, thee, thee, thee—"

In the middle of that last *thee*, she would reach out and slap my jaw upward, forcing my mouth to close, my teeth slamming down on my tongue, often drawing blood.

These days, I don't look back on Grandma Lucy quite as fondly.

LITTLE FREDDIE KERGAN, JR.

I don't know all that much about my dad's youth. He was largely a quiet man, so stories are few. One of my favorites involves a holiday program at his church. He was sitting in the audience with his parents, when the pastor stepped up to the podium, saying, "And now we will have a poem recitation by little Freddie Kergan." All eyes turned expectantly towards my dad, but he sat perfectly still, eyes wide, shocked at having completely forgotten his assignment. Lucy nudged him sharply out of his stupor. Finally, he stood, finding his voice and gathering courage. "I'm sorry, Pastor, but I forgot." As he sunk back into his seat, tremendously embarrassed, Lucy seethed, so upset with him for having publicly embarrassed the family. I just wish I could give Little Freddie a hug.

My dad was born in Ft. Smith, Arkansas, but as a teen the family moved to Long Beach, California, and it is Long Beach that Fred thought of as home. He liked tinkering with cars and as an adult bought a metallic gold Corvette. My sister and I loved it when he would take the rear window out, and we would sit backwards, our legs tucked into the storage compartment, and watch and wave as the world went past in reverse.

During World War II, he enlisted in the Air Force, but was too young for boot camp. Instead, he was sent to Stanford University, where he studied so hard, he almost ruined his eyes, dampening any chance of being a pilot. In the fall of 1945, he was sent to Germany, where he almost died—though not in battle. He and some other men were in the back of a truck, moving furniture, with my dad holding onto a refrigerator. The truck swerved, throwing my dad out onto the pavement, with the fridge landing right on top of him. He was in the hospital for eight days. Later, he served in the Korean War, though he never engaged in battle.

My dad's primary characteristics are decency, kindness and quiet support. He didn't often talk about his feelings, but it was clear to my sister and I how he felt about us. His love, unlike Dottie's, was never in doubt.

My parents met in Long Beach through a church singles group, and he was quite smitten with Dottie's beauty. After a year of dating, they married, and I showed up roughly a year later. With my arrival, safe to say, their lives would never be the same.

SIGN #1 THAT I WAS PRECOCIOUS

Me, age 3.

Dottie: "Why did Lisa cry?"
Me: "Oh, she just cried. I can't talk about it anymore."

SIGN #2 THAT I WAS PRECOCIOUS

Age 3.

Me: "If you swing me any higher, you'll hurt my feelings."

SIGN #3 THAT I WAS PRECOCIOUS

To my female cousin, both of us then four-years-old:

Me: "I've got a penis and you don't."
Her: "Yes, I do."
Me: "Where is it?
Her: "At home."
Me: "Does it come off?"
Her: "No."

THE EARLY YEARS

For several of their early married years, Fred worked in construction with his best friend, Pat, before they transitioned into accounting. Their first office was smack in the middle of an arid field of oil rigs. In the back lot sat a golf cart, which my cousins and I enjoyed driving.

One memorable afternoon, my dad and I drove through McDonald's to grab lunch before returning to the office. Apparently, on the way inside the office, arms laden with food, I neglected to properly close and lock the front door. We were in a back office eating when my dad suddenly bolted out of his chair, shouting obscenities at the top of his lungs and running as fast as he could down the hall, as a man darted out of the office with a typewriter. We all ran out into the street, only to see a car speeding off in the distance; billowing dust the only reminder that a robber had been in our midst.

Fred and Pat soon moved, with their construction company occupying a run-down lot adjacent to the Long Beach freeway, where old equipment littered the outer yard. As a kid, it was a wonder to explore that yard and when we were old enough, we'd "work," pulling weeds or such, before taking our winnings to the corner store to splurge on Hostess and Dolly Madison snack cakes, with Raspberry Zingers usually winning out.

PEE WEE'S PLAYHOUSE

Growing up, my fondest moments involved creative, free play. I used to love puppets, and twice a year, a traveling puppet theater troupe would perform in the open space in front of our local grocery store. They had different kinds of mobile theaters, built on wheels, which they'd pull into the center, drop off, and—*voilà!*—instant showplace. My favorite was a theater that looked like an old paddlewheel steamboat. While it had one main stage area, each of its many doors and windows could open, so you never quite knew where a puppet might pop out.

Couple that with regular visits to Bob Baker's Marionette Theater in Los Angeles, where backstage visits offered a peek into the magic behind the spotlight, and I guess you could say that puppetry was my first love.

Imagine my surprise, then, to find my dad in the backyard one day, hard at work, constructing my very own puppet theater. The experience that he and Pat had gained building schools, houses and shopping centers was put to good use, building the theater of my dreams. It was tall enough for an adult to stand inside, with a stage area facing out into the yard. It had curtains that opened and closed, with spliced fabric at the back, accommodating both hand puppets and marionettes. There were pegs to hang puppets on and a slanted roof to keep out the rain.

Just imagine the look on my face that final day, after all hammering and painting was done, when my dad carefully applied shiny gold lettering above the stage: Freddy's Puppet Theater.

It is one of the first amazing things I can remember my dad doing for me, but it certainly wasn't the last.

"I am a puppeteer. I'm creative. I have a puppet theater that my daddy built me. And a playhouse. It's two-story and has a balcony upstairs. And you can sleep in it," so Dottie recorded me saying, in a journal.

That two-story playhouse would later get me into trouble—big, *sexy* trouble—but that's another story.

LIFE LESSON #4

At age five, when invited to your best friend's house, who is a girl, to play with her Lite Brite, do not suggest that each of you take off your clothes and jump up and down naked on the bed. I can assure you that it will not go over well when her mother walks in.

THE START OF SOMETHING BIG

My love of puppetry and theater jumped into hyperdrive in kindergarten, when our class put on a stunning production of *Three Little Pigs*. The main reason I remember this particular production was because it was where I first fell in love, with a boy who played the straw seller. Jimmy Hayforth had the most beautiful teeth, always gleaming, and I set about to become his best friend. For a while, I succeeded.

I remember going to his house one afternoon, and his bedroom looked like it had been decorated by a teenage boy: walls painted black, rock posters on the walls, and a lava lamp. Not the room of your typical kindergartener. Nothing remotely sexual happened, and I can't tell you anything else about that interaction. It was just nice, being with someone I loved, and having him be nice enough not to kick me out.

I knew there was nothing wrong in my love for him, for it felt entirely right. But I also knew he felt nothing for me, and that was okay too. Pretty prescient, for a kindergartner.

And even though my love for Jimmy never led anywhere, my love for theater took me on journeys near and far, and for that I am grateful.

THE ESSENCE

I've always been creative. In 2nd grade, I was the one spraying pine-scented Glade into the audience, trying to establish the proper forest mood for my production of *Snow White*, my riveting directorial debut. Perhaps, to some, it would've been wiser to have spent less time on such 'non-essentials' and more time rehearsing the actors. But in my view, it was far more important that our dwarves looked the part, with dwarf-like shoes (i.e., bedroom slippers) and cute pointed hats, than that they learn their dialogue. Who cares if little Billy knows his lines, if everyone looks onstage and still sees little Billy?

For great art, you need the magic, the essence—the *scent*—more than anything. Which brings me to my next production...

THE WIZARD OF OZ

What an ambitious play selection, you might be thinking, for a third-grade production—and you'd be right. But there was an entire rationale for picking this particular play, even if it wasn't an actual play.

Number 1: I loved the movie and knew it by heart, so I already knew most of the dialogue.

Number 2: I wanted to play the Scarecrow.

Number 3: I already had a set piece perfect for Auntie Em's house.

For our earlier production of *Snow White*, my dad had again put his carpentry skills to work and built a wood-framed house façade, with cardboard walls. It had a working door and window, and while it had been pink for *Snow White*, I insisted that we repaint it yellow for *Wizard*, as I felt certain that otherwise people might recognize it from the prior production and be transported out of the moment. Again, the *essence*.

And, again, just like with *Snow White*, I kept rehearsals to a minimum, instead focused on ensuring that when the tornado hit, the house's front door would burst open and bits of torn newspaper would fly into the air—hence much time was spent working with an electric fan, borrowed from home.

If you happen to have been in the audience that day, I sincerely apologize. Yes, the tornado effect came off as intended, eliciting *"ooh's"* from the audience, but as Dorothy and I, along with the Tin Man, Cowardly Lion, and a stuffed Toto skipped around the audience, singing "We're Off to See the Wizard" again and again and again, in screeching acapella, I saw your eyes. I knew how badly we sucked. But there was nothing I could do. I could give up, and acknowledge we were awful, or proceed down that yellow brick road, smile on my face, and pretend I didn't know. I chose the smile. The Dottie Kergan smile, plastered firmly in place, ignoring negativity and reality... In the many years since, that smile has rarely failed me.

The essence is indeed key to making the magic, but as I learned the hard way that day, your content better be bone solid. And I made sure that it was in future creative endeavors. At least, those projects under my control.

LIFE LESSON #5

Sharing that you know what kind of underwear each of the boys in your neighborhood wears is a sure-fire way to ensure you are never invited to any more sleepover's.

ANGEL IS A CENTERFOLD

Life wasn't solely "theater" growing up. Sure, I went to see every play possible, and me and the neighborhood kids would put on lip-synched concerts for our parents to Partridge Family albums (yes, I was always Keith.) But there was so much more to elementary school, such as sex.

I was a precocious child, if you haven't already gotten that point, so it should come as no surprise that my first time "playing doctor" came at an early age, in second grade. But it wasn't *doctor*, specifically. It was photographer.

To say that Teddy was the gayest 7-year-old I have ever met would be underestimating just how gay Teddy was. With his sashay, pouty lips, and fluttering eyelashes, it was clear even at an early age that Teddy would have a lifelong career in cosmetology. There would be no discussions between his parents over how suited Teddy might be for construction, law, or the medical profession. Teddy was born to rock the runway. He had style and personality to spare, with a determination and headstrong zeal that even adults admired. There was no stopping Teddy when he wanted something. And, soon enough, it became clear that he wanted me.

We became fast friends, and in no time, we had our clothes off. The location would vary, but the routine was always the same. He would be a Playboy model, as in female, and I would be the male photographer, shooting the centerfold. But rather than having a camera in my hands, there were actually hidden cameras embedded all over my body, which, by necessity for a successful shoot, required that I remove all of my clothing. Thus, we were two naked kids, rubbing up against each other, going *"Click! Click! Click!"*, over and over and over.

One time, we were just starting to disrobe in the second floor of my playhouse, when my dad pulled himself up into the window, scaring us.

"Boy, it's so hot today," I insisted, trying to rationalize our shirts being off. Luckily, my dad didn't notice that the zipper on Teddy's pants was somehow down as well.

But almost getting caught didn't stop us. It was only when Teddy's family moved away that our experimenting came to a sad end.

Years later, I ran into Teddy in the theater department of UCLA as fellow students. When I brought up our shared past, he looked at me blankly, as if he didn't recall a single moment. From that point onward, whenever we encountered each other, Teddy pretended to be straight. But I knew otherwise—*Click, click!*

BUTCH ME UP

I don't think that I was ever particularly effeminate, but it seemed that my parents were continually trying to butch me up. Not that they would have ever said it. But the attempts were often and varied. They signed me up for a Cal State Long Beach '49ers Summer Camp, with promises that it would be fun, only to find myself forced to play every single sport known to man, including golf and archery. Considering that I was—and to this day continue to be—lousy at sports, I hated every minute.

Soon after, they employed a neighborhood boy to help me become better at sports. However, they picked a high school boy who lived across the street who wore the tightest white pants imaginable. He was also dreamy, in a Bobby Sherman kind-of-way—except he had a better tan. We met twice-weekly after school, during which time he would show me how to bat, and throw, and catch. It never helped. But that might be because, while he later married a woman, all of the clues pointed to him likely being gay, without having a clue as to the sports he was supposedly teaching me. I blame my poor throwing on him, not my limp wrist.

In a fifth-grade parent-teacher conference, my then-favorite teacher told my mother, under hushed suggestive tone, that I had no male friends and spent "too much time with girls," leading me to be pushed ever further into athletics—not that it ever helped.

In fact, as the years passed, I would be bullied so much by both teammates and adversaries, calling me "fag" more times than I can count, that my esteem did indeed suffer. I always knew there was nothing wrong with me, but that hatred—in their eyes and venomous tongues—was hard to ignore. Having no one in whom to confide, I let those vile epithets pile up inside my chest until I was old enough, with the help of a therapist, to finally confront and banish them forever.

I FOUND MY SPORT

Eventually, I found a sport that suited me, mainly because I liked the outfit: swimming. For several years, I was a member of the Los Alamitos swim team and held local records for my age group in the breaststroke, my best event. I excelled at it and really loved the sport, particularly as I'd previously thought myself athletically stunted. It was also fun to be hanging around in Speedos, just me and the beautifully sun-tanned hunks. Having to change in the high school boys' locker room, with all the sights to be seen, was an added bonus.

There was a sense of pride that came from success in a sport, as if I'd finally be able to make my parents proud. (To clarify: my dad was always proud of me; my mother, not as easily apparent.)

I'm not sure why I ever stopped swimming. It could've been the freezing cold mornings where, regardless, we dove into the pool, or the endless practices, or perhaps it was just a general feeling of "been there, done that." Regardless, after a few years of competitive swimming, I was done.

Still, that sport helped my esteem, even today, when someone offers to race. Upon each proposal, I smile a bit inside. They have no idea of the gay-shamed, poor-at-sports, but great-at-swimming beast they've unleashed—until I soundly beat them.

LIFE LESSON #6

If you were ever our babysitter and happened to find yourself on trial for being the worst sitter ever, complete with a judge (me), a prosecutor (my sister) and a witness stand made from cardboard boxes, please don't take it personally. We only did that to the vilest of sitters.

LIFE LESSON #7

If you were ever our babysitter and found a way to make rain fall from the clear sky by doing an Indian rain dance, you will forever be exalted as highest of the high—even if we knew it was likely a garden hose.

STARS ON THE NIPPLES

The L.A. Free Press was a counter-culture newspaper published in the 60s-70s which was miraculously sold in ultra-conservative Orange County from a vending machine next to my beloved Thrifty Drug, which then offered three scoops of ice cream for fifteen cents. For just three quarters, this radical mag with its two-color cover and black and white pages could be mine. I'd stand near the newspaper racks, watching shoppers leaving the grocery store and Thrifty's to make sure no one I knew would see me, then scurry over to the kiosk, drop in my change, and bolt away on my bike, the paper clutched tightly to my chest until I was safely at home.

Once there, I'd stash it in a cubby behind my bed, which would later officially become my porn cubby. But in those early days, just having a newspaper like that was intoxicating. I would read about boring things like politics and culture, and then quickly skip ahead to my cherished classified ads. It was there that the women with stars on their nipples appeared, advertising strip clubs and escort services. While they took up the prime advertising spots, I was more interested in what I would discover within the copy-only personal ads. There, scrolling past endless "heterosexual seeking sex" ads, I would occasionally find an ad that would pique my interest:

Straight-acting, curious man (30) seeking younger men for pleasure and adventure. Send replies to Ivan at 6214 Dix St., Hollywood, CA 90028.

The copy of the ads and the names would vary, but inevitably there would be the same address, 6214 Dix St. *"Who lives there?"* I wondered. Was it some hot baseball team, sharing digs? Was it a club of like-minded men, all using the same address to protect their privacy? And how in the world did they all end up on Dix Street?

I would fantasize, thinking about this amazing house/apartment/world at 6214 Dix St., where you could be your authentic self, no matter how distasteful some might find that to be. Looking back now, it was likely a porn company, using their ads to entice young men into the world of pay-for-sperm acting, but back then, I saw 6214 Dix St. as an "out." Someday, I thought, I'll join them. People like me were out there—somewhere. Even if we had nothing in common but sexual orientation, it was comforting to know that I wasn't alone.

WILD HORSES

It was the Christmas gift that I had valued most that particular year: a silver necklace with a running stallion charm, which my Aunt Jewel had bought through Avon. I'd always liked their glass cologne bottles, shaped like cars, but given that I was only 13, a necklace was much handier than cologne, and so cool! Those were the days of Ocean Pacific shorts, shirts with rainbows, waves, and boats sailing across one's chest, and that perfect deep-summer tan. (This was also pre-skin cancer awareness, where we'd find any excuse to lie by the pool or beach, slathering on a homemade mixture of baby oil and iodine. Such a concoction resulted in deep tans that last, which is why those of us who grew up in Southern California have major skin damage. But I digress.)

Unwrapping the necklace, I was so engaged and delighted with the gift that I didn't notice my Mother's reaction. If I had, I likely would've been prepared for what came next: the cajoling. "You don't really want that necklace, do you? Wouldn't you rather give that to your sister and I can get you something else?"

When I protested that I loved the gift and began wearing it, *cajoling* turned into *procurement*. "What if I pay you for the necklace, hmm?" Dottie prodded. "I'll give you $15. For that, you can get a lot of candy down at Thrifty's. Or ice cream! That Bing Cherry you love—imagine how many scoops you can buy!" (Thrifty's prices had risen, but you could still get a triple scoop for a quarter.)

Time and again, I turned down her offers. Then, things got weird.

"If someone, a man—a particular kind of man—sees that. Sees you *wearing* that," she offered, eyebrows knowingly raised, "He might get the wrong idea."

"What do you mean?" I innocently asked, knowing full well what she meant.

"I just... They might get the wrong impression," she intimated, as if I should know what that impression was.

"Impression of—?" I enjoyed any opportunity to make my mom squirm.

"Well, there are men—you know—who wear trench coats and hang out in dark corners. They might see that necklace and think—that you're one of *them*. They might see that and snatch you off the street. To do God knows what..."

She'd finally said it. What she thought they'd do to me was most likely something she knew I'd consider, even if neither of us had the words to communicate just that.

What she didn't know is that I would have given almost anything to have run off with a man in a trench coat, taking me to his lair at 6214 Dix St., and doing God-knows-what to me. In my eyes, that would've been just fine.

But I didn't get abducted. Or molested. Or anything else, for that matter. For a few years. But one day, my wild horse charm necklace mysteriously disappeared.

I'm pretty sure I know who took it.

LIFE LESSON #8

What you see in a junior high locker room may leave a lasting impression.

As a seventh grader, I recall entering into said locker room at Oak Junior High, only to walk straight into an aisle where ninth-grader Craig was pulling a jockstrap up over his full bush and astute penis. It was the single most erotic encounter of my life.

OUR TOWN

In eighth grade, I appeared in my first real play—as in, there were actual sets and costumes, rather than the poor excuses I'd created in my early years. Our junior high school drama teacher was Jack Schlatter, whose claim to fame was that his brother George was the producer of TV comedies *Laugh In* and *Real People*. While Jack would never quite match his brother's heights, he would later go on to write stories for the *Chicken Soup for Dead People's Souls* series, so I guess that might qualify as fame to some.

Jack would call each of his plays a GLY Production, which stood for *"God Loves Ya!"* How he got away with this, I do not know, but he uttered that phrase incessantly, and insisted others do the same.

To put it mildly, Jack was an over-the-top personality, and at that stage in life, he was worshipped by most of his students. He had drive and passion, and made kids care about theater. More than once, I would perform a song or monologue in class, and he would then have me stay with him for the remainder of the day, repeating my performance for each subsequent class. Such encounters put stars in my eyes: I must be a good singer. I must be a good actor. He has me performing for these others—I must be good, right?

For the GLY production of *Our Town*, I knew I was a shoe-in for the role of George Gibbs, the play's lovable, stereotypical small-town hero. Why did I know I was "it"? I had the hair. It was the early 80s, and my feathered locks were so beguiling, there was no one who could compete with me on that level. The role was *mine*.

But, shockingly, it was not to be. Instead, I found myself playing Joe Stoddard. *"Who?"* you might ask, *"is Joe Stoddard?"* You and I were asking the same question. It turns out that I was cast as Joe fucking Stoddard, the town's fucking undertaker, ancient as the fucking hills, who doesn't come on until the end of the third fucking act. Can you tell that I loved the role?

Aside from getting to wear a suit, the only other thing that was fun about the part was spraying my hair gray for each performance. In this role, I was also required to walk with a hunch and raise my voice into a shaky, old man quiver. It was not my finest hour.

What was particularly fine, however, was watching the hunk who did get cast as George in each rehearsal and performance. With his dark feathered hair (almost as nice as mine) and arched eyebrows, he really did exude the boy-next-door quality of George, and he was a ninth grader, so Schlatter probably just gave him the role because he would soon be promoted. Not that he was any better than me!

What matters more is that I finally had a part in a play, which an audience would pay to see. My love for theater grew exponentially, consuming me, and fueled the trajectory of my life. Plus, I later got a second shot at playing George in high school—and nailed it!

YOU CAN'T TAKE IT WITH YOU

Following my triumph as Joe Stoddard, undertaker to the stars, I next appeared in the GLY Production of George Kaufman and Moss Hart's comedy classic, *You Can't Take It with You*. I understand that I played the part of Boris Kolenkhov, an eccentric Russian ballet instructor, but I couldn't tell you a thing about it. I don't recall the plot, or anything about my character, or what my Russian accent sounded like, as I have no recollection of having ever appeared in the play. But there are pictures to prove it.

SPEW CHICK AND SCUM BOY

Throughout the years, my best friends have been those I bonded with in ninth grade, Spew Chick and Scum Boy (AKA Sandra Young and David Diaz.) I was never cool enough to get a nickname, but I absolutely loved these two. Sandra exuded a toughness, with a don't-fuck-with-me attitude, and scared a lot of people—me included. With her short-cropped black hair, olive skin, tight black jeans and sauntering stride, Sandra made an impression on all she encountered.

She lived with her dad, as her mom had abandoned the family, which is likely where some of Sandra's walls came from. Her dad let her perform at the midnight movies each weekend, where she would assume the role of Magenta in *Rocky Horror Picture Show*—which seemed rather scandalous to the rest of us ninth graders, who had earlier bedtimes.

Tall, lanky David was funny, giving, and kind. We appeared in several plays together over the years, the most amusing of which was when David played my father in that later high school production of *Our Town*, despite being several months younger.

While we'd all met earlier, I think the friendship was cemented on one day in particular. Sandra and her friend Michelle were always talking about guys they liked, whom they'd given nicknames.

"Oh my god, did you see Jelly Bean this morning?" Michelle would ask, with Sandra replying, "Was it on the right side or the left?"

I naively inquired if they were talking about on which side Jelly Bean had parted his hair, which wasn't at all what they were referring to... That moment of realization, shock, and humor is what bonded us together forever.

Without telling their own, fascinating stories, I will say this: Spew Chick and Scum Boy are more like family to me than my own flesh and blood. Even if years pass without contact, all it takes is one seamless reunion and the years dissipate. Thick and thin, good and bad, these friends are the real deal. And I treasure them.

JO: A MUSICAL VERSION OF LITTLE WOMEN

In ninth grade, I finally got a theatrical role I deserved, or at least that I was physically built for: the dashing Laurie Lawrence, Jo March's beau in a musical version of *Little Women*. This time it *was* primarily due to my hair, feathered to perfection, and as I was one of the only boys in the ninth grade remotely able to hit a musical note.

This play is worth mentioning for three reasons:

#1. It starred Katherine Britton, who would go on to appear in the hit film *Back to the Future* and star in a TV comedy series called *Safe at Home*, replacing the original lead actress. While born Katherine Habenicht, Katherine changed her professional acting name to Britton, but is now Katy Cable, a fun, pug-inspired pet reporter and blogger. And it was she whose Lite-Brite I was playing with, jumping up and down naked on her bed, when her mother walked in.

There is a scene in the show where Jo and Laurie quarrel, and as I dash out, she cries out, "But Laurie, where are you going?" My reply closed the scene.

In each performance, this scene always got applause at the end and, inspired by that, my acting got bigger and bigger and bigger, building dramatically at each performance until, as she cries, "But Laurie, where are you going?" I would scream at the top of my lungs, exiting, *"To the devil!"* I'm just glad there is no video.

#2. The best singer in the show was Anne Runolfsson, who played Beth, Jo's sickly sister. It is her character's death that gives the story any sense of poignancy. Unfortunately, in this particular rendition of the tale, her character had only one song, so it was Mr. Schlatter's inspired idea to have Anne sing a curtain warmer, "Corner of the Sky," from the hit musical *Pippin*. Why that song, as an opener for our humdrum musical that no one had ever heard of? Who knows? But it was the single best moment of the entire show.

Anne would go on to understudy Fantine in *Les Miserables* on Broadway, play the lead, Roxanne, in Broadway's musical *Cyrano*, as well as understudy the iconic Julie Andrews in *Victor/Victoria*. I'm sure it was simply an oversight that in her bio for that show, she failed to mention playing opposite me in *Once Upon a Mattress*, where I played Sir Harry to her Lady Larkin and wore a great deal more makeup than she.

And, #3 in the list of reasons why this play is even remotely worth mentioning is that my girlfriend at the time, who sang in the show's chorus, during breaks would put the moves on me, encouraging me to touch her—uh— everywhere. It was the closest in my life that I ever got to pussy and, predictably, that woman is today a born-again Christian.

OUTDOOR ADVENTURE

Most schools offer an outdoor science camp in middle school and Oak Junior High was no different. Our ninth-grade class got to venture to Yosemite National Park for a week, where we camped in tent cabins, went snowshoeing, hiked our asses off, learned about flora and fauna, and generally ran amuck. We were told there were bears in the area, but the biggest creatures I saw that trip were raccoons, raiding the trashcans.

Those of us who were "gifted" were placed together, which meant that all the smart kids bunked together, and figuring out room assignments was challenging at best, given the various personalities at play.

In ninth grade, no one was smarter than Missy Sprague—I mean, *no one*. Picture this: Brainiac, bar none; long red hair, with bangs pulled straight across her forehead, into a rosette, clasped tightly with a bobby pin, with the rest of her hair twisted into two severe braids, trailing down her back. She knew everything—*everything!*—and was every teacher's star pupil, except in P.E. Looking back, I'm sure Missy must've hated dodge ball, and anything else sports-related—but especially dodge ball. I'm sure you can understand that everyone hated Missy. *Everyone.*

As the trip approached, an idea was hatched—I'm not sure by whom—that we conspire to make Missy pay for being smarter than the rest of us, once and for all.

These tent cabins had one light in each: a bare bulb from which hung a pull-string. We decided that, in the middle of the night, one of us would sneak into Missy's room, cut off her awful braids, and tie them onto the pull-string. Thus, at some point in the middle of the night, Missy would awaken, cross to the light string, and pull down on her greasy braids.

It was a hateful, ambitiously-inspired goal, even if ultimately unrealized.

And the reason I feel so comfortable now, using her actual name? In the years since, Missy has changed her name and become a pastor, all goodness and light, so isn't likely to sue.

HIGH SCHOOL/MUSICAL

I couldn't wait to get out of junior high. I instinctively knew that high school would be better. That I'd make more friends, be the center of everything, and finally become popular. How wrong I was.

Getting promoted from Oak Junior High felt amazing. In my final year, I won awards for my acting, was editor of the yearbook, and received the Principal's Award, the highest honor bestowed at the school with non-specific criteria. (Again, it was most likely my hair.) At our end-of-year drama banquet, I closed the show singing *A Chorus Line's* "What I Did for Love" solo—as my duet partner, future Broadway star Anne Runolfsson, with whom I'd rehearsed several times, didn't bother to attend. The show must go on, I told myself. So many highs, so many lows, so much time feeling alone and hated. High school, I imagined, could only get better.

Part of me believed that I'd easily meet more gay people in high school and perhaps actually make more friends—"musical" friends, shall we say—discovering a tribe of my own in which to belong; boys who never cared much for the women with stars on their nipples, but lusted mightily for the men of 6214 Dix Street. While I did make friends who'd eventually turn out later to be gay, in 1983, absolutely every gay man I knew was fully closeted. Everyone, that was, except Bobby Kiker.

Bobby was flaming, both in bright red hair and spitfire personality. Bobby was ahead of his time, fierce and forthright, rocking the tightest pair of white Jordache jeans possible, highlighting his form and function. Those pants were so tight, he must've needed a pro-NASCAR pit crew to pull them on each morning. Bobby was a force of nature, managing to shirk off every poisoned arrow slung his way, like Wonder Woman with her bracelets, using a sarcastic, biting response, designed to maim and kill.

He walked the campus of Los Alamitos High School like he had somewhere to be, impervious to the verbal darts aimed his way. We all knew what and who he was, though that reality was never verbalized except in taunts, and thus the reality of who Bobby was as a person was never fully explored. No one talked about what it meant to be gay in those days. While "queer," "pansy," and "faggot" were the derogatory terms spat our way, usually being gay was discussed only in hushed euphemisms. "Is he a friend of Dorothy's?" alluding to gay men's love for Judy Garland. "Oh, he's 'musical'!" Being gay was almost always a negative trait or "illness," not worthy of exploration, discussion, or even consideration. That message was clearly received by the rest of us in Bobby's orbit, knowing that his fate would be ours if we revealed our true selves.

In our junior year of high school, Bobby disappeared. I was never clear on where he went, or even if he was indeed still alive, as to simply have *asked* that question would've opened up myself to other questions I wasn't yet prepared to answer. Bobby was a cipher, an idea worth being, but the cost to be so was ever-so-clear.

Did we young gay men at that school really want to be ostracized? Were we ready for finality? Here we were, hoping and waiting to bloom, faced with the reality that being out might mean being other. The questions percolated inside of me... How much was I willing to endure, to give up, in the pursuit of honesty and forthrightness? At the time, it seemed an unseemly bargain.

Many years later, after repeated online searches for Bobby, I discovered through Facebook that I had common friends of his sister. I reached out to her in 2015:

Hey Susan,
I have thought about reaching out numerous times, but never have. I assumed you were Bobby's sister, but as you and I were a few years apart, I was never entirely certain, so never followed up.

I cannot tell you how many times over the years that Bobby has popped into my thoughts. He was unimaginably fearless at a time in which very few of us were. When I think of high school, I think about Bobby strutting across campus, being fully authentic, and not giving a damn about what anyone thought. I wish that I had been that strong.

The truth is, Bobby's bravery kind of scared me. I wasn't yet out, and there was a part of me that was concerned that any association with him would reflect badly on me. Chickenshit, I know.

I witnessed so many others being cruel to him, and never stepped in. I so wish that I had.

I have googled him many times over the years, hoping that he somehow survived the years of high school torment, but never found any clues. When I was looking through your profile and saw your post with the panel from the AIDS quilt, it all fell into place.

I had a partner who died in 1995, and fully realize what Bobby went through. I would love to know more about him and his years after Los Al, if you ever have the time. I have always felt like there was a puzzle piece missing, related to him, and I would be grateful for any information you may want to share.

I can't recall any actual conversations or major interactions with him, but of course I realized that he was gay, which piqued my curiosity. He was incredibly brave and confident, though I'm sure inside he felt the arrows directed at him. I wish I'd been more fully aware of myself, so that I could've reached out to him. For some reason, he's held a bit of a mythical presence in my memories, and anyone who holds that kind of power is worth knowing and remembering.

His sister responded, and we ended up speaking via phone, with her filling in some of those missing puzzle pieces. It turns out that the bullying had indeed taken its toll on Bobby, and he had dropped out of high school, with a string of failed jobs and love affairs to follow. From the sound of it, there wasn't much happiness in Bobby's life, which broke my heart a little. After our phone call, I wrote back:

"Thanks again for sharing some of your memories with me. Bobby touched so many people, whether or not he knew it, simply by living his truth. He gave others the power to live more honestly, in an era in which that wasn't encouraged. I'm grateful to him, and you for your time and compassion on his behalf."

Her final reply:

"Thank you! Just hearing the nice things you have said about him has made us very happy."

I'd wished for a better outcome for Bobby. He'd burned so brightly, that while it made poetic sense that his flame would've been just as quickly extinguished, I really had hoped that he'd have made it. That he could be here, standing up to those who had mocked and tormented him, saying *"Look, motherfuckers: You hated me. You made my life hell. But I am still here. I rose above. I fucking lived an amazing life. And you poor shits deserve every unhappiness."*

But that was not to be his narrative.

His name is now one of many, sown of cloth, one name barely perceptible in the endless NAMES Project AIDS Quilt. A quilt so large, containing so many people and stories, that it can no longer be displayed in its entirety. So many fucking people died who didn't have to, had the government done its job. Act up, knowledge equals power, silence equals death...

To all those who were "musical," especially in high school, I offer my deepest and heartfelt thanks.

MY FIRST HEADSHOTS

In high school, certain I would become a star, I had my first professional headshots taken. Not knowing any better, we used the first and only photographer my new agent had recommended, who was likely ripping off unsuspecting kids and parents right and left. All photos were shot indoors, against a white backdrop, and I am wearing virtually the same clothing in every single shot.

My favorite photograph from the shoot is one of me smiling into the camera, holding a string, pulled taut, on which spins a gyroscope. Because I did that all the time.

FALLEN ANGEL

That first headshot must've been successful, gyroscope be damned, as I was soon cast in my professional acting debut, as an extra in a 1981 TV movie called *Fallen Angel*, starring child star Dana Hill. She played a young innocent lured into the dangerous world of child porn by Richard Masur. This was during the era when TV movies were big, and the more lurid, the better. Titles like *Dawn: Portrait of a Teenage Runaway*, *Born to Be Sold*, and *This House Possessed* were de rigueur.

At 16, I wasn't cognizant of any of that. I was just excited to be making a movie! I got to get out of school and shoot at a pinball arcade in the Valley. And in my *big scene*, they shot me playing a pinball game, just behind Dana, who was seated in an auto racing game as Richard Masur leaned into the game, seductively. Thus, in the shot, due to the camera angle, you basically have my butt just behind and to the right of Dana's head.

Probably the finest acting of ass cheeks in a TV movie that entire year.

OUR TOWN 2: OR, WHERE KERGAN IS AN ASS

The vision stays with me, even after all these years. I'm in junior high, looking into the eyes of an overweight girl, having just delivered a devastatingly cruel blow about her physique. Truly shitty, I know. Her bright blue eyes, haunted and broken, serve even now as lingering reminders of just how destructive my words can be, and I've often wished I could take that moment back.

Little did I then know that the girl, Elizabeth Emken, would years later run for public office in an attempt to unseat California Senator Dianne Feinstein. Today, she campaigns on an anti-gay platform and in 2016 was actually a spokesperson for candidate Donald Trump, forcing me to wonder if my cutting remarks played any role in influencing the awful person she would become, and how she could come to take such a rigid right-wing stance, given the many gay friends she once had.

As alluded earlier, during my first year at Los Alamitos High School I auditioned for—and finally got—the plum role of George Gibbs in *Our Town*, of which Elizabeth would be the student director. Knowing that I couldn't continue to act as if I didn't remember the pained look on her face when I'd uttered my awful remarks some years prior, I got up the courage to finally apologize. When I did, Elizabeth pretended she didn't remember the incident, though her piercing blue eyes told me otherwise. Shutting down to prevent oneself from being hurt is a trait with which I'm inherently familiar, and I couldn't blame her for doing the same.

Despite this awkward start, Elizabeth and I would go on to become friends, and she introduced me to what I called the "choir gang." This rag-tag band would never be uber-popular, but instead was united by talent and outsider status. Almost every single male member of the group would later come out as gay. And as play rehearsals progressed, I was relieved that Elizabeth and I were able to move beyond our painful initial interaction.

The girl playing my sister in *Our Town* had some kind of disease which kept her short, in addition to suffering from diabetes and hypoglycemia, requiring her to eat all of the time—much like Dana Hill of *Fallen Angel*. Thus, my "sister" was short, stunted, and fat, which were apparently the only qualifications necessary for nabbing the role. She could also be extremely annoying, which can be helpful when playing someone's little sister. In fact, she was so annoying that one night, after playing a scene on a raised platform, I was rushing to get to my next mark and almost pushed her off the platform, as she was moving like molasses. She's now dead, so I'm trying to be charitable and not list any more of her lovely attributes.

The lead role of the Stage Manager was played by Marty Robinson, who would later become a professional actor named Martin Kildare. Some years in the future, Marty and I would run into each other again in the UCLA theater department, where he was getting his MFA and me my BFA. His girlfriend at the time, Lisa Darr, would go on to play the lead in a Paramount sitcom on which I would work, *Flesh 'N Blood*, as well as to play Ellen DeGeneres' girlfriend on that final, groundbreaking season of *Ellen*. In other words, I've mingled with actors who are ten times better than I will ever be. Which brings me to the highlight of my performance in *Our Town*.

In the third act of the play, the romantic lead, Emily—my childhood sweetheart turned wife—is dead from childbirth. Before undertaker Joe Fucking Stoddard—finally not being played by me—can put her in the ground, and just after she delivers one of the theater's most iconic monologues, hubby George visits her graveside. The audience is supposed to be highly emotional, watching as he approaches from afar, his grief palpable, until he lies sobbing, prostrate on her grave.

As great an actor as I believed myself to be, I could never muster up sufficiently believable grief as to be "palpable." That's probably because I'd never really known what it was like to suffer such a loss, on any level. (Today, however, intimately knowing such grief, I can cry at the drop of a hat). Still, then, not being able to cry was a sticking point.

One day, however, I hatched a plan. I nabbed a container of Vick's VapoRub from my parents' medicine cabinet and tucked it into my jacket pocket. Each performance, just prior to emerging from the wings, I'd dab some of the rub beneath my eyes, which encouraged tears, making it difficult to even find my way to the stage. During one performance, I kept applying more and more of the ointment, until my eyes were completely on fire, blurring any sense of what was in front of me. But—as I've noted—theater is all about the *essence*, and in this one and only instance, this particular trick of theatrical deceit worked out just fine.

Tears were shed, by the audience and uncontrollably by me.

I AM A POET

In a high school English class, a guest teacher, Jack Grapes, came in as part of California's Poets in the Schools program and attempted to illuminate the world of poetry for us. We wrote countless poems, but nothing I wrote ever got more than from a *"meh"* from him. Quite simply, I didn't understand poetry or why people even read it. Seemed like a waste of time to me.

Mr. Grapes did give me good marks for this heartfelt poem:

GREEN ELEPHANTS
Ice cream strangled on her neck.
Blue trees crying out for grapes.
Blood pouring out of the hair.
Tomorrow's another yesterday.

Yellow monkeys smashed under thumb.
Bones breaking in two.
Skull fragments for dinner.
Tomorrow's another yesterday.

After weeks of thinking that I was an awful poet, I had finally figured out how to be successful: simply throw together a bunch of random, quasi-disturbing images and you are a poet. No over-thinking or searching for meaning:

just vomit up whatever comes forth and put it on paper. That is poetry. This technique certainly worked for me.

And I'm sure my parents were thrilled, reading my poem, to realize they'd likely raised the first school shooter.

THE MAGICAL BOOKSTORE

The minute I had my driver's license, I knew where I had to go: Dodd's Books in Long Beach. I had spotted it one day, from across the street, as my mom and I were at our optometrist for back-to-back appointments. After I was done, and she heading into hers, I told her I'd kill time in the bookstore. I was shocked at what I discovered upon entering.

In the front, by the checkout, were magazine stands, with the top row consisting entirely of gay porn. Titles like *Blueboy*, *Honcho*, *Inches*, and *Uncut* peeked out at me, beckoning. It was a young gay boy's wet dream. And a sign hanging high at the back of the store also drew my attention: "Gay Studies." *Um, who were these gays*, I wondered, *and what were they studying?*

That initial visit, I was so terrified of being discovered that I couldn't even pick up a single book, but with each subsequent visit, circling closer and closer to the Gay Studies section, my determination solidified.

One day, feeling sufficiently brave, I finally bought a book, then hugged it closely until I'd safely reached my car. It was a classic, Andrew Holleran's *Dancer from the Dance*, and that tale of gay life in New York prompted endless dreams of a world so different from my own. It was a world to escape to and I was desperate to be a part of it.

After consuming that novel, on each visit, I would buy

another classic. And another. But it wouldn't be for an entire year until I had enough guts to purchase a Gordon Merrick romance novel with its racy, seductive cover, let alone Larry Kramer's scandalously-titled novel, *Faggots*. After all, I had to be prepared with a believable excuse, should I unexpectedly run into someone I knew.

Even with all of this, buying one of the enticing porn magazines seemed a step too hard to take. But one day—gathering up enough courage—I called Dodd's, asking in an incredibly fake deep voice, "Um, how old do you have to be to buy the gay porn magazines?" The tired queen who answered paused, gave a long sigh, then responded dryly, "Old enough to read." And with that, I was on my way back to Dodd's.

MY FIRST TIME

The summer before my senior year, we took our annual family vacation, this time to Maui, Hawaii. Far from the Valley Isle's more crowded western towns, on this trip we journeyed east down a winding road, past endless waterfalls, to a magical expanse known as Hana. Our digs were at the luxurious Hotel Hana Maui, today called the even-more-luxurious Travaase Experiential Hana, which meant that my dad, usually reliably cheap, had spectacularly outdone himself with this superb choice of hotel. The rooms and grounds were immaculate, the food exquisite, and the picture-perfect private beach proved the ideal backdrop for my long-awaited deflowering.

At 17, with many trips to my magical bookstore under my belt, and its resulting stack of porn hidden in my bedroom, I was more than sexually primed. From my gay studies, I knew the basics on the anatomical gymnastics gay sex would entail, as of course I had never been taught such elsewhere, but I was far more interested in what my sensory experience might be. *What would a man taste like? Smell like? What would it feel like to be fully embraced, held, comforted, and loved?*

The year prior, our local newspaper, the Long Beach Press Telegram, had run a groundbreaking series documenting the city's gay community with a different element explored each day for an entire week—which was particularly insightful for this young person, curious about the world I'd soon be entering. As one day focused on gay bars, helpfully noting the address of each, I quickly broke out my Thomas Brothers map book and charted routes to the bars that sounded most promising. As soon as it was dark, I headed out, clueless to the notion that gay bars wouldn't be popular until much later at night, and sat in my car outside each, watching the few men entering and departing. *"Who were they?"* I wondered. *"What did they do during the day—did they have jobs? If so, doing what?"* and—most importantly—*"What must it be like to be able to walk into such an establishment, confidently and without fear?"*

Sex may have been important, but it was a longing for connection and empowerment that I most desired.

Upon arrival at the Hana beach, I immediately noticed the Speedo-wearing blond downwind as my sister and I staked out two chairs in the sand. Eyeing him covertly from behind my sunglasses, I was keenly aware that his eyes were locked on me as well. My eyes darted about, ensuring that my sister was oblivious and that no one else around could feel the heat emanating from the sexual energy burning between us.

A little while later, his eyes still on me, he rose, grinned knowingly, and disappeared around the corner of the cove. Intrigued, and fairly certain that I was meant to follow, I rose, stretched, and told my sister, as casually as I could, that I was going for a walk. I followed his path and, rounding the corner of the cove, almost ran right into him. He'd been waiting... for *me*.

This was it. I knew what was coming. He led me up onto a gentle slope, overlooking a secluded cove. We were alone. It was a picture-perfect day—sunny and warm, with a 99% chance of semen.

I don't remember what was said. It was clear that he wanted me, and I wanted him, and that was really all that mattered.

We were soon kissing and groping, with a ferocity that comes from a lifetime of waiting, hoping, praying. Our bathing suits came off, and we took each other into our mouths, bobbing passionately, until I finally began to feel nervous. What if someone were to see us? We were perched on the hillside, no barriers, and all it would take would be one person to turn the corner, exposing us, and my parents would surely be told.

We hadn't yet cum, but I begged off, telling him I had to get back. Reluctantly, he let me dress, and I hurried off, back toward the other cove, only to run smack into my sister, who'd come looking for me. If we'd continued even one minute longer, my goose would've been cooked.

Back at my chair in the sun, horny as hell, I watched as the man also returned. Tanned and muscular, he exuded Southern Californian self-confidence. He continued to sneak glances at me, and I knew he wanted more. He wanted me. Again... proving that gay life wouldn't be a struggle, or empty, or sad, as I'd been told. Finding love would be possible, after all.

Seeking release from the scorching sun, I finally went into the water, letting it envelop me. Rising, shaking out my hair, I suddenly realized he was beside me. Glancing over to ensure my sister was dozing, I smiled at him, feeling increasingly confident.

"Are there any showers here?" I queried with a smile, knowing full well that there were.

"Yeah," he grinned. "In the bathroom."

I nodded, then sauntered up toward them, gently grabbing my beach towel so as not to wake my sister.

Entering, I saw that there were two shower areas with multiple shower heads, which had shower rods over the entrances, but no curtains or doors. I put my towel up over the rod on one, creating my own curtain, then took my suit off and began showering. It wasn't long before he joined me, and we finished what we had set out to do.

Looking back, any number of people could've walked past that impromptu shower curtain and correctly assumed what was going on. We could've been caught. And while that wouldn't have been remotely ideal, there is a part of me that wouldn't change a single element of my first time. Erotic and fulfilling, that experience was everything I had hoped, and just having had that made moving forward into my senior year of high school a bit easier.

I do wish I remembered more about the guy. I don't recall his name or much about him. I remember that he was 35, and me only 17. But age didn't matter to me much then, as hormonally-driven as I was to complete the act of sex. Just having the touch of another man was so all-important that the person himself didn't much matter.

Today, however, that age difference gives me pause. I can't imagine having sex with a teen, and the mere thought makes me a bit queasy. The 80s, however, were a different era with different norms. In this situation, there was no abuser. There was just me and the man who made my dreams come true.

I wanted it. I wanted him. I needed that moment—that touch—that explosion. And I don't regret a single thing...

LIFE LESSON #9

Should you want to start your senior year with a bang, *after* your big bang, do not let the girl at another Hawaiian resort ply you with Sun-In. Those senior photos of you with orange hair will follow you for a lifetime.

FUMBLING DESPERATELY IN THE DARK

Back at high school, a younger guy on the cheer squad and I had been flirting for weeks. As a senior, I knew that the class system meant we shouldn't have interacted, but I was intrigued. He was sweet. He was hot. He was a yell leader like me. Still, I was a bit taken aback when he started hitting on me.

Okay, maybe "hitting" isn't the correct word, but his actions made clear that he was at least curious about me and all that I was. We started out as friends, but as more time was spent together, the attraction steadily increased.

One evening at sunset, walking along the beach, shoulders bumping, I finally asked the obvious, "A lot of people think I'm gay... Why do you still hang out with me?" He didn't answer at first, looking away, but as he finally turned to look into my eyes, it was clear. He was just like me.

It wasn't long until things moved forward, on the night prior to a ski trip with another friend. Given our early morning departure, this guy stayed over at my house. I was to be in my bed, and he on the floor in a sleeping bag, but that arrangement didn't last long. Somehow, despite the differences in our positioning, our hands miraculously found each other. This initial clasping of hands, showing that we were somehow united, quickly moved on from there. It was a pivotal and profound moment, united by love or sex, and only altered the next day by the unwelcome intrusion of our common ski friend. It was incredibly painful to have had such an intimately profound sexual experience and yet mere hours later to be acting as if we were nothing more than buddies. It had been a moment of idyll, only to end as estrangement.

It would be some time before we interacted again, given his supposed confusion around what had taken place, and what his decision to engage in our sexual interaction said about him. But we would later "interact," time and again, until he finally determined that he was indeed straight and moving on with his life.

However, he wasn't straight. And he didn't move on. He's out there now, living the free-wheeling West Hollywood life.

You've heard it here first, folks: Penises rarely lie.

THE PIANIST

It was my senior year in high school. We were to perform *Once Upon a Mattress* as our final class play, and The Pianist was the roommate of the man hired to be our musical director. The Pianist was to accompany us. Given that he was cute, muscular, and friendly, with a nice brown mustache filling out the package, I couldn't help but take notice, despite my being 18 and him 23.

The musical director was straight, or at least reported himself to be, and his girlfriend at the time seemed entirely scandalized that his roommate The Pianist and I were dating. She and the musical director were Christians, or reported to be, so perhaps that we were gay and doing evil nasty things in that Pianist's bedroom might've been what bothered her. But that didn't stop her, or any of them, from sharing their wine with me; Riunite on ice—so nice! And that didn't stop any of them from sharing their hopes and dreams with me.

One day after The Pianist and I had split up, due to The Pianist's supposed confusion around his sexuality, the musical director and I went swimming in the community pool. We'd just pulled ourselves out of the pool, toweling off our toned bodies before perfectly positioning ourselves onto chaise lounges, when the musical director leaned toward me, intimately, seductively, and confided, "I am straight. But I'm not saying that the idea—that if I met the right guy—"

He let the idea hang in the air...

We were so close to each other; both young and beautiful, dripping wet. It was clear that he was offering himself to me. And I hesitated, being both attracted to his "straight" Christian ass while also still caring about The Pianist. While intrigued and turned on, that wasn't a line I felt comfortable crossing.

In my freshman year of college, The Pianist made repeated efforts to contact me to reestablish that fire. I wasn't very nice in my response. I'd come to a point where I wanted someone open about their sexuality, unafraid, willing to proudly take my hand and journey forward into the world as a gay couple. From where I then stood, it didn't seem that hard of an *ask*.

Today, the musical director and The Pianist are both married to women. I wonder where such same-sex longing goes? It can't entirely disappear. That throb, that desire... One can't simply wish it away.

As I learned long ago, Pianists rarely lie.

LIFE LESSON #10

Late one night, should you hear your doorbell ring, and your dad running out into the darkness, yelling for someone to stop, don't panic. Don't be upset when your dad reenters, dragging your "friend" Scott into the house. Just listen as Scott offers an apology—for what, you don't yet know.

Don't overreact when you learn that he and your other "friend" Bill have left a glass jar, full of pennies and piss, on your front step. Don't over-think why they would do it or just precisely *what that meant*. Just know that one day, you can take that pain and the turmoil of emotions you felt, and turn it into a pivotal plot point in your first novel.

A LETTER TO MY BULLY

Dear Dirk,

I have hated you almost every day since we first met. But for different reasons altogether than you might expect.

I still remember the terror I felt, every time I approached the soccer field. It was junior high, a difficult time for almost everyone, but for me, especially so.

You see, I'd always known I was gay. Even in kindergarten, just looking at Jimmy Hayworth's smile would make me happy, and I knew, intrinsically, that it was alright to feel this way—to love other boys—as everything about it felt completely natural and unforced.

In junior high, however, once placed on the same soccer team with you, everything changed.

What I had seen as natural and good, you were suddenly calling abnormal and detestable. Every "faggot" you spit towards me hit directly between the eyes, and the whispers, taunts, and dirty looks you and Mike Baker continually sent my way unnerved me, affecting my sense of self, as well as my performance on the field. Because of you, questions about my masculinity hovered over, and I would feel physically ill at the thought of another practice or game. I would choose different, roundabout paths to my classes, just to avoid where I knew you'd be.

In high school, while I went on to be active in theater and

academics, you and Mike continued to rise socially, becoming the big men on campus that I longed to be. You were even voted onto the homecoming king's court, and as you took to the field, flashing your charming smile, all I could see was the sneer on your lips when you turned and glanced my way.

But that isn't why I have hated you.

Just prior to our senior year, during summer break, word came that you'd tried to commit suicide and were in a coma. No one knew what had happened, but you eventually returned to school for our senior year. You were just as popular as you had been before, and perhaps even more so, now that you had this added sense of intrigue about you. But despite your outright hatred of me, I still wondered about you and about what could have possibly led you to try to take your own life. You, more than anyone, seemed to have it all, and despite the way you continued to torment me, I felt a pang of pity for you.

The following summer, after graduation, I got another call. You'd again tried to kill yourself, tying a noose from the garage rafters—only this time you succeeded. Your mother discovered you upon her return home, hanging there as she opened the garage door.

How lonely you must have felt, Dirk, as you tied that rope. Could you really see no path forward? Was there no one you could have reached out to? Was there no friend, family member, priest, counselor—not one single person you could've trusted with your pain?

Later, I heard that you'd left behind a note, writing that although you did not like girls, you did not want to like boys. And suddenly it became horribly clear to me. You and I were exactly alike. That anger and venom you directed at me, you were also directing at yourself.

How I wish, Dirk, that you'd allowed yourself to connect with me. I'm not saying that a friendship between us could have altered your path, but just knowing that we weren't the only ones could've made our lives easier. For me, discovering that there were other gay people out there did help. I found a progressive bookstore, not too far from where we lived, and I'd covertly journey there as often as I could, just to lose myself in reading about a world which I knew I'd someday enter.

And even if a friendship between us wasn't possible, given our differing social status, imagine how less torturous you could have made another's life, simply by being kind.

While in school, my hatred was based solely upon how mean you were to me, now my anger is reserved for the lack of value you placed upon yourself. Clearly, you didn't think you were worth loving. Where did you get such a message? You were smart, personable, an exceptional athlete, and beyond handsome. Even with all of the venom you sent my way, I still admired your more affirming qualities. Regardless, despite these many gifts, somewhere along the way you were taught that instead of acting on your love of other men, you'd be better off dead.

I hate that you hurt so, Dirk, and hate just as much that you listened to those who filled your head with such thoughts.

I also hate that I was so absorbed in and blinded by my own situation that I couldn't see your venom for what it really was. What if, one day, instead of running the other way when I saw you, I had instead offered you a smile?

Dirk, you might be surprised to know who I ran into at our 10-year high school reunion---your old pal, Mike Baker. Imagine my shock, spotting him across the room, when we suddenly locked eyes. I immediately went to that same junior high school place of fear and panic, but that lasted only a moment, when I saw him break out into a big grin and make a beeline toward me.

I was shocked when he warmly clasped my hand in his, as if we were longtime friends. "I've been looking all over for you," he said, intently. "I've really been wanting to say 'hello.'" While he never brought up our shared past, it was clear to me that he was making amends.

Did you know, Dirk, that Mike's younger brother had come out as gay? Would it surprise you to know that Mike is totally okay with it? If you had known back then that your best friend might have been accepting of you, could that have possibly altered your decision?

People loved you, Dirk—then and now.

I wish I could have held you, Dirk, comforted you, and told you that everything would be alright. Our individual uniqueness' are a gift, given by our maker, which we then get to share with the world. Your void is noticeable, even 20-odd years later.

You could've done so much, Dirk, if only you'd realized that each one of us is deserving of love and respect.

Wishing you peace,
Kergan

Written in 2012. Though innocence for all was lost some years ago, in respect of their families, all names have been changed.

TROUBLE BRUIN

On my first day of college, moving into UCLA's Sproul Hall, I got onto the elevator, only to find myself face-to-face with TV star Loni Anderson, of famed comedy *WKRP in Cincinnati.* Looking impeccable, wearing a cowboy hat and tight denim jeans, she bore in her hands a single potted plant, whilst her daughter huffed and puffed beside her, arms full of trappings.

This was L.A., I told myself. This was to be expected. And I wasn't far off.

Moving into my dorm, I was pleased to find that I had arrived before my roommate, allowing me time to arrange the room as I desired. I put the beds atop each other, kindly leaving him the top bunk, as this configuration allowed the other side of the room to be utilized by a fridge, TV, and lounge chair. I'm sure my choice of posters—one Judy Garland, one Norma Scherer, and two of *Flashdance* star Jennifer Beals—might have been confusing to some, including my Asian roommate, but he seemed to speak little English so couldn't complain.

Soon after moving in, I jumped into an ill-considered affair with a dormmate, who was not yet out. As my roommate spent virtually 24/7 studying at the library, one day my lover and I were going at it quite furiously in the bottom bunk, when suddenly we heard a key in the door and my lover darted beneath the covers. I attempted to act as if everything were normal—as if I always took naps naked in the middle of the day in a very lumpy bed—but I could see the look of both embarrassment and fear in my roommate's eyes. He clearly knew what was going on, and that it was not a woman beneath the sheets, so quickly did he dart about, grabbing what he needed before again vanishing to the library.

Almost every day, I would lock myself in my dorm room to watch *All My Children*. I would sit quietly, glued to the set, and ignore any knocks that might come between noon and 1:00 p.m. The stories of Greg and Jenny, the Martins, the Chandlers, and kick-ass Erika were my stories. I loved these people and their devious ways, which continually kept me in suspense. I hated Fridays, as you always knew that something terrible was going to happen, leaving you to spend the entire weekend worrying as to the outcome.

Several years later, one of my favorite actors from the show moved into the apartment next to me. His scenes with his leading lady were among the show's best acted, and I enjoyed getting to know him off-screen. At 60-something, he was then dating an actress from the same show who played a teenager. She was very sweet, if not the most talented of actresses, but I fondly recall evenings in our courtyard, bougainvillea intertwined over the arching light fixtures, sharing red wine as they smoked and reminisced about their years on the show.

When I finally moved out of that apartment, the actor hadn't worked in ages and had become an alcoholic. I ran into the actress sometime later, then working a makeup counter at a shop in the Beverly Center. It was a sobering lesson for me, to see how quickly and deeply these once-prosperous and dear people, whom I'd idolized and watched daily for years, had fallen from stardom. What had happened to them was disheartening, but not enough to veer me off my own acting path. I would bang my head against that particular wall time and again.

The theater department at UCLA was where I spent most of my time during college. It contained the usual assortment of the brilliantly talented, mildly demented, and utterly useless faculty and body of students.

There was one pretty girl who would occupy a perch in the student lounge, where all would come, if only to check mailboxes. She was loud, obnoxiously so, desperate to be noticed, and seemed to have no talent. I don't recall her ever being cast in a play, yet, as the daughter of 60s bombshell Jayne Mansfield and boxer Mickey Hargitay, she knew how to command a room. I can see her now, cracking jokes to those entering the lounge, trying to connect, but few did. Spotting her in the lobby, most stepped slightly off-track to avoid catching her eye. But Mariska Hargitay would go on to star in *Law & Order: Special Victims Unit* for 20 years, winning an Emmy for Best Actress in the process, so I guess she had the last laugh.

My first several performances at UCLA were in one-acts, where I struggled to make myself known. I was so excited to finally get cast in a mainstage production that I never once questioned the quality of the production; I was just happy to be in it. Essentially, in the middle of this tale set on a South American plantation, an earthquake occurs, ripping the hacienda into two. As the set pieces fly offstage, two tribes tumble out: the Sun and Moon Mayans. For about 20 minutes, the play's narrative is interrupted as these tribes battle it out through dance. As a Moon Mayan, I energetically jumped and danced about in my blue loin cloth, my severe black wig pinned tightly to my head and my spray tanned limbs flailing about. After our dance concluded, the Mayans retreated offstage, the house miraculously began to repair itself, its fractured pieces flying back together, and the story meandered on to its forgettable close.

After the show, with me still wearing my costume, my parents and their friends met me in the hallway. Dottie was absolutely mortified that I hadn't warned her that I'd be clad in little more than a dance belt; if I had, she wouldn't have invited her friends to join them, saving her from embarrassment. We said our awkward hello's before going our separate ways. My mom remained entirely scandalized by this particular acting endeavor, which would become a recurring theme with us. Nothing I could do was ever good enough for Dottie.

LIFE LESSON #11

Should you, as a freshman in college, decide that the best way to let others know you are gay is to carry around a colorful children's lunchbox, do not do it. It will not work as intended. You will become an object of ridicule in the process, making any other gay men fearful of being seen with you. Trust me.

MY FIRST LOVE

Once at UCLA, I was incredibly desperate to find other like-minded people. It was during this time that I first laid eyes on Steve at the original Cheesecake Factory in Beverly Hills. He was wearing a cream-colored Irish fisherman's sweater, with a deep tan and sparkling eyes. A group of us theater folks had gathered for dinner, and while he wasn't in theater, all of his friends at the time were. Steve had an easy laugh and genuine warmth; our attraction was immediate.

We dated for several months and he eventually asked me to live with him over the summer. As his straight roommate wasn't remotely hospitable, we soon found ourselves in a beautiful old apartment on Laurel Avenue, just up the street from West Hollywood's longtime staple, The French Market restaurant. Our pristine white 1920s apartment building was surrounded by flowers in bloom, and our one-bedroom contained cute customizations and intricate design motifs. It was a picture-perfect apartment, and should've marked the beginning of a beautiful relationship, but I wouldn't be there long.

Soon after we'd moved in, my parents came to visit and, following a quick tour, which included the sole bedroom containing a queen bed, my mom turned to Steve and remarked, "Thank you for sharing your bed with Fred."

My dad just grimaced, knowingly, and looked away.

Had I been more mature, or more patient, or more giving, perhaps the relationship could have survived. Steve loved me so much, it felt suffocating. I'd never been in a true relationship before and didn't know what to expect. To find myself at 19, waking and falling asleep with the same person, as I also tried to balance my studies, was overwhelming. I began to feel trapped, blaming Steve for "smothering me" when he was doing nothing of the sort.

This led to fights, and unnecessary dramatics—I *was* a theater major, after all, and had a certain reputation to uphold—and ended with me pulling out of my sophomore year of college and moving back home with my parents.

I went into an emotional tailspin, torn by my mixed emotions. I felt such love for Steve, certain he had been "the one," but I chafed too at how I'd felt as if I were drowning. My parents were aware of none of this, and I put my energies into working at night as a waiter at a local Mexican restaurant and during the day, traveling up to Hollywood for acting classes.

Stuck living an hour from Los Angeles, back behind the then-solidly Orange Curtain, I set about finding some new friends and discovered the gay bars in Garden Grove, particularly one called DOK West. Only a twenty-minute drive from my parent's house, I soon began going there almost nightly, hoping to make friends and meet "the one." My parents rarely inquired where I was or what I was doing. While they may have had their suspicions, they also weren't yet at a point where they felt comfortable bringing it up, though that moment quickly came—much sooner than I'd expected

I'M COMING OUT: PART 1

January 4th, 1985. That night, I'd gone to L.A., dancing with friends, and had come home very late, at 3:30 in the morning, to be exact. So I was not altogether surprised when my parents—still up—called me into their room. This entire passage is taken directly from a letter I wrote to Steve soon after, without editing.

SCENE ONE: THE PARENTS

Dad: "We're concerned about the late hours you've been keeping lately."
Me: "Okay, I'll make sure I come in earlier. Goodnight—"
Dad: "Wait just a minute! Where do you go until 3:30 in the morning?"
Me: "I went dancing in L.A."
Dad: "Where?"
Me, fully aware he won't know the club: "Rage."
Dad: "When you go to these clubs, who do you dance with?"
Me, fully knowing where he is headed: "My friends."
Dad: "Boys or girls?" (Yep, I was right!)
Me: "Boys."
(a long period of silence ensues.)
Dad: "Does this mean... you're a homosexual?"
Me: "Yes, I'm gay."
Mom: "Ohhhhhh!..." (like a knife piercing her heart)

Dad: "Hmm..." (knowingly)

Me: "Surprise!"

Dad: "Not really."

Mom: "For me it is..."

Dad: "How long have you been—?"

Me: "I've been attracted to men for as long as I can remember. I've never liked girls."

Mom: "Are you an active homosexual?"

Me: "Do you mean have I had sex before or am I active now?"

Mom: "Both."

Me: "Yes, I've had sex before but I'm not going out with anyone right now."

Mom: "You need help. I think you should see a therapist."

Me: "I'm happy the way I am. It's not a disease. I'm not sick."

Mom: "To me you are."

(dead silence)

We talked a long time. They set up the following rules:

1. Curfew—12:00 p.m. on weekdays, 2:00 a.m. on weekends.
2. No friends can spend the night.
3. If I have a friend over, the door to my room is to remain open.
4. If they don't like my friend, I don't get phone messages.
5. My friend Greg, who is flaming, is not allowed in the house.
6. I'm now seeing a therapist.

SCENE TWO: THE THERAPIST

Setting: The basic therapist office, comfortable, with a large armchair and table across from a sofa. On the table rests a Bible, precariously poised for instantaneous use. We open the scene in the middle of the discussion.

Therapist: "Well, it's obvious that you're happy and well-adjusted to your sexuality. I cannot make you straight, but if you want, I can stop you from acting on your homosexual fantasies."

Me: "Does this mean you are advocating celibacy?"

Therapist: "Well, celibacy is not that bad, you know."

Me: "Maybe for monks, but not for me. I don't think you realize what being gay means to me. It sounds as if to you, being gay is equated with promiscuity. That may be true for some gays, just as straights can be also. But for me, being gay means loving, and being loved. I want the simple things—to be held, to go for walks on the beach... If you ask me to stop being gay, you are asking me not to love, not to live. I couldn't live a lie, because if I tried to change, I'd be hypocritical. I've got to be true to my feelings—I'm sorry if neither you nor my family approves, but I've got to be true to me, only I am responsible for myself and my actions. I like who I am. And I won't change."

(After a period of silence, the therapist reaches for the Bible at his fingertips and reads five passages that condemn being gay as a sin.)

You can guess where it leads from there.

THE AFTERMATH

A short time later, on the way to her Winter Formal, my sister asked my friend Ed, her escort, if he was gay and he lied, telling her "No"—*Chicken!* Then she asked about me. Ed's response? "I don't really know. You'd have to ask him. Besides, if he is, does it really matter? You should be concerned with his happiness, not his sexual preference."

A few days later, my sister did ask me. I told her, and she seemed to take it well. Though initially hesitate, my dad turned out to be great, reading books I gave him on the subject and trying to keep the lines of communication open. My mom, on the other hand, continued to be the Queen of Tears, presenting me with literature on "gay conversion camps" and praying for me at every opportunity.

As soon as I was able, I headed back to UCLA to resume my education—and my openly gay life—without fear of judgement.

WE ARE FAMILY

Restarting my sophomore year at UCLA, my parents happy to get rid of their newly-out gay son, I soon booked my first commercial, a local spot for Honda, filmed at an actual Honda car lot in Hollywood. Local commercials, unlike nationals, don't pay very well, and that showed all the way through from director, to videographer, to the cast. We were a rag tag bunch, playing a family, and we filmed several different versions of the ad, focusing our "family" shopping together for Honda XRs, an off-road motorcycle line.

I was 19 at the time, with my trademark feathered brown hair and tan. The girl playing my sister was a pale, curly haired red-head. And the actor playing my dad was blond, a bit more than effete, and only 10 years older than I. The woman cast as mom, a vivacious brunette, showed up on shooting day with gigantically swollen cheeks, having had root canals the day prior, and was promptly sent home. Trying to save the day, my gay dad called up an actress he knew who would "be perfect," and when mom arrived, she turned out to be Hispanic.

Thus, our "family" journeyed through a day of shooting, being coached by the director to not only chew, but digest, the scenery. So unbelievable was our acting that I was later mortified to find the commercials running on local channels, seen by my fellow UCLA acting chums. Inevitably, walking into the Theater department lounge, someone behind my back would snicker, repeating my overly sincere and poorly-acted line, "Dad and I go trail-riding on our Honda XRs— *together!*"

DYNASTY

When I first started at UCLA, I really wanted to be an actor. The truth was, though, that I hadn't yet fully explored my soul and I wasn't very good; I was all artifice and posing. My favorite shows at the time were *Dynasty* and *Knots Landing*, and when they were on, just like with *All My Children*, I'd hide in my dorm room with a towel blocking the bottom of the door, so no one would see the light beneath and disturb me.

I was convinced that it was my destiny to end up on *Dynasty*. If only the casting director would see me, I was certain that they'd write a role for me as the teen son of Alexis: a brooding, sexy, tormented young man. I was so confident that this would occur that I actually practiced my *Dynasty* title sequence, walking and turning to look directly into camera, smoldering, as if caught unaware.

As luck would have it, I heard about a special day-long Cold Reading class on campus, taught by none other than the casting director of *Dynasty*, Tony Shepard. I knew that once I made an impression on him, I would find myself on the show. I spent much time picking out just the right outfit and concentrating on this brooding character I'd conjured in my imagination.

There were 100 actors in the class that day, held in a large lecture hall. While there was very little chance of me even meeting the man, let alone reading for him, I still felt certain.

The entire morning session, Mr. Shepard talked about the key points to cold reading, which requires one to not have any preconceived ideas about the scene, as there is no time to even read it. It is all about being "in the moment." Finally, as we broke for lunch, he announced that upon our return, one guy and one girl would be selected at random to cold read for the entire class. *My chance*—at last!

Despite Mr. Shepard's very clear instruction not to "overthink" and let the moment simply transport you, all throughout lunch I ran imaginary scenes in my head, each more emotive than the last. I probably even practiced my squinty "sexy pout" a time or two. After lunch, Mr. Shepard asked for volunteers who wanted to read, and every hand in the class shot up, including mine. And he picked me! (I knew it!!!)

As the woman he'd selected and I stood up and walked to the front of the room, we were handed our sides. We began to read, and I tackled it with all the force and passion I'd been storing up since my early days of first watching *Dynasty*. I was intense, in a really bad way—but entirely befitting an Aaron Spelling production. I was a dark and brooding Hamlet, only to find out mid-scene that the piece I was reading was witty, light Noel Coward-quippy comedy. I was utterly mortified, having so fully committed to my acting style, yet had no choice but to see my folly through to the bitter, painful end.

After we had finished and returned to our seats, I could feel the other actors shirk away from me, fearful of catching my bad-acting bug. I was truly terrible, and they all knew it.

Which is why I'm a writer today.

THE CONDOM GUY

The most famous I've ever been, or likely will ever be, is as "The Condom Guy." I earned that title by appearing in a condom ad. (Don't quit reading—I wasn't *wearing* it.) This was a legit, professional photo shoot for a national print campaign for *Today Condoms*, featuring me dressed in a tux, my arm around my "prom date," in front of a fake fireplace and mantle.

The shoot took forever, as my right arm was taped against my side with duct tape in the back, to ensure no unsightly wrinkles should appear on my suit jacket. For hours I stood, arm taped in place, grinning stupidly into the camera. The look on my face was not so much "Hi, I'm the guy taking your daughter to prom... Aren't I innocent?" as "I'm gonna get some action tonight!"

The ad ran for months in GQ, Esquire, and Rolling Stone, to name but a few magazines. It became so famous that when walking the campus, I'd hear people say, "Hey, it's the condom guy," which happily erased any memory of "My dad and I go trail-riding on our Honda XRs—*together!*"

Across town, at USC, my sister's school, that very ad photo would end up being sent to my sister's sorority in a party invitation, as an example of how big brothers and little sisters should groove. (By fucking each other safely?!?)

Much later, I'd again become known as "The Condom Guy" for my appearances at countless pride festivals, where

I'd give a comedic spiel about the importance of safe sex, and end my routine by pulling a guy from the audience, equipping him with a strap-on dildo, and rolling a condom onto that big sucker with my mouth. That, my friends, takes great skill. And tremendous acting talent. (I really would've been wonderful on *Dynasty*.)

WHEN KERGAN SAW THE LIGHT

The crowning achievement of my college career were four plays I directed, all written by the same playwright, Michael Sargent. Prior to attending UCLA, Michael was already considered a child prodigy, having been shepherded in writing workshops by renowned playwright John Steppling. When we first met, Michael had his hair swept into a pompadour and dressed in punk rock-meets-rockabilly style. Black boots, tight jeans, a penchant for graphic T's, and obscenely talented—I was immediately hooked.

Together, we would go on to create our first show which totally rocked the UCLA theater department, *Rat Songs*. Dark, trenchant, and impossibly funny, the production immediately put Michael and I on the map with its perfect dialogue rhythms, Brechtian-theatrics, and bravado acting performances. I believe it was the first time at UCLA, or perhaps anywhere, where an actor licked a foot-long stretch of stage floor. (She was a real trooper.)

At UCLA, I'd been coached in directing by the wonderfully charming Michael McClain (a specialist in Russian theater), the legendary *Pillow Talk* film director Michael Gordon, and the future chair of the theater department, Michael Hackett. Apparently, being named Michael was a mandatory requirement for UCLA theater department success.

Michael Hackett was an educator extraordinaire, then teaching all theater majors in the obligatory first-year introductory theater class, but he was also the brilliant mind behind our Moon Mayan fiasco, and entirely to blame for not only my dance belt appearance, but all subsequent issues with my mother. He, in particular, encouraged me to embrace a more theatrical approach to theater.

One scene study I directed for Mr. Hackett, from the ground-breaking gay Holocaust play, *Bent*, starred my then-lover actor/dancer who would end up being "straight", and another guy I cast just because I wanted to see him with his shirt off. Under Hackett's encouragement, the scene changed dramatically from first reveal to last, as I began to incorporate his Brechtian philosophy, in which theater means THEATRICAL, with a capital *T*.

In the scene I'd selected, the two men are in a concentration camp, unable to show any sign of affection for each other, and are forced to do mind-numbing physical busy work, spending all day, every day, moving rocks from one area of the yard to another, then back again—all while feeling a yearning for each other they're unable to express. Under Hackett's suggestion, what had started out as the actors moving imaginary rocks (as I didn't want to deal with dragging heavy stones to each rehearsal), morphed into stacked pieces of 2x4, which made a loud clacking sound each time they were stacked. What had started out as a muted siren turned into lights flashing around the theater and a blaring, shrill whistle. And, for my pièce de résistance, I went into the men's locker room shower with my cassette tape recorder, and chronicled the drip-drip-drip of the showers as I banged methodically on the pipe of a shower head. This recording is heard in the background throughout the scene, and that monotony—combined with the men's longing—interrupted only by a shrill whistle and startling, piercing lights—resulted in me getting an A.

This approach of fully theatrical stage moments informed my directing-style moving forward. My next show with Michael Sargent was called *When Esther Saw the Light*, and it would go on to win the American College Theater Festival award for Best Play, and me an award for Meritorious Direction, and we traveled to Washington, D.C. to perform it at Kennedy Center.

One young 18-year-old stoner kid had auditioned and was brilliant. Up until our show, he hadn't been cast in anything at UCLA, primarily because he was such a unique type that no one yet knew quite what to do with him. Jack Black wasn't then the plump comedian filmgoers would later fall in love with, but instead a scrawny teen with perpetual smirk and lead-brick eyebrows.

Yet in this play, there came a moment in which his character needed to deliver a corny line, and he nailed it as only "Jack Black" could. Arguing in a chaotic scene with his crazy wife, she finally demands, "Call me a cab," to which Jack replies, *"You're a cab!"* His delivery never failed to bring down the house.

It was after this play, which begins with a woman in skimpy lingerie hanging on a huge wooden cross, thinking she is the scarecrow from *The Wizard of Oz*, that my mother told me that my work was sacrilegious and she would no longer attend any of my shows. Which I was totally okay with.

Years later, after starting a relationship with my now-hubby, Russ, we celebrated a Valentine's night at the restaurant Jar in Los Angeles. When we walked in, we saw actress Anne Heche, seated in the middle of the restaurant, clearly hoping to be recognized, yet totally eclipsed by Jack, seated in a banquette with his soon-to-be-wife, Tanya. After Russ was sat at our table, I moved past, approaching Jack, not even certain he would remember me now that he was a huge movie star. I'd told Russ my "Jack Black story," and it would be more than a little awkward if Jack were to meet my approach with a blank stare. Upon seeing me, however, Jack immediately jumped up, hugged me, and promptly offered me a seat at their table. We chatted for a while, leaving Russ alone for 15 minutes solid minutes on Valentine's.

When I finally returned to Russ, a waiter came over to ask who I was, assuming that I must be an agent or a producer whom he could blow for an acting job. I then noticed that, all over the restaurant, eyes were turned towards us; even more so when Jack and Tanya made their exit from the restaurant, stopping at our table to introduce themselves to Russ and apologizing for monopolizing my time on this special evening. Kind, humble, and a great actor, Jack Black is a singular talent, and I'm proud to have played however small a role in his acting career.

Jack would also appear in my third play at UCLA with Michael Sargent, *Locust*, about the dirty underbelly of Hollywood, in which I both acted and directed. In that play, my embrace of Brechtian techniques was most fully on display, with the actors in underwear onstage as the audience entered, changing into their costumes and putting on their makeup while being scrutinized by theatergoers, to making all sound effects with their mouths (from jacuzzi bubbles to car sounds), and also acting as furniture, so when in one scene two characters lie in the sun on chaise lounges, there were actually three actors under each, propping them up. While my mother wouldn't come to that, my dad did, driving an hour to the theater just to see us perform. His well-intentioned words upon seeing me afterword? "Well, that was *something!*"

Jack would not appear in our final production, *Don't Fence Me In*, which would go on to truly shock the entire theater department due to its rampant nudity and sexually explicit acts. Produced in a black box space with wooden floors, theatergoers entered to find the black room eerily illuminated only by blood red spotlights, hitting the center of dead body chalk marks on the floor, on which a character's name was written, with a naked actor strewn out atop each outline. These "dead" bodies would become the characters who became HIV-infected from our lusty, non-discriminatory and ethics-free protagonist, and it would be the first time—and likely last—in which naked actors at UCLA simulated anal sex, blowjobs and cunnilingus onstage. I was one of those actors, as we had a hard time getting anyone to perform naked, which led to many months of hard gym workouts and low-calorie meals—not that I was ever satisfied with my naked body.

Michael Sargent played the lead character, and both he and I were naked throughout the entire play. Our past history as off-stage lovers was recreated in scenes in which he both blew me and tried to fuck me.

To this final play with Michael Sargent, I did not invite either parent.

MR. RIGHTS

Throughout my twenties, I dated a lot of men, but was never a whore. Well, I guess that depends on how you define "whore." I did sleep with a lot of people—*a lot*—but there were never any one-nighters. Well, there were no "one-nighters" in the sense that there were no drunken nights at the bar, wandering home with whomever was closest. Each and every person I slept with was essentially a test-drive, following a respectful dinner date, to determine if that person could actually be Mr. Right. But, yeah, in my quest, I fucked a lot of people.

One guy took me to a touring production of the lavish musical *La Cage Aux Folles*, and immediately followed it up with a wholly unexpected declaration of undying love for me. I gracefully declined, and he went on to star in a long-running home improvement TV show.

Another guy, I ended it after finding out that he had an oil painting of Barbra Streisand hanging above his fireplace.

A waiter I dated a few times cheated on me, which ended the relationship, only for me to discover some weeks later that he had a new career, and would soon be starring in such gay porn flicks as *Butt Boys from Outer Space: Blasting Out from Uranus*. (I should've known that porn might be in his future when, during our first sexual encounter, he whispered to me that he really didn't let guys fuck him, but then proceeded to promptly plop himself right down on my dick without lubrication. That should've been a clue.)

A waiter-artist seduced me with his beautiful paintings, only to later find out that he'd also bestowed crabs on me.

A waiter-actor I'd been seeing rolled over in bed one beautiful sleepy Saturday, propping himself on his elbow with a grin, only to say, "You know, you repulse me."

An actor-dancer I'd been seeing rolled over after a particularly energetic sexual romp, only to say, "I'm sorry, but I'm straight."

I dated one guy, an avid runner named Phil, who could only cum if he ground up and down against my body. Afterward, he said, "I'll bet no one's ever done that to you before, right?"

Another guy, also named Phil and also an avid runner, also loved rubbing against me until he came. And he also proclaimed, overconfidently and incorrectly, "Bet no one's ever done that to you!"

I dated a guy who turned out to have only one ball, of which he was endlessly ashamed.

I dated a guy who portrayed Prince Charming at Disneyland, whose dick was shaped like an incredibly short stubby pencil—like something Pixar would animate—with a small head where the pencil lead should've been.

Another guy's laugh, half horse neigh, half machine gun, made me want to gouge my ears out.

And another guy I dated a few times, Jon Cantonwine— an impossibly cute man who looked great in a tank top— would go on to become the first person I intimately knew to die from AIDS.

MR. PEACOCK

With doe-like eyes, shy smile, and abundant knowledge of the entertainment industry, it was easy for me to like Mr. Peacock. We'd met through common friends and begun dating. While he was extremely rich, it was never his wealth that attracted me, though I'll admit that I did like the comfort his generosity provided in terms of life experiences. Mr. Peacock had been a precocious child and had never felt at home in his own skin. Endearingly awkward in social situations not involving his profession or politics, there was something about Mr. Peacock that made me feel extremely protective—as if he were an orphaned bird.

I quickly embraced his circle of friends and soon Mr. Peacock and I were "a couple." There was something intoxicating about rubbing elbows with the Barry Diller and David Geffen's of the world, even tangentially. But I was still extremely cognizant that to this extreme stratosphere, I was little more than a starving actor, a piece of meat, who few took seriously.

When Mr. Peacock was traveling, I would often stay at his palatial estate to house sit. I'd enjoy his pool, workout room, screening room, and opulent kitchen, and feel as if all of it were my own. Someday, I thought, I'll have all *this*. Whether with Mr. Peacock or through success on my own, the opulence he'd acquired spoke to me and I felt as if it were only a matter of time before I was part of that illustrious world.

Some months into our relationship, cracks began appearing. It began with small annoyances and petty comments. There was nothing tangible that I could easily identify, but something was definitely off, and I knew our time together was limited.

That summer, knowing that I had little money, Mr. Peacock asked if I'd join him as his guest on a trip to Boston and Provincetown. Despite a growing sense that something wasn't quite right, I agreed, and we set off on what promised to be a fun adventure.

Storied Provincetown proved to be as wonderful a destination as I'd imagined, and I was glad to be experiencing it with Mr. Peacock. His love of fine food, arts, culture, and wine meant that I was exposed to new tastes, and his love of such opened my eyes to unimaginable new sights. Still...

During that trip, I began to see us more fully as an outsider might: young, cute boy and rich older man. While the difference in age didn't bother me—he was only 10 years older—I began to see that he viewed me as a project, rather than as a person. To him, I was property, to be improved upon as one might a house. That critical emotional bond, essential for a relationship, was missing.

This became more noticeable as our vacation stretched on, and a rich friend of his arrived to stay with us. The friend clearly saw me as a mere toy and treated me as such. Throughout his stay, the friend repeatedly made coy remarks about my desirability and "jokes" about me being a "hired boy," and I found it bewildering that Mr. Peacock never stood up for me. As the days of catty comments stretched on endlessly, I began to chafe.

One day, tension mounting, I finally broke, spewing a vicious barb at Mr. Peacock, falsely insinuating that he was cheap, only focused on the dollar, and didn't care about me at all. As my words tumbled forth, I instantly saw the hurt in his eyes. He turned and began to walk away, his head hanging downward, like a sad old dog. I ran to him, apologetic, but it was too late. The damage was done. Here he had been, desperately wanting to be loved and afraid of getting hurt, and I hurt him, likely more than he was even aware.

I'd used my words to inflict harm, purposely and felt awful about the damage I'd caused.

Later that night, Mr. Peacock wandered off, making it clear that I could now date his rich friend. And as soon as Mr. P left, his rich friend entered my bedroom, without query, and lay down beside me, offering himself. He proceeded to paint a vivid picture of the life we might have together, traveling the world in style, if only I were to choose him. I was sickened and mortified that he thought I could be bought. I don't know how I rebuffed him, but I somehow did, and from that moment on, I couldn't wait for this "vacation of a lifetime" to end.

On the flight home from Boston, Mr. Peacock upgraded himself to first class and boarded the plane ahead of me. As I stepped through the plane's entry, heading to my economy seat, I spotted Mr. P, sipping from a porcelain tea cup in his comfy leather chair, purposely averting his eyes so that ours would not meet.

In the months that followed, I tried numerous times to patch things up with Mr. P, continually extending olive branches. We still had some contact, working on TV shows together, mingling at social events, and I would continue to housesit for him, but our interactions were purely perfunctory.

In fact, when the Rodney King/L.A. riots started, I was watching it all from a drop-down screen in the living room of Mr. P's Beverly Hills estate, as a friend and I were housesitting. Earlier that day, I had been at Paramount Studios working on some schlocky sitcom, when we got word that "rioting crowds from Compton might come your way." Of course, the very idea was ridiculous. That this swarm was burning everything in their path and were headed directly for Paramount Studios...?

Nevertheless, upon leaving the studio, I could see smoke due south, and, feeling fearful, immediately drove to the West Hollywood Pavilions on Santa Monica Blvd. before heading up into the hills. How many weeks might we be held up? How much food would we actually need? Was Mr. Peacock's prior trip to Whole Foods enough to sustain us? What would we need to get through this hellish nightmare?

The grocery store itself looked like a war zone. Endless rows of people, carts full, hoping to check out. I thought I spotted Connie Stevens amongst the bedraggled, wearing a disheveled wig, but I could've easily been mistaken. Everyone in line pretty much looked like they could've once been Connie Stevens or Troy Donahue.

Roaming the store's aisles, most shelves were empty. Why is it so hard to plan for the apocalypse? At the bread aisle, the only brand left on the shelf was King's Hawaiian. Really, people? A full-blown crisis, and you can't live without bread—save for King's Hawaiian? What beef could one possibly have against sweet bread?!?

That horrific night, back at Mr. Peacock's estate, a few friends and I watched on Mr. P's huge TV screen as L.A. burned, snacking on organic popcorn. The next morning, lying on chaise lounges aside Mr. Peacock's pool, helicopters circling above, we speculated as to the Barbarians who might soon be storming our enclave. As if the crowds of people miles away, closely filmed by the very helicopters hovering above, whose every move was announced to the entire metropolis via TV, might suddenly change course and swiftly barrel up our road—pitchforks high and guns loaded—breaking down Mr. Peacock's perfectly sculpted wrought iron electric gate and leaving us in a pile of rubble. As a group, we were both entirely stupid and entirely naïve. Death is never that certain, and rarely so quick.

My final falling out with Mr. P was due to his new object of affection. This new gent appeared suddenly, having been offered a free guest room in Mr. P's house, and I instantly recognized that he was there only to benefit from Mr. Peacock's generosity and bleed him dry. I tried to warn Mr. P as to his intentions, but Mr. P wouldn't listen. Realizing then that this wouldn't end well, I immediately began extracting myself from his inner circle.

I recall a final dinner party at Mr. Peacock's, where all conversations were centered exclusively on his new boy toy. I was in Mr. P's dining room, in his kitchen, in a home I'd somehow begun to think of as my own, and yet felt entirely alone, prompting me to leave. I hovered outside for a few moments, next to my car. I had become the old, rundown automobile rusting in the yard, while everyone else was focused on the new, red-hot Mustang. In the darkness, through the windows, I could see the party continuing on— without me. I so wanted someone within to feel my absence. I hoped that any one of them might come outside, shout my name, and beckon me to come back.

But that never happened.

Several years later, having yet again attempted to reignite our friendship, Eyes and I invited Mr. P to a party at our house, to which Mr. P came bearing three very impressive and expensive bottles of wine. Mr. Peacock clearly knew his wine, as evidenced by the wine cellar he'd built at his home, where each bottle bore a circular collar, noting its year and attributes. That knowledge gave Mr. P comfort, allowing him to talk about wine as confidently as he talked entertainment and politics.

At this particular party, Mr. P proceeded to head outside with his three bottles. He set them up next to the buffet and stationed himself there, talking to anyone who approached and offering him tastes of wine and commentary, as if he were a hired sommelier. None of these people knew that Mr. P had once headed television networks and been one of the most powerful people in entertainment. No one asked about him or his life, and he didn't volunteer. Instead, once all three bottles had been consumed, Mr. P quietly snuck out through our side gate without saying goodbye, and it would be years before I would see him again.

Fast forward 30 years, to a news article: Mr. Peacock had been charged with sexual molestation of a minor in a salacious lawsuit involving several Hollywood notables. At first, I was shocked. I couldn't envision Mr. Peacock doing any of the things alleged and the tales of drug and alcohol-fueled sex parties didn't seem like any event Mr. P would attend. He wasn't a brute, or conniving, or manipulative, or even all that sexual. He was more like an affectionate pup, looking for love.

Still, the question of guilt or innocence lingered. Mr. P did have a history of attraction to younger men, hopefully all of legal age. Still, when I think back, where one person might stash one's porn, Mr. Peacock tucked away old VHS tapes of young male wrestlers, in singlets, wrestling. There was no sex in the videos, just wrestling. Could this person I had once known so well, whose aims were almost childlike, have turned into the salacious manipulator of which he'd been accused, plying underage boys with pills and alcohol? It didn't feel right to me at all.

Mr. Peacock would later claim exoneration, as the young man proved a problematic witness. But for me, the questions lingered: were Mr. P and the other Hollywood A-Listers actually innocent? Or was their power so great and pockets so deep that they were able to change the expected narrative? To that, I have no knowledge.

The last time I saw Mr. Peacock in person was one summer in Laguna Beach, at the very-gay West Street Beach. He was fully dressed, wearing khaki shorts, a Polo shirt, and Topsiders, sitting in the sand, surrounded by sycophantic twinks, who seemed not to know who he was or why he was in their midst, ruining their meticulously coiffed aesthetic with his obvious middle-agedness.

In that moment, even before I approached him, I immediately realized that life for Mr. P would always be a disappointment. He wanted, quite simply, to be loved and valued. And he was willing to pay cash for it, to someone not remotely his peer.

Those of us who truly loved and cared about Mr. P would always be kept at arms' length, beyond the waves. Forever in sight, but just out of reach.

CASTING COUCH – EPISODE #1

I was thrilled when I learned I'd be auditioning for the head of casting at NBC. It wasn't for any part in particular, but more of an introductory meet-and-greet, at the end of which I'd do a monologue. Just pulling into the NBC lot in Burbank was a bit intoxicating, and walking alongside a well-known local news anchor into the building, with her "natural" streak of gray prominently featured in her beautifully styled hair, immediately put a smile on my face. "I've made it!" I thought. Oh, so young.

Ushered into the Casting wing, I passed framed photos of all of NBC's stars. As this was in the early 80s, big hair ruled the day for both the women and men.

I'll admit it. I was excited. And I more than matched the framed photos in terms of gorgeous hair. It was clear that NBC and I would be a perfect fit.

Meeting Mr. Casting was completely uneventful. He was nice, fairly attractive in a blond, nondescript, mid-Western kind of way, and seemed completely receptive to my canned chatter. And I nailed my monologue. Nailed it. After I was done, he told me how great I'd been and mentioned that I'd be perfect to play George Michael in a bio-pic, should there ever be one. Well, *Wake Me Up, Before You Go Film!*

As I said my thank-yous and goodbyes, in my head I was already picturing my future at NBC. Maybe I'd get a role on one of their daytime soaps, to start. With my looks and talent, there was no question I'd quickly become a fan favorite. And once that happened, it would only be a matter of time before I'd graduate to primetime. Maybe they'd even create a night-time soap just for me!

A week later, Mr. Casting called, inviting me to join him for a night at the Ringling Bros. Circus, as he'd been given comp tickets. (Since when do casting directors scope out the circus for acting talent?) I knew during the call that this was the put out or shut up moment. Nonetheless, I went, hoping to salvage my George Michael bio-pic or Dynasty-like soap.

On our "date," I tried to be friendly and open, but keep clear boundaries. On that, I wasn't entirely successful. When walking, his hand would brush mine, and I'd not-so-subtly steer dramatically off course, finding something fascinating to attract my attention. His knee rubbed mine at the show and I practically shoved myself against the opposite side of my seat. I knew from my experience with Mr. P that I wanted to be valued for who I was as a person, and it was clear that Mr. Casting just saw me as someone to fuck.

At the evening's end, he walked me to my apartment door. That night in the courtyard was dazzling, with rare starlight visible in the skies above, the bougainvillea in bloom draped over the archway, and the strings of café lights zigzagging across the walkway, all conspiring to create a night meant for romance. It was the La La Land version of *La La Land*, but long before film director Damian Chazelle was even born. He stole my romantic L.A. evening.

I can't remember what excuse I gave when Mr. Casting made his move, but it was likely something along the lines of: "I already have a boyfriend, but you're a really great guy! I'd love to be friends and, of course, still be considered for roles..."

Crickets chirped. Literally and figuratively.

Mr. Casting smiled, ever the professional, and wandered back out of the courtyard, toward his car. And I never heard from him again.

And that, folks, is showbiz.

LIFE LESSON #12

Being hired as a lowly assistant director for an L.A. Free Clinic AIDS education play, working under TV director Harry Winer and doing most of the work as he rarely showed up to rehearsals, is worth it, if only because you'll be able to meet his beautiful, bad-actress wife, *Charlie's Angels* star Shelly Hack.

NEVER MEET YOUR IDOLS: MISTAKE #1

The hit movie *Flashdance* debuted on the big screen my senior year of high school, and I was there in a United Artist Theater opening night to witness it. It was fucking amazing. I couldn't get over the music, the kick-ass dancing, and the entrancing performance of Jennifer Beals. At turns tender, tough, seductive and sweet, she centers the implausible film and makes you believe in her character and the film, though I'm still wondering how she learned to weld.

I fell in love, hence the choice of those two posters for my college dorm room years prior.

Cut ahead 10 years and I am a production assistant on a truly low budget flick called *Blood and Concrete: A Love Story.* (Yes, that was the title. Totally marketable, right?)

If you know anything about Hollywood, you are likely aware that production assistants are the bottom rung, lowest of the low—and I was happy to be one. I'd gotten the job through a referral from Mr. P. He had once been the boss of the reptilian man producing this sad movie, and I'd had to go to dinner with the grossly unattractive man just to land this poorly paying job. Still, it *was* a job, nonetheless, in the movie business, so dinner was easy enough to suffer through.

My first few days at work were spent before production started, helping out in the production office and meeting all of the key players. Director Jeffrey Reiner would go on to win a Golden Globe and Peabody award. Cinematographer Declan Quinn, brother of actor Aidan, went on to win three Independent Spirit awards for cinematography. Star Billy Zane would later anger countless female *Titanic* fans worldwide by famously coming between Kate and Leo. Needless to say, *Blood and Concrete* did not reflect any of these professionals' best work.

But I didn't care about the quality of the movie at all. I had a job! A job, in Hollywood, which didn't entail waiting on tables or blowing someone in order to get it.

As shooting approached, I began to get very excited. I would be on my first film, as a hired hand. I learned that my first official role would be to ferry star Billy Zane to and from the set each day. On bigger budget films, there is usually a professional driver who carts the stars around in a Lincoln Town Car, but in this piece of shit, I was to drive Billy to the set in my bright yellow 1968 Volkswagen bug, which—despite being bright yellow—was actually two different shades of bright yellow, due to various bad paint jobs.

On the big day, I pulled into the drive of a nondescript Hollywood bungalow and went to the door. Billy emerged, toupee glued firmly in place, and confidently introduced himself. Then, his eyes went to the driveway and my car.

"What—? You're driving me in *that*?"

I nodded, smiling, very certain that I didn't have another nicer car lurking about. "Yes, they said to bring you to the set."

He scowled, returned inside the bungalow to grab his backpack, then reluctantly stomped over to my car. It would be the only time I would ever drive him.

The minute we arrived on location, he ejected himself diva-style from my bug, vaulting directly over to one of the producers. "You expect me to ride in *that*?" he gestured to my car. "I need more car around me! I can't ride in that little thing!"

The producer tried to reason with him, but it was not to be. He was the star of this shitty movie, and so they made him happy and gave the "privilege" of driving him to some other poor production assistant. But I was okay, as the producer quickly made his way over to me... "Don't worry about Billy. He's an ass. Jennifer starts next week. You can drive her."

And so it was that I would come face-to-face with my once-crush, Jennifer Beals.

On her first day of shooting, I picked up Miss Beals at the Chateau Marmont and was grateful she didn't complain about my car. But then again, she really didn't have much to say at all. I had spent hours rehearsing how I'd tell her how much I loved her work, about the posters in my dorm room, and how underrated I thought she was. I was sure that, upon hearing my declaration of support, we'd become fast friends.

But after our brief but cordial introduction, she settled into the passenger seat and closed her eyes, which remained shut until we reached the set.

We went on this way for weeks. As we were shooting six days out of every seven, I had ample opportunities to chat her up, which I repeatedly attempted. I asked questions about her day, about the movie, about her day off, and would receive sentences of one, two or three words in return. Clearly, she didn't have time for the help.

On one of our last production days, we were to shoot in Lancaster, an hour north of Los Angeles. As my car radio wasn't working, Jennifer climbed in the tiny back seat and closed her eyes. I focused on the road, but quickly realized that the transportation team had not given proper directions to the location. As this was before the days of cell phones, and given that we were in the middle of nowhere, there was no place to make a call from, and no place to call either, as the entire production crew was en route to the set.

Luckily, as I had been to Lancaster before, I was somewhat familiar with the area and, after much time driving around with comatose Jennifer, finally found the location. We arrived only a few minutes late, while others similarly lost would be pulling up for the next several hours.

Rousing herself from the car, Jennifer sleepily smiled at a producer standing nearby.

"Have trouble finding us?" he queried.

"Oh, no—Kergan knew exactly where he was going," she nodded at me, and I nodded back. It was better than the truth, and for once I was glad for her sleeping.

There were two other notable driving-related stories on this fun-filled flick. One day I had to drive Darren McGavin, the dad in the classic movie *A Christmas Story* and TV's *The Night Stalker*, home. Upon seeing my car, he also glared and refused to talk to me. Maybe it's just that celebrities have an aversion to Volkswagen...?

And on another day, I had to pick up comedian Harry Shearer, then famous for *Saturday Night Live* and TV's *The*

Simpsons, who was shooting a single scene. I was given his address near Venice beach but, upon arriving, I was faced with a row of what appeared to be duplexes or apartment buildings. Walking to the front door, I knocked, but no one answered. I knocked again and got no response. I tried peering inside, as the front door had panes of glass with a sheer curtain, but couldn't quite make out what lie within. After knocking a third time, and still receiving no answer, it occurred to me that maybe this really was a duplex or apartment building, with a central hallway or staircase. It was then that I decided to go in and find Mr. Shearer's apartment. Opening the door and stepping inside, however, I was shocked to find myself standing face-to-face with the comedy legend. Let's just say that he did not take kindly to me walking unwelcome into his living room.

After the film had finished shooting, Mr. Peacock accompanied me to the wrap party, which none of the talent attended. There, I learned that the reptilian producer who had hired me had told everyone to be nice to me, because I was his "boy." I took that opportunity to drag Mr. Peacock, who had once been the lizard producer's boss, over to confront said lizard, giving him the full Julia Sugarbaker, "rip-him-a-new-asshole" take-down that he more than deserved.

Later that night, a producer asked me how my experience had been, squiring Jennifer Beals to the set. I explained that while she wasn't mean to me, she wasn't really nice, either. As a person, she was totally lukewarm, milque toast. I didn't really care that she didn't want to be my best friend, but I was surprised that she couldn't even attempt to carry on a conversation with me, simply out of courtesy, if nothing else.

The producer eyed me knowingly. "I spent quite a bit of time with her myself, and, you know, I don't think there's any *there* there."

CASTING COUCH – EPISODE #2

The agent's building was on world-famous Sunset Blvd. I had no money for the valet and thus parked several blocks away, given the area's street parking restrictions. As I made the trek to his office, forever the optimist, I was sure I'd be returning to my car a winner. After all, this was the agent of renowned child star Ebony Scrooge, whose TV sitcom catchphrase "a little dab'll do ya!" had taken the nation by storm. And the agent wanted to see me.

I still remember my shirt. I was wearing a bright blue polo shirt, which I was sure made me stand out.

As I waited in the reception area, I noticed the pretty girl seated across from me. She couldn't have been more than 16, with soft features and long, dirty blonde hair, which kept falling into her face. I smiled. She smiled back as I was called into the agent's office.

I don't remember my introduction to him, but soon after we went over the requisite pleasantries, he buzzed the receptionist, asking her to bring the girl waiting in. I was puzzled, as he hadn't asked me to do my well-rehearsed monologue or even chat about my resume.

As she entered, he introduced her to me and it was clear they'd met before. He told us that he wanted us to do some improvisation and that he would coach us through it.

It started out benignly, with us playing a young couple

having an argument over something stupid, but soon he had us make up, and in that making up he asked us to kiss. We did, and he didn't ask us to stop. Now, being gay and wanting our make-out session to end, I kept waiting for his next instruction to move the scene forward. He gave it. "Play with her top."

Um, excuse me? Like, tease it with my fingers? Twirl it around? What does "Play with her top" even mean?

But I tried. I really did. Because he was a big-time agent, with a kid on a hot TV show, and I was in his office and thought he'd make me a star.

"Now," he encouraged her, his voice a bit deeper than before, "unbutton his pants."

She pulled back a bit, startled and confused, as if she hadn't heard him correctly. But she bit her lip slightly, looked in my eyes, and it was clear that she had. She was just like me. She saw stardom in her future as she reached slowly downward, her hand grazing the fabric of my bright blue shirt.

She unbuttoned the top button of my jeans and again, I waited for him to stop her. As she kept going, I gulped then grabbed her hand, stopping her. I tried to smile, as if nothing had happened, before I turned to face him. "Thank you, Mr. Show Biz, but I think I've had enough." He grinned, as if this were an ordinary audition, "You were great! Thanks for coming in."

As I gathered my things, the girl stood there, not moving. I nodded goodbye. As I exited, his office door closed behind me, with he and the girl remaining alone inside. The receptionist eyed me, reading my flushed face, and I knew that she knew. She knew and she sat there, greeting aspiring actors and actresses coming in and out each day, fully aware of what they would experience once inside.

It was all I could do to make it to the elevator. Staring as the numbers flashed, counting each floor and urging it to quickly descend, I only remembered to breathe once the elevator hit the ground floor.

On the walk back to my car, all thoughts of stardom were miles away. I was an entirely different person than I'd been just a half hour prior. I felt dirty. I had done nothing wrong, had tried to make a graceful exit, and yet I still—even knowing what he'd done was awful—felt like a failure. Had that been my chance? Had I blown any hope of having an acting career? And had Ebony Scrooge, who was older than he looked, been asked to do dirty things too?

The thought of turning the agent into the police never crossed my mind, and I don't recall ever telling anyone what happened to me that day. In my mind, I somehow felt complicit, ashamed.

Years later, long after Ebony's fame had flamed out, I read in the newspaper that the agent had died. I wondered what had become of his receptionist and the young girl. Did that moment scar them, as it had me? Did they too feel dirty? Or were they remorseless, simply focused on survival or a quest for stardom? Either way, I knew how I felt. I was glad he was dead. I didn't know what his kink was, or if he got his jollies from me or the girl, or if anyone ever reported him, and I don't really care. I was simply glad he could never hurt anyone again.

LIFE LESSON #13

If you are ever lucky enough to capture lightning in a bottle, don't attempt to repeat it. Lightning can't be captured twice.

THE FLAME AND THE FURY

Tired of the mindless TV and film work I was doing, and frustrated by the rate at which I was climbing—or sliding down—the Hollywood ladder, I made the decision to take the cash scholarship award I'd received in my senior year at UCLA and invest it in myself. Or, rather, invest it in a local theatrical production, which I was certain would gain attention, thus launching me on a trajectory high into the entertainment stratosphere.

I contacted my old flame, Michael Sargent, suggesting that we take our two hit plays from UCLA, *Rat Songs* and *When Esther Saw the Light,* and produce them in a local Hollywood theater under the umbrella title of *Fury!* Since both had received superlative accolades in college, I was certain that they would also succeed in real life. I was wrong.

To get these off the ground, I borrowed money from Mr. Peacock and a writer-producer friend, Mike DiGaetano, and, adding in my scholarship, promptly invested in a sinking ship. (It would take me years to pay them back.) We cast several of our UCLA acting friends in the show (Pamela Silverman—always deadpan brilliant, Cathi Skillman— always hysterically brilliant), as well as hiring an array of professional actors. (I'll never forget calling in Roz Kelly to audition, simply because she'd once played Pinky Tuscadero on *Happy Days.*) Eric Close, a friendly and handsome guy, was cast in one of the leading roles. He would go on to star for several years in the CBS series *Without a Trace*, but will always be remembered by me as the guy who showed me a photo that his brother had taken, of Eric sitting on a toilet, showing the camera his used toilet paper, full of shit.

We used essentially the same production crew as in school, the same blocking, similar performance style—but the plays never worked. In college, almost every line was met with laughter. But in real life, lines that would've once been met with gales of laughter fell entirely flat, despite similar performances by the actors.

At some point during our run, struggling to pay bills and dealing with bad reviews, it hit me: in college, these adult characters were played by young actors, making the plays a commentary on real life. In this production, with actors roughly the same age as the characters, a level of ennui mixed with despondence was added that I hadn't anticipated or experienced. In college, we poked fun at the characters. As adults, we were forced to look at ourselves, and what we saw wasn't nearly as entertaining.

"NBC'S 'BEST' NOT TOO GOOD"

That was one of the kinder review headlines to greet a TV show I worked on, *Sunday Best*, in 1991. Though our friendship still had not resumed to the degree I'd have liked, Mr. Peacock had kindly hired me for this gig, and I was excited to be working on the NBC lot, where *The Tonight Show* with Johnny Carson was filmed. If you don't recall *Sunday Best*, it is likely because it was the first show in TV history to receive a negative Nielsen viewer rating. We premiered on Sunday opposite CBS' *60 Minutes*, during the Gulf War. Now, what would you rather watch? Interviews with key movers and shakers of Operation Desert Storm, or past-his-prime TV legend Carl Reiner?

The idea for the show was flawed from the beginning. It was to be a roundup of the best television that had aired the previous week. Kind of like the Cliff Notes version of TV. In that pre-YouTube era, host Reiner would highlight funny or profound moments that viewers might have missed, which kind of made sense—until you factored in that aside from NBC, no other networks would provide clips of their shows, for competitive reasons. And not only did other networks refuse to provide content, but NBC's own most prominent talk show hosts, Johnny Carson and David Letterman, also chose not to participate, robbing the show of sharing their best jokes from the week. Thus, even before airing, the show morphed into kind of a review of past iconic television moments, and current made-for-the-show content, which resulted in one of the most hodgepodge series to ever hit the air.

The brilliant and satiric Bruce Handy, of *Spy* magazine fame, was one of the producers. I believe the idea to promote Jane Pauley's new weekly show, *Real Life*, by dressing each member of a dance troop as identical Jane Pauley's, complete with matching JP wigs and outfits, for a musical number, was his idea. Serious TV journalist Linda Ellerbee was somehow convinced to jump aboard this bullet train to hell and present funny moments from the news. *(Um, were there a lot of funny moments from the news each week?)* David Letterman's former head writer Merrill Markoe was an on-air talent, producing quirky comedy bits. My former lover/drivee/restraining-order-giver, Harry Shearer, also was on the show, though happily he didn't remember me from *Blood and Concrete*. And Bossy Blonde was a producer as well, because a TV series as bright and uplifting as this one needed a serious, unfunny lesbian running the show.

Still, given all this, I had a ball, working and laughing alongside the various segment producers and fellow production crew. I was sad to learn of its untimely passing, as not only was I immediately jobless, but more notably, the comradery that we'd quickly established was snuffed out as quickly as it had been established. The show lasted on air for a whopping three episodes before being canceled, relegated to the trash heap of TV history; a perfectly fitting ending for a show entirely made of recycled footage and ideas.

A little while later, Mr. Peacock asked me to work on

another show with him, a new talk show starring a woman who was then the editor of a popular teen magazine. *"Who will watch this shit?"* I wondered. His ask meant me moving from West Hollywood to New York, which—at that time—I wasn't willing to do. A mutual friend, however, decided to take that production assistant job, and went on to not only quickly become a producer on the series, which switched hosts to a hot young actress, but eventually even landed a talk show bearing his own name as the result. At the time, I was admittedly jealous of his fame and import. *"That could've been me!"* I would scream into my pillow. But today, looking through the lens of growth and wisdom I've gained in the ensuing years, I wouldn't change a thing. As I have gradually come to accept, that "right place, right time" shit is actually true.

SONDHEIM, ETC.

Soon after dating Mr. P, I met Mr. C, as in *Chicago*. Short, smarmy, squinty-eyed, and always schmoozing, Mr. Chicago was Mr. Peacock on steroids. I'd first become aware of Mr. Chicago through his biography on the phenomenal Stephen Sondheim, my theater idol, which immediately placed Mr. Chicago on a higher level than most in my heart. I mean, if a person can write such a perceptive tome on Sondheim, he's got to be a great guy, right?

Sadly, Mr. Chicago and I didn't last long as a couple, because I never once trusted him. Soon after our connection, I mentioned that Bernadette Peters, whom I absolutely adored, was giving a solo concert performance in Orange County. Mr. Chicago immediately bought four tickets, to which we'd bring his close friends.

Imagine my shock, after Bernadette's amazing performance, to find ourselves ushered backstage and into her dressing room. That shock quickly turned into something else...

"Oh my gosh, Bernadette—you were wonderful!" Mr. Chicago gushed. He was a *big* gusher.

"Oh, C, how you exaggerate!" Bernadette laughed, as if that were not completely true.

"You remember Dean, don't you?" Mr. Chicago continued, gesturing to Academy Award-winning songwriter Dean Pitchford, standing to my right.

"Of course! Oh my god, Dean, I recorded your song, 'I Never Thought I'd Break,' on my first album." Their joint squeal was long and powerful.

Mr. Chicago ignored it, continuing on. "You might also know Richard Kramer?" he offered, gesturing to another man at my right. "Richard produced *Thirtysomething*, and wrote that recent amazing episode, where the two guys kissed in bed?"

Bernadette offered him a hug. "Of course, Richard! Such a ground-breaking moment."

"And this," Mr. Chicago said, all eyes turning to me, "is Kergan."

My moment as the focus of their attention was painfully long and silent. They were staring at me, a lowly production assistant, with no follow-up from Mr. Chicago about any positive attributes I might have. Everyone just stared.

The resigned sigh, as those present went back to the important people in the room, may have been real or imagined. But that moment was the beginning of the end for me and Mr. Chicago. Once again, it seemed that I was nothing more than bought and paid-for, though no money had changed hands.

One night, having decided to break things off, I met Mr. C at an upscale L.A. hamburger restaurant. I had with me a few books he'd lent, as well as a screenplay on which he had asked for feedback. As his eyes landed on the assembled items, I could tell that he knew this was *the moment*. That I was actually breaking up with him. But that didn't stop him from one last feeble attempt.

"Steve's coming into town in a few weeks," he offered.

"Steve...?"

"Sondheim," he smiled. "I thought that maybe you and I could host a dinner party. Maybe invite Bernadette, Barbra, Madonna—?"

I couldn't believe that he was resorting to such a cheap ploy, offering me the dinner party of my dreams.

Me, the queen of Hollywood? Me, mingling with first-namers? If I chose to stay with him for that single opportunity, what would that that say about him, and what would that say about me? Others may have looked at me as a whore, but that isn't how I saw myself.

I smiled, then got up from the table, slid the screenplay and books toward him, and bid him farewell. Self-respect matters.

Some months after we had broken up, I ran into him and his latest boyfriend at a Chinese restaurant. "Kergan is going to do great things," Mr. Chicago solemnly stated to his beau. "He is going to own this town."

I didn't believe him then, as Mr. C could pile it on, but his words actually meant something at the time. That someone who "is worthy" verbalizes that you too are worthy as well can motivate you to climb mountains you never even knew existed.

It would be years before we saw each other one final time. Mr. Chicago and his producing partner were being honored at a Century City hotel for their many years of achievement in film and television. My now-hubby Russ and I had gone to the event with some friends, dressed up to the nines, but I never imagined that Mr. Chicago and I would actually cross paths at said event, given the many hundreds in attendance.

Still, as Russ and I stepped out from an elevator, we ran smack into Mr. Chicago and his producing partner. Awkwardly, introductions and schmooziness ensued, prompting knots in my stomach. *"I am not this Hollywood person anymore. This is not me!"* I wanted to cry, yet kept my lips sealed shut. Happily, Mr. C and his partner were quickly ushered off toward the dais, and Russ and I made our way toward our table.

Dinner and awards were given, gushy platitudes were tossed out by Mr. C to the audience, left and right, and sitting there, amongst the tossed shit, it was clear to me that I'd made the right choice.

Mr. Chicago created a lasting impression nationwide by singularly reviving the stage musical as an art form. It is because of him that we have the recent TV interpretations of *The Wiz*, *The Sound of Music*, and so many more. Varying quality of said productions aside, I hope we can all agree that more music in our lives is a positive thing. For that alone, thank you, Mr. C.

CASTING COUCH – EPISODE #3

In the world of Hollywood agents, Mr. Pansy was among the top, the crème de la crème. He represented Alec Baldwin, then a young actor on *Knot's Landing*, who would go on to greater acclaim impersonating America's most hated President on late-night TV. Mr. Pansy ensured Baldwin's future triumphs by preaching to him the importance of training, specifically staying active in live theater, as the key to success in the craft. Mr. Pansy was known as the actor's agent, and it was my goal to make him mine as well.

Ironically, his office building was located on Sunset Blvd. directly opposite that of Ebony Scrooge's agent, which should have been a clue. But no clues came as I parked and entered the lobby. I was a starving actor, willing to do almost anything to get my foot in the door. Mr. Pansy was the head of a small prestige agency bearing his storied name. Even just announcing to the receptionist that I was there to see him made me feel important.

Sitting in the lobby, I ran the lines of my monologue, the character of Ronnie in *The House of Blue Leaves*, which Ben Stiller had played so well in the 1987 Broadway revival. I'd been rehearsing daily, coached by my upstairs neighbor, a fellow actor, who kept insisting, "No, no, no—You're *indicating*, not acting!" I never did understand what he meant.

Finally, a woman appeared, ushering me down the elegant hallway and into the impressively large office of Mr. Pansy. Dark wood paneling and strategic lighting helped create a refined, mannered room, at the end of which was an ornate desk, behind which sat Mr. Pansy.

"Do come in," he implored, noticing my reticence.

I inhaled, putting on my best smile, and crossed. He rose, shaking my hand, and gestured to a chair, on which I sat.

We exchanged pleasantries, both of us doing our best to schmooze and entertain each other. The entire time, a sly smile never left his lips. Finally, it was time for my monologue.

I rose, walked to the center of the room, then turned again to face him. I began. Never before, in the history of Hollywood, has there ever been a more impassioned display of Herculean acting. I hit every note, blowing through the speech with drive and determination, acting the hell out of it, Neighbor—*not* indicating!

When I'd finished, I breathed deeply, so happy to have nailed it, yet not willing to show my satisfaction. Mr. Pansy just looked at me, his elbows resting on the desk and fingers intertwined. "Take off your shirt," he said. It wasn't a question. It wasn't a comment on my performance. It was *"take off your shirt."*

I didn't move. I thought back to Ebony Scrooge's agent, and to the humiliation and disgust I felt at myself. I tried to figure a way out, to save myself and this audition, but ideas were fleeting.

"Take off my shirt?" I repeated, stalling.

"Yes."

This was it. This was my moment. Did I really want to go down this road? I knew if I acquiesced, he'd then ask for my pants. How badly did I want to be an actor? How much was I worth?

"Look, Mr. Pansy," I started. "I appreciate your time. I really do. But—I don't really feel comfortable taking my shirt off. I mean, if you were a casting director and you were hiring someone for a beach scene, and you wanted to see what I looked like, fine. I get it. But this doesn't feel right to me." I kept his eye, and he kept mine, his fingers still intertwined, posed at his chin.

"Great. I was hoping you'd say that," he offered, with a warm smile. "I like to know what the actors I represent will do when confronted with—uh, certain situations."

I nodded, wondering if his famous client had been asked to take his shirt off, and whether or not he'd consented. Just how eager was Baldwin to "make it?" Eager enough to let Mr. Pansy suck his cock?

I don't recall much else, except—once again—walking back to my car in total disgust and in need of a shower. The casting couch walk of shame is one veil that clings to me still. Actors are vulnerable. We are emotional people, yearning for attention, vying and jockeying for the spotlight, hoping to gain the slightest of toeholds in the toughest and most unsympathetic of industries. Such people are ripe for the picking. Happily, my cherry wasn't plucked by those vultures. They may have tried, but at the end of the day, I can hold my head and butt high.

GARY KALKIN

As a young actor, trying to make it in Hollywood, I had the great fortune to become acquainted with producer Laurence Mark and his one-time romantic partner Gary Kalkin. They'd been together for years. At the point I met them, however, they had split yet remained the closest of friends. They still shared a beautiful home where I enjoyed some memorable dinner parties.

Larry is famous for his involvement with such iconic films as *Terms of Endearment, Broadcast News, Dreamgirls, As Good as It Gets*, and *Jerry Maguire*, to name but a few. My favorite story of Larry was when I phoned and inquired how his day had been. "Oh, you know—just hanging out in Malibu with Shirley MacClaine, being photographed for the *Day in the Life of Hollywood* book, eating bananas on the beach, because that's all I do each day."

Gary was the senior vice president of domestic marketing for Buena Vista Pictures (Disney.) As such, he oversaw the creation of the marketing campaigns for *Aladdin, Down and Out in Beverly Hills, Good Morning, Vietnam, Who Framed Roger Rabbit, Pretty Woman* and *The Lion King*. I'm not sure why Gary took such a liking to me, but it was nice, after all of the Casting Couch Slouches, to have another gay man want nothing from me, aside from friendship. He soon put me on the studio's sneak preview list, inviting me to screenings of every Disney movie released during his tenure.

As a starving actor, it was a wonderful gift to receive. I can still vividly recall the magical movie premiere for the animated *Beauty and the Beast*, at the newly restored El Capitan Theater in Hollywood, preceded by an elaborate stage show.

One of the best nights of my life—*ever*—happened in February 1993 and also involved Gary. Having been a fan of Stephen Sondheim for as long as I can remember, when I heard they were doing a one-night-only, 20th anniversary original cast reunion performance of *Company* at the Long Beach Terrace Theater, I immediately bought two tickets. My good friend at the time, Cheryl Dolins, was also a Sondheim fan, and we couldn't wait to go.

Gary called shortly after we'd bought tickets and invited me to Disney's Golden Globes after-party, scheduled for that very same night; I was crushed at the conflict. I told him about our prior engagement, and he said to stop by afterward, if we could, and at least say hello.

Cheryl and I loved the performance of *Company*, particularly the astonishing performance by Dean Jones, who had quit the original cast early on, given the play's relationship themes hit home as his own marriage was crumbling. He was truly remarkable, revisiting the role all these years later. Completely exhilarated from this once-in-a-lifetime theatrical experience, Cheryl and I rushed back to L.A., hoping to make it to the Golden Globes after-party. Walking up the red carpet at the Beverly Hilton, there were a few photographers straggling about, trying to figure out if we were "someone" and, to us, we felt as if we were.

When we got to the check-in desk, the woman helping apologized, saying the party was just about over, but if we wanted to go in for a quick drink, we could. Dejected to have gotten there so late, we still went in to look for Gary. Entering, we found that there were only about 12 people in the huge ballroom. But aside from Gary, those people included Anthony Hopkins, Emma Thompson, Al Pacino, and Rodney Dangerfield. Cheryl and I were completely beside ourselves, hovering with the others around the few platters of food left, acting as if hanging out with this particular crowd was an everyday occurrence.

Two years later, Gary was gone, another talented and caring soul lost to AIDS. He'll never know just what an impact his simple generosity had. He was directly responsible for some of my best "life moments." In a town not known for kind acts, Gary's sweet gift of access to film to this young actor provided me with endless opportunities to soak up the movie business, for which I'm eternally grateful. I missed him then, and I miss him now. RIP, handsome Gary.

IT IS PARAMOUNT

One of my most menial jobs in entertainment was on a cable show called *Wild & Crazy Kids,* hosted by, among other teens, Omar Gooding (younger brother of Oscar-winning and alleged serial-groper Cuba Gooding, Jr.), during which the overly-enthusiastic young hosts would encourage competing troops of children to execute all manner of physically-challenging tournaments—none first tested by professionals. We would basically show up on location—a park with a steep hill, for example—set up a stunt, and pray that the Gods would be willing. To my knowledge, there were never any fatalities.

Given my illustrious entertainment career thus far, I was thrilled when Mike DiGaetano, who'd unwisely invested in *Fury!,* asked me to work on a new sitcom that he and his writing partner were developing for Paramount. The famous Charles brothers, Glen and Les, had signed on as producers for a show entitled *Flesh 'N Blood.* Known initially from their work on *The Mary Tyler Moore Show, The Bob Newhart Show,* and *Taxi,* they then connected with renowned sitcom director James Burrows and created *Cheers.* With this television pedigree, I was convinced that there was no way this comedy gem could fail.

The premise of this show, unlike *Sunday Best,* had promise, if lovingly borrowed from *The Beverly Hillbillies*: a

District Attorney adopted at birth, Rachel (played by Lisa Darr), searches for her birth family, only to discover that her brother, Arlo, is a total redneck. Laughter ensues when Arlo brings his hillbilly children, King and Beauty, to live with Rachel in the big city.

Someone must've been under the mistaken impression that David Keith, so wonderful in his dramatic role in *An Officer and a Gentleman*, would be equally adept at comedy, as he was cast as the star of our show. I can assure you that while a good actor, comedy is not his strong suit. I'll always remember one taping day, with audience arriving, David running up to me and telling me to drive across town to the Chateau Marmont, through Friday rush-hour traffic, to pick up his contact lens, which he'd mistakenly left in his hotel room... Fun. No pressure at all.

The show was mildly funny, if mainly for the dry delivery of Peri Gilpin, who played a receptionist. She was so sweet to me, and I loved hanging out with her after taping days at a local restaurant with the cast and crew. I knew her boyfriend was gay before she did, from the way his eyes followed me around as I worked onset. For several years after, Peri and I would exchange Christmas cards, until she was cast on *Frazier* as producer Roz and the cards stopped.

Flesh 'N Blood didn't last on-air a full season, but the comedy powers that be still felt that David Keith was destined for comedy greatness, and the same producing team of Charles-Burrows-Charles came up with a new show to star him, *Buck and Barry*, also known as *Local Heroes*, also known as *Glory Boys*, also known as a sitcom so good, it filmed several episodes but never made it to air. The premise was basically borrowed from *Taxi*, which made sense, given that *Taxi* producer Ken Estin was brought in to create the show, but rather than setting it in a taxi cab garage, this version was set in a gas station garage, so it was *totally* different. Bill Nunn of *Sister Act* fame and David Keith played former high school football buddies who ran a gas station together, complete with convenience store, manned by Peri Gilpin, wise-cracking as always.

Daniel Davis portrayed the funniest character on the show, basically giving his inspired take on *Taxi*'s oddball mechanic, Reverend Jim, and I was happy to see him go on to later find fame as *The Nanny's* butler, Niles. He was always kind to me, which didn't jibe later when I heard scandalous reports of his firing from Broadway's *La Cage Aux Folles* for bad behavior.

David Keith never did go on to become a comedy giant, though he's continued acting ever since. *Flesh 'N Blood* would be the last TV show or movie I'd ever directly work on. After years of banging my head against the wall, and tired of the craziness of the entertainment industry, I finally decided to make a change. That decision fully transformed who I'd then been to who I am today.

LIFE LESSON #14

Should you decide to write a coming out letter to everyone you have ever known, having copied your parents' Christmas card mailing list, please know that it might not go as well as planned.

I'M COMING OUT: PART 2

It had been a long time coming. When I first came out to my parents, they had made a request, which to that point I'd honored: I was to not tell their friends or our extended family that I was gay. My parents were embarrassed and ashamed to have a gay son, as to them it demonstrated just how fully they had failed as parents, and they wanted to keep that "Parents of the Year" trophy on the mantle. (I'm sure my sister and I never actually voted for that.)

But after years of obedience, I'd finally had *enough*. Enough of my parents, enough of not being able to freely present myself in their community, and enough of working on shitty TV shows and low-budget movies. I'd begun to sense that the work I was doing was not only beneath me, but downright awful. More importantly, I had come to realize that people were dying—my own people were dying—and I needed to do something meaningful.

Through the guidance of my therapist, I'd been on a path, a journey, realizing that my self-centeredness, which I'd once seen as confidence, was actually a crutch, designed solely by me to hold others at bay. I began to see that I held others at arm's length through my biting wit and cruel, purposeful sarcasm, in order that they might not get too close to me, as they would quickly discover just how fully flawed I am. I had held that shield for years, and putting it down required that I start connecting fully and authentically with others.

Prior to leaving the TV and film production world, I got up the guts to begin volunteering at AIDS Project Los Angeles (APLA), which at that time was in its original location. But the disease was moving so quickly, they would soon move twice before landing at the colossal old ABC studios on Vine. My time there was initially focused on the Speaker's Bureau, traveling to schools and organizations to share the facts about HIV and safer sex. I spoke to elementary schoolers, fraternities, the Louisiana State Department of Health, and anyone else who would listen. I manned informational tables, answering questions and giving information to those brave enough to stop at our table, emblazoned with the word "AIDS" on it.

It was during this period when I decided to come out more publicly by writing a mass letter, combining my acknowledgement with a plea for donations for the Los Angeles AIDS Walk. I purposely wrote the missive so that it would be unclear to the reader if I was coming out as gay or if I were HIV-positive as well. I wanted people to grapple with that tension, so that the personal connection we'd had in the past might help influence the size of their donations in the present. That I was HIV-negative, I kept to myself, and let the donations roll in, raising several thousand dollars for the cause.

To put it mildly, Dottie and Fred were not pleased. They were angry and felt betrayed, and I could see their point. However, I felt that my honesty, and the resulting donations, would make an actual difference, both in my life and the lives of others. They, however, would take vengeful retribution later.

I would continue as a volunteer for two years, until I finally took a full-time position at AIDS Project Los Angeles, leaving the world of entertainment behind, at least for a while.

THE EXPERIENCE

The first time I laid eyes on Eyes was at The Experience, a gay and lesbian empowerment weekend, originally run by The Advocate Magazine. Encouraged to attend by my therapist, I was fully open to embracing the weekend, hoping to make new friends, connections, and tapping into my soul, which was so desperately in need of intimacy.

Held at Beverly Garland's Holiday Inn near Universal Studios, there were approximately 100 people in attendance. The weekend's two leaders were a woman who'd largely devoted her life to The Experience and a man who'd written for *Star Trek*. After an overview of the weekend's goals, we broke into a series of smaller group exercises and at some point, I found myself face-to-face with Eyes. With chiseled frame and sparkling eyes, he was an astounding presence, and I couldn't believe that he seemed to only have eyes for me.

We went to lunch together and I felt an immediate connection. He was open, honest, warm, and inquisitive, and I was so grateful to finally have a multi-layered, authentic connection with someone. Eyes shared that he was recently out of a long-term relationship and I shared that as I had recently begun dating someone, I needed to see that commitment through and hoped Eyes would be respectful of that choice. Throughout the rest of the weekend, we continued to have *moments* together, and it was all I could do to focus on the workshop itself, so taken was I with Eyes and our attraction.

In the last exercise of The Experience weekend, we participants were to write a letter to our parents, living or dead, expressing who we were and how we felt about them. We were instructed to be as honest as possible, and I took that objective to heart, despite feeling manipulated by the sentimental theme from *Out of Africa* playing in the background as we scribbled. I wrote of my sadness and frustration, having been made to feel ashamed by my mom's attempts to change me. I was filled with anger and resentment, and my many years of emotional stress effortlessly flowed through me to pen and paper.

After everyone was done writing, we again gathered in small groups and were told to read our letters out loud— which had not been explained upfront, or else I might have written an altogether different letter. Going around the circle, as each relayed their writings, it became clear that everyone in our small group had an entirely different experience with family than I'd had. Their notes were full of love and gratitude, thanking their parents for their endless support. *Who the fuck are these people?*, I wondered. When my turn came, I didn't want to read, but had no choice. And so, I began. My face became flushed and tears sprung to my eyes as I recited the litany of misdeeds and hurts lobbed my way by my mom, in particular, and by my dad, for simply standing by his wife. I am not sure that any of those gathered quite knew what to do but nod and murmur, "There, there..."

As The Experience concluded, the room was suddenly flooded with supportive friends, lovers, and fellow Experience graduates, enveloping those assembled in hugs. I saw a tall man approach Eyes, pulling him into a close embrace, and the look in the tall man's eyes told me that while that may have been the "ex," their story wasn't over. I know love when I see it.

Eyes called me a few weeks later and invited me to dinner in Orange County. "We're just friends," I told myself. "You're dating Martin. Eyes is a good guy. Give him a chance."

As I walked into the El Torito Grill, I spotted Eyes and immediately lit up. Over dinner, I inquired about his ex, he affirmed that they were indeed broken up, and I believed him. I had no reason not to... Eyes seemed so moral and ethical, and his attention on me so focused, I felt that I must have thoroughly misinterpreted the stolen moment I'd witnessed at the Experience, and pushed any thought of potential disingenuousness from my mind. That decision I'd later regret.

LOVE ME KNOT

In the months following The Experience, I continued to run into Eyes, most often with his "ex," and his greetings were always warm and sincere. Still, we eventually drifted apart. I continued to practice my serial monogamy, drifting from one short-lived relationship to another, hitting the bars with my best friend, always feeling like if I didn't go out that particular night, it would be the one and only night that Mr. Right would show up. The fear that I might actually miss him sent me scurrying out almost every night of the week.

Throughout the years I auditioned many nice guys for the role of Mr. Right, but none ever quite fit. Tom Day, however, seemed like he might work out nicely. He was medium build, great legs, with blonde thinning hair which receded in the corners of his hairline, creating a severe widow's peak, which he tried to disguise by tousling his hair so that the hair still on his head looked eternally windswept. Tom was an academic, which normally would have bored me, except his field was Film & Television, which provided us with ample opportunities to attend free screenings and hob nob with Hollywood elite, semi-elite, and losers. Tom was witty, smart, politically-savvy and a lot of fun to be with. But he also thought Sharon Stone, who had just appeared in *Basic Instinct*, was the best actress he'd ever seen.

We'd been together for six months, and as we approached Valentine's Day, I hemmed and hawed over what to get him. Flowers didn't seem right, and neither did chocolates. Finally, it hit me: I'd spice up our love life.

That had been the one area in which Tom, while not exactly deficient, needed help. He was incredibly controlling in bed. As in, he would take my hands by the wrist and put them where he wanted them. He would instruct me in all aspects of what, when and how. There was no room for spontaneity or deviation. It was Tom's way or no way.

But this desire to control provoked a thought: what if he couldn't coach me? What if he were forced to give *me* control?

Yes, long before *50 Shades of Grey* became a national sensation, yours truly brought in the kink.

We'd dined that night at Palermo's, a kitschy Italian restaurant on Vermont. It's the kind of place with murals on the wall, the scent of garlic permeating the air, where they serve complimentary box wine while you wait for your table. It's nothing fancy, which is part of its appeal.

Following our meal, feeling satiated, full of food and wine, we drove back to his apartment in West Hollywood. There, I told Tom I had a surprise and needed to get ready. In his bedroom, I hauled out my bag and began to set up. Candles, check. Incense, check. Dildo, check. Leather ties tucked under the bed, check.

Ready, I ushered him in and told him not to speak. He nodded, expectantly and eagerly, taking in all that surrounded him. I explained what I was going to do. Why I was going to do it. And the pleasure he'd receive at my bidding. Again, he nodded. He was clearly aroused.

I moved in, kissing him. Every time he'd reach for me, I

pushed his hands away, continuing to kiss him, moving down his clothed body, my hands, mouth and tongue everywhere, making sure the foreplay was hot as hell, keeping him on edge. Slowly, I rose and began taking his clothes off, my mouth and hands in active motion. Finally, he was naked and I stood, taking my clothes off as well.

"Lay down," I ordered, and he did. Again, I went to town, keeping him on the brink. And every time he tried to give direction, I pushed his hands away. "Just go with it," I urged, certain that this was just what Tom desperately needed. Again, he nodded.

Giving him a grin, I reached under the bed and pulled out the ties. Eyeing me, I could sense he was hesitant, but intrigued. "Come on," I plied. "It'll be good for you. We don't have to do anything you don't want to... But I promise, you'll enjoy it."

Tom smiled shyly, then rolled onto his back, holding his hands together obediently. I slowly began to wrap the ties around his wrists, when Tom abruptly rolled over, bolting upright. "I can't," he muttered, then ran from the room.

I followed, talking to him, trying to reassure him, but it was as if he'd become another person. I couldn't tell if he was mad at me or himself, but a wall had come up and nothing I said made any difference. I tried to get him to talk, to try to salvage our relationship, but Tom clammed up entirely. I went back into the bedroom and packed away my things before returning to the kitchen, where Tom was making a cup of tea.

"This isn't going to work," he flatly stated. This time, it was my turn to nod. He was right. A switch had been thrown, from which there was no recovery.

It was a long walk home that night, schlepping my backpack a few miles across town to my apartment. Here I had thought I was creating a fun escapade, potentially something that might dramatically transform this man who so desperately needed to dominate, creating a more layered, nuanced personae, only to find it backfire spectacularly.

Everywhere around me, happy couples wandered. But I was, once again, miserably alone on Valentine's. Clearly, Mr. Tom Day had ruined my night.

WRITE ON

While continuing my volunteer work, I'd take jobs allowing me maximum freedom, such as waiting tables. I'd decided to put my creative efforts into writing screenplays. My first made it all the way into the semifinals of the Nicholls' Fellowships in Screenwriting, and I thought, *"Hot damn—I'm gonna be a screenwriter!"*

I must've written eight spec screenplays, which my agent insisted would get sold, but none ever did. Writing, however, gave me a place to channel my artistic impulses, even if it wasn't paying the bills.

Soon, a position opened up at AIDS Project Los Angeles which played to my creative skills, as well as my interest in activism. A new educational program was being created, with the goal being to keep HIV-negative gay men from sero-converting. We called it Sex Essentials. I was selected to run the volunteer and curriculum creation portion of the program, and a perpetually sad-sack man who ended up being a crystal meth addict was chosen to graphic design a free 'zine called SexVibe, which I wrote and edited, and which we regularly delivered to the local gay bars. I trained volunteers on what HIV was and how to prevent it, which included doing safer sex shows at Pride festivals everywhere. Each weekend, we'd head to the WeHo bars, wandering Santa Monica, distributing free condoms to anyone who wanted one, and trying to cajole people into coming to our weekly safer sex workshops.

While we had many cute gay male volunteers, Sex Essentials had two volunteers who made an indelible impression on me, both of whom were straight women:

The first, Véronique Ehinger, lived in Lausanne, Switzerland. Twice each year, she would journey from Switzerland to Los Angeles for a few months at a time, happy to help us in any way possible, from doing paperwork, to making phone calls, to registering people for our workshops. Véronique would do whatever necessary to ensure we succeeded. That she would dedicate so much time for our cause, and travel so far to do so, meant the world to me.

Later, Eyes and I would go to Lausanne and connect with Véronique, who showed us around the city she called home. While she had confided in me that she had been battling cancer, I had no idea how far it had advanced until we visited. Her face was gaunt, her bald head covered in a scarf. I kept insisting that we didn't need a tour of her town, that she needn't exhaust herself on our behalf, but she would simply smile and nod before leading us on to our next destination.

The other volunteer I really loved was Janis Martin, a grandmother, who was so filled with love and compassion, and with an infectiously joyful attitude towards life. It was from Janis that I learned how to give expert blowjobs—a trick she'd learned from working with prostitutes. Thank you, Janis. It is because of your committed teaching that thousands have benefited.

Although they volunteered for an agency largely focused on assisting gay men through their battle with HIV, both Véronique and Janis died from cancer. Véronique died October 9, 1997, and Janis died September 10, 2015. Both were treasured by me and both are sorely missed.

For Sex Essentials, I created two characters who led our safer sex workshops, Biff Boffum and LaToya Latex—not-so-subtle rip-offs of a popular local lounge act, Les Stevens and the Lovely Carol. I portrayed Biff, hair brushed high and wearing flashy 70s TV game show host attire, and a variety of volunteers rotated through LaToya Latex. It was cutting-edge and hip AIDS education done in a down-and-dirty, outrageous way.

For our first issue of our 'zine SexVibe, we created a step-by-step safer sex pictorial on proper condom usage, commandeering a men's bathroom in our building as the set. Our photographer and I coached as we captured photos of one of our staffer's hands reaching under a toilet stall and professionally rolling a condom onto an obliging porn star's friendly dick. I can tell you that, as director, I had no idea my UCLA theater skills would come in so handy.

Crafting a SexVibe article, I created a pseudonym for a fictious drag queen, and wrote this piece:

BOOPSIE GIVENCHY: THIS I BELIEVE...

I believe that "gay" still means "happy."
I believe that good will always triumph—Unless, of course, we're talking *Melrose Place.*

I believe that Latoya Latex could benefit from a nice full-length mirror.

I believe that one day Richard Simmons will rise up and lead us.

I believe in fairies.

I believe that Stephen Sondheim should be deified.

I believe that the Rev. Fred Phelps should not.

I believe in the Golden Rule (and anything else made of gold.)

I believe that rimming is next to Godliness.

I believe that Pamela Sue Martin is due for a comeback.

I believe that O.J. needs a better acting coach.

I believe that Susan Sarandon is the only woman I'd ever sleep with.

I believe that in Newt Gingrich's next life, he'll come back as Connie Norman.

I believe that in Mel Gibson's next life, he'll come back as a blow-up orifice Ken doll.

I believe that the seven deadly sins should've included bad hair.

I believe that no one will ever hand you anything—except a subpoena.

I believe that *Saturday Night Live* should have been canceled long ago.

I believe that Calgon can take you away.

I believe that one day there will be a cure for AIDS.

And I believe that I will be here to see it.

I'm happy to note that today, aside from the line about Sabotage Susan, I wouldn't change a word.

SHANE MICHAEL SAWICK

If it weren't for his love of denim overalls, Shane Sawick would have fit perfectly into a 1940s Cary Grant movie. I can see him now: tall, dapper, great smile, smoothly trading quips with Rosalind Russell, unflappably.

Shane was a coordinator of the Southern California AIDS Hotline, overseeing and training volunteers. We'd met when I first started volunteering at APLA, but hadn't seen each other much until I transitioned to full-time employee. We shared the same boss, a smirking psychopath named Glenn Buttinski, who loved causing trouble between his charges.

At some point, a co-worker told me that Shane had a crush on me, which piqued my interest. While I'd thought Shane attractive, I didn't sense an immediate connection, and his overalls certainly didn't help the matter. Still, I thought—why not? That he was HIV-positive didn't so much matter, but the fact that his T-cells were dropping significantly, triggering an AIDS diagnosis, did give me pause.

I wasn't afraid of contracting the virus—I was far too educated for that—but I was concerned about allowing myself to fully love him, as there was then no cure or drugs effective at slowing down the disease. That evil PAC-MAN virus could mow down anything, destroying everything in its path. Still, I knew that allowing myself to love Shane would change me, and that I desperately needed changing. I didn't yet know how it might alter me, but it wouldn't be long before I found out.

Shane was raised in upstate New York, along with his older brother and a younger sister, Jill, whom he adored. Jill was quite shy in those days, and Shane was a very loving, protective brother. Winters were filled with snow play and skiing, and he loved nothing more than hanging out with his best friend, Vivian Alexopolous, grabbing pizza at DeLeno's.

A big lover of theatre, Shane treasured his trips into the city to see shows, and it was a surprise to no one when he decided to become an actor, eventually moving to Hollywood, like so many before. When we met, he was working at APLA and taking acting classes at night. His job gave him flexibility, allowing him time off to film commercials whenever he booked them.

Meeting Shane, I was immediately drawn into his tight circle of friends; funny, smart, caring, attractive—these guys had it all, turning just about any hum-drum event into an occasion. And Shane's English Springer Spaniel, Clementine, sweet and gentle, quickly became my best friend.

After we'd dated for several months, Shane asked that I move in... As much as I loved him, I still hesitated. Lovers was one thing. Living with him—and potentially becoming caregiver—was another. I was a selfish prick, even if evolving, and I knew that this decision was the biggest I'd ever make—one with profound ramifications. Scared, uncertain, but knowing he needed me, I finally decided to take the leap.

Shane loved to cook and attempted multiple times to

duplicate his beloved mother's chicken and dumplings recipe, but could never get it "quite the way mom did." We would alternate from ordering delivery from Louise's Trattoria to trying out other new recipes. The easiest, which became a weekly staple, was pasta puttanesca, the name of which Shane loved. It translates roughly as "pasta of the whores", because—as Italy's "women of the night" weren't allowed to shop daily at the fresh markets—it was made with all-canned ingredients.

Through Shane, I learned to love his favorites, Bette Midler and Bobby Short. Seeing Mr. Short's show one night at the Café Carlyle in New York, we were surprised when he came up to us, waiting at the door, and welcomed us into his "home." Shane's love for both Bette and Bobby would later help give shape to my first novel.

Christmas was Shane's favorite time of the year and on this we shared a special bond; I was a Christmas-aholic as well. At a young age, his mother gave Shane nutcrackers at Christmas, which quickly grew into an amazing collection. But Shane was very particular—they had to be German nutcrackers, because they were, quite simply, the best. I've continued this tradition to this day, giving Russ and my boys nutcrackers every Christmas Eve, though I've often cheated and given them cheaper, sub-par non-German nutcrackers. When I die, you'll be able to see their bonfire from miles away.

On our first Christmas together, a bomb was set off, from which it would be difficult to recover. It came in the form of my parents' annual Christmas letter. Each year, they would devote individual paragraphs to me and my sister, filling in our family and friends on our activities throughout the year, but this particular year was quite different. My entry read:

Our son lives in Los Angeles, has a new apartment, and loves his new job.

Now you might think, "what is so awful about that?" What is awful is not so much what is said, as what is missing. I'd recently changed my name, hating the name Fred, and my parents felt as if they couldn't possibly say that my name was now Kergan, our last name, as that might thoroughly confuse our dear loved ones. And if they had such an issue with just a simple name change, imagine telling everyone that my new apartment was actually the apartment Shane and I shared, or that my new job was at— gasp!—AIDS Project Los Angeles. There I was, a 28-year-old adult, and they were sugar-coating my life for safe consumption. I was livid.

Calling them and hearing their excuses, I finally realized that far from simply an oversight, or an attempt to paint over that which they didn't like, this letter had been purposely scripted. That dawned on me when Dottie pushed back on me: "You wrote what you wanted to write in that coming out letter, so we wrote what we wanted. You didn't think about how that would affect us at all!" My coming out/fundraising letter a few years prior had hurt her so deeply that she had decided to do the same to me. That decision led me to be away from my family for the first Christmas ever, instead flying with Shane to spend the holiday with his family in New York, and it would be a full year before my parents and I would speak again.

THE FIRST TIME I SAW PARIS

In our second year together and with his health on a slow decline, Shane opted to sell his life insurance policy and take me on a five-week trip to France and Italy. I'd always wanted to go to Europe and I couldn't believe that the historic places I'd read about would soon be right in front of me.

Given our love of food, we packed nice dress suits so that we could treat ourselves to the finest dining possible. At the world-famous Jules Verne, situated on the mid-level of the Eiffel Tower, I could not read the menu and mistakenly ordered sweetbreads—a mistake I would never make again. At Les Tour D'Argent, overlooking Notre Dame Cathedral, known for numbering their famed ducks, their exquisitely tasty $50 bowl of Lobster Bisque became an ongoing joke.

I remember the bees-a-Pisa and the Pitti-kitties. I recall the floral-scented grapes in St. Remy-de-Provence. Italy's lake region where we would sit at cafés on the lake's shore and try to like Campari. The breathtaking and quaint fishermen's villages of the Cinque Terre, where an old shopkeeper—realizing we were Americans—interrupted our conversation with her son, only to say: "Bill Clinton?", she gave a thumbs up. "Monica Lewinsky?", she grimaced and spat onto the floor.

And I clearly recall Rome, our final stop, where Shane began tiring easily, and would go out only once per day, by taxi, to see a sight, and each night I would bring us dinner from the McDonald's near the Spanish Steps.

Back home, Shane quickly declined and began losing control of his motor skills, veering off course when walking, experiencing a slurring of words, his reflexes not reacting as quickly as they should... I took him to endless doctor's appointments, with umpteen medical tests, until he was finally diagnosed with Progressive Multifocal Leukoencephalopathy (PML)—essentially a growing lesion on the brain. There was no cure.

There was, however, a fun unproven drug that could do one of three things: #1. Reverse the disease's course, #2. Halt the disease from progressing but leave the patient in whatever state they were presently in, or #3. Nothing. And it required having an implant inserted onto one's skull, just under the skin, to administer the medication directly to the affected site.

As the chances of success were slim, Shane held off and hoped for the best. But his decline only accelerated. He could no longer work, and as I had to continue working, nurses were brought in to care for him. APLA case workers continually stopped by, checking on their co-worker. Friends gathered, his family came out, all knowing that his time was limited.

One day, with his sister and mother by his side in our bedroom, Shane looked up at me and said, "You're enjoying this." I instantly went from shock to hurt and back again. How could he think any part of this was remotely enjoyable? I knew he was angry—at the disease, at facing death—and was likely sick of my hovering, but he'd somehow come to interpret my efforts to greet our friends and family with a degree of warmth as some sign that I was enjoying my role as caregiver. Like I was a party hostess, twirling about in my cocktail attire, showing off the charming invalid in bed before rushing everyone out and onto hors d'oeuvres. That couldn't have been further from the truth, and that wound still hurts.

AIDS IS REALLY SHITTY

I focused first on the wall. It was an inspired shade of yellow, bright and cheery during the day, warm and welcoming at night. Shane and I had discovered it during our European trip, where bright spots of golden color dot the landscape, popping up now and again, welcomingly. Upon our return, Shane and I scoured paint shops, trying to duplicate it, only to finally find the exact shade at Sears under the name "Straw." That designation doesn't remotely do its muted brilliance justice, but our apartment soon glowed, just the same.

I tried to keep my voice calm, like the measured, reassuring voices of NPR's radio hosts. As if this were any typical day, and we were doing any typical act.

"Shane's muscles are shutting down," the hospice nurse had said. Of that, we were well-aware. He hadn't left the bedroom for several days, other than to be helped to the bathroom. "His bowels are obstructed, as he's unable to push..." She let that sentence hang, hovering as I struggled to understand the meaning. "He needs a manual extraction," she nodded, prodding. "I can do it, of course. But I thought... He might prefer you."

I nodded, partly because it was expected and partly because there was no other option.

"If left as is, blocking and disrupting his flow, the stool basically turns toxic, allowing his body to be poisoned."

Again, I nodded; this time, because there was nothing left to say but, "I'll do it."

She walked into the bathroom, laying out latex gloves and Vaseline.

I stood in the bedroom doorway, leaning against it for a moment, looking at Shane, so thin, lying inertly on the bed, eyes closed. The nurse appeared beside me and together we propped Shane between us, gently ushering him through the bathroom door and next to the toilet. As she left, holding eyes with me and nodding as she closed the bathroom door, I turned back to Shane. We'd propped his arms out, hands gripping the counter to try to ensure he stay steady, and I held his face in both hands as I gave him a quick kiss.

"Do you understand what we're doing?" I asked. He gave a vague nod. "Alrighty, then." I exhaled, realizing his pajama bottoms were still on. I worked them down his body, made sure he was still propping himself up, until they were at his ankles. I looked to the wall, that beautiful golden shade, then exhaled again, seating him onto the toilet. I moved his right hand onto the shower door handle, wrapping his fingers around it. "Hold tight to this, okay?"

Standing, I went to the sink, washing my hands first, dried them, applied a bit of powder, then awkwardly pulled on the gloves. I methodically applied the Vaseline to my right hand, then turned to face him. His gaze fell downward. It was then that I began truly channeling NPR. "So, now... Everything is ready," I smiled, as if we were about to have tea.

I knelt next to him, spreading his knees apart. Reaching between them, my fingers found their destination, and I gently inserted one. Shane's eyes widened a bit, slightly wincing as I inserted another finger. I extracted some stool, then inserted again, more deeply. I proceeded methodically, talking continuously throughout.

"Are you okay, sweetie? Am I hurting you? Okay, we've got one. But there's more, okay? I'm trying to be gentle, see? Don't worry, my love. This will all be over soon..."

I concentrated on the task at hand until we were through, and only then did I look again to Shane's face. He glanced away, eyes glistening, and I realized then that this would indeed all be over soon. Our relationship. His life. It would soon evaporate into the void. The fight he'd had, the strength he'd shown, it was almost gone. This proud man, once so vain about his appearance, had been reduced to having his lover pull shit out of his ass. He couldn't protest, or help, or curse me out. He could only acquiesce, as any measure of resistance had been stripped clean. He knew it, too—I could see it in his eyes—and that was what hurt most.

HAPPY BIRTHDAY TO ME

On the day of my 30th birthday, I admitted Shane into the hospital. It was time; we all knew it, even if we didn't want to admit it. We loaded Shane into my car and drove to Western Medical. He would not come out alive.

I'd called my mother earlier about this change in plans, as—having finally patched things up after the Christmas newsletter debacle the year prior—my family had planned to come up to L.A. to celebrate my birthday. My mother seemed to take it personally that we needed to cancel, as if this entire episode was simply a ploy, instigated to annoy her, rather than that a sick man who needed proper care in order to make it through his final days.

Still, to my family's credit, they showed up at the hospital, cake in hand, and tried to act as if everything were actually alright. That it was perfectly normal to be celebrating my birthday in a hospital room with my lover barely able to blink once for yes, twice for no. No, this wasn't normal. Nothing about this situation was remotely normal, but what else could we do?

Once in the hospital, against my better judgment, the doctors implanted that fun medication device under Shane's scalp, administering the unproven drug to the affected area of his brain. Shane had changed his mind after his initial opposition and assented to this last-ditch attempt to save his live. *"Good God,"* I wondered, *"what if it leaves him like this, in this impossible state?"* We'd all come too far and too close to the inevitable. His decision, while entirely reasonable from his point of view, weighed on me, and no doubt on his sister and mother. None of us were remotely equipped to deal with him in an almost-catatonic state.

For the next two weeks, every night, I slept in the empty hospital bed next to Shane's. I didn't want him to be alone. I didn't want him to think he'd been abandoned. Still, as anyone who has stayed overnight in a hospital can attest, it is almost impossible to get sleep, given the lights—never fully off—and the nurses' continual prodding, poking, checking. I was emotionally drained from the many weeks of his declining health, continual conversations with his doctors, and trying to keep myself upbeat without much sleep—all of this was taking its toll.

During the day, Shane's many friends and colleagues would stop by, attempting conversation—both with Shane and me—but it was challenging, at best. I'd have gone crazy without my friends, prompting me repeatedly: "Have you eaten?" "Why don't we grab a quick bite—*outside* the hospital?" "I'll watch Shane while you go home and shower—Don't worry—I'll call you if anything comes up."

My trips to our now almost-abandoned apartment were always lickety-split fast. So many of the reminders of Shane were still there. Pillows propped just so. Syringes in the bathroom. His slippers, next to the bed. I'd run in and out: walk our dog Clementine, shower, check voicemail, get mail, pay bills, and back out the door. I knew Shane's time was brief, and I didn't want to miss a moment. And that apartment, where we had crafted so many memories, suddenly didn't feel like home.

Upon my return to the hospital, I'd immediately fly into my list of daily questions: "Who came by? What did his doctor say? How are his stats? Anything new to report?"

After one of my daily trips to the apartment, I returned to the hospital, only to find that Shane's older brother and his wife had visited in my absence. Shane had come to detest his brother, as he had never been accepting of Shane being gay, and the brother's wife was nothing but a moocher. While they'd been relatively pleasant to me, it was also apparent that they didn't view us as their equals.

I'm not entirely sure how they knew what was going on with Shane, as he'd made it clear that he didn't want them visiting, or just how they knew exactly when a window would open when I would be at our apartment, but they arrived during that window and were gone before my return. And, apparently, their sole purpose in visiting was to inquire as to what would happen to Shane's beloved baby grand piano upon his passing. An inquiry, it should be stated, that would come again soon, this time to me, not long after Shane's death.

On Sunday, March 19, 1995, after conferring with his doctors, his sister, his Mom and I agreed to that it was time to take Shane off all of his drugs, and instead give him morphine, to dull the pain.

That afternoon, over a week since Shane had last spoken, I was alone with him in his room. Shane's sister, Jill, and his mom, Mary Ann, had stepped outside the lobby so Mary Ann could grab a quick smoke. It was a habit Mary Ann kept saying she was going to quit, but—quite frankly—at this particular moment in time, I didn't blame her. I was sitting beside Shane, blathering on about God-knows-what, when I lifted up his oxygen mask to wipe his face and he said, "Mom."

Unbelieving, I locked eyes with his, which also hadn't happened in days.

"Your mom?" I asked. "You want your mom?"

He didn't speak, but his eyes were so tightly focused right on me, I felt certain of what he'd said and intended.

Tears came to my eyes. This was a man who couldn't talk, walk, or even swallow anymore, and he'd somehow found it within him to ask for his mother. A desire so dear, so primitive, so understandable.

I didn't want to leave the room, so fearful was I that this moment of lucidity would soon be gone. I ran out into the hallway, summoning nurses, explaining that someone needed to be with him. That he'd responded. And that I had to go find his mom.

A nurse told me that she knew where Mary Ann was, and not to fret—that she'd be right back. I returned my attention to Shane, but his eyes no longer focused on mine. I tried to get him to grasp my finger, to use our "once for yes, twice for no" squeeze, but he was unresponsive.

Several minutes later, Mary Ann came in, crossing to him. I sensed no urgency in her. As if her son speaking after days of not, and asking for his mother, were an every-day-occurrence. She took his hand, perching herself on the side of the bed beside him.

"I'm here, sweetie. I'm here, Shane," she softly murmured, gently rubbing his hand. He didn't respond.

I don't recall how long they sat like that, or how that moment ended. What I do know is that I was struck by two things...

Number 1: It wouldn't be long now. While we'd been in the hospital for almost two weeks, which made those endless hours/days/nights blur into one, there had been no improvement. The experimental drug hadn't worked. Shane just continually declined, and those who were caring for him—our energies and spirit had declined as well.

Number 2: Shane wanted to live. He wanted so badly for that he somehow summoned the strength to reach out, telling me to get his mom.

But had he? Had I imagined it? Had I wanted it so badly, for him to rally, that I'd invented something? But, if I had created that moment, wouldn't I have had him calling out for *me?*

When Mary Ann walked in, there had been no, *"Oh my God! My son who hasn't spoken in days called my name!"* I'd have thought that she'd be joyful, emotional—but no.

Perhaps Mary Ann's nonchalant reaction was perfectly normal. Perhaps she knew that Shane loved her and longed for her, but couldn't give herself over to the idea that his speaking might mean there was "hope." Like me, I think she knew it was time and was focused on the practical, not the sentimental.

Still, in my heart and in my memory, he spoke that word. And I felt that longing. Simple as that. He was a dying man, and he wanted his mother.

That night, lying in the bed next to Shane, I couldn't sleep. I was agitated by a jumble of sentimental, stupid and senseless thoughts running through my head, one after the other. As exhausted as I was, as much tossing and turning as I'd done, I simply could not turn off my brain.

Finally, moved by something in the back of my head, I stood from my bed and slid ungracefully beside Shane in his. I kissed his cheek, pulling him close against me, trying as best I could to spoon him. Snuggling in, I first reminded him how we met. About his overalls. His humor and sense of style. His love of Christmas, and that amazing European trip on which he'd taken me.

I walked him through every step of my sexual fantasy of him, wearing only a jockstrap, and me—well. As I've always said, rimming is next to Godliness.

I walked him through each remembrance, good and bad. I really had no pre-set agenda—I was just talking—but as I kept blathering, it became clear that I was giving him permission to let go. It wasn't what I wanted—but it also was. I wanted peace for him, even if it meant turmoil and grieving for me. I wanted release—for both of us. This wasn't feasible, hanging on, day-by-day, unable to forecast, or plan, or dream. Something had to change.

From my journal, depicting the day before his death:
"Monday he was pretty doped up, but I kept talking to him anyway—telling him how I felt and trying to get him to visualize a calm, quiet place for him to rest. I told him to picture a sidewalk café that served coffee and cognac, and wonderful foods, and peaceful surroundings—with all of his

favorite people there. It was hard—it hurt—to tell him to let go, but I had to make him understand that he needed to think of himself now and not worry about us—that we'd be okay. And I'm not sure if that's true or not—that I'll be okay. Some moments I'm fine, others I just want to die. And I feel like I could sleep for years."

On Tuesday, his family and I decided to pull him off his ventilator.

Friends gathered, both in and outside the small hospital room, to say their goodbyes. At some point, we'd snuck in Clementine, laying her on the bed beside Shane, so that she too could say farewell.

I'd brought in a CD player and on it we played Bette Midler albums until the time drew close. Everything had been turned off. There was only a steady drip of morphine for comfort. The room was almost silent, save for the whispering of friends outside, and, inside, Bette's quiet singing and Shane's labored breathing.

His favorite Bette Midler album had been hard to pin down, as there were several that he loved. But he and I had most discussed one of hers, *Songs for the New Depression*, as there was a song on it, Tom Waits' "Shiver Me Timbers," which Shane absolutely loved. It speaks of leaving family and friends, as one's heart's in the wind, charting a new course, moving on alone...

I can't be certain that song is indeed what was playing as Shane took his final breath, but in my memory, it was. As Shane's breath drew in and out, ever so slowly, the entire room would inhale and exhale with him, so focused were we on his passing.

As the clock ticked, endlessly, a thought entered my head, which unfortunately I then blurted out: "That's Shane, stubborn to the end." Whether I'd intended it as a stupid crack to ease tension or as an insensitive proclamation of fact, the minute it came forth I felt like a heel.

It was getting late—very late. Only me, Mary Ann, Jill, and a few friends remained, as most had left, having to work the next day. I leaned up to Shane, kissed him on the cheek, said "I love you," and with that he was gone.

From my journal:
"I don't know how to describe the torrent of emotions running through me at that moment—horror, anger, relief— and total sorrow. Sorrow for the life extinguished and sorrow for my new one begun. While the guys gathered up our belongings, I dealt with the nurses and signed the necessary paperwork."

Shane Michael Sawick was proclaimed dead on March 22, 1995, at 12:22AM, surrounded by his family and friends. And let me make this promise to you and to him: As long as I am alive, Shane will never be forgotten.

THE WOMAN IN RED

The very next day, having barely slept, I headed to the mall with two friends in search of scrapbooks, as I wanted to integrate our photos, journal pages, and European memorabilia, and share that France and Italy journey with the attendees of memorial, set for the following weekend. As we walked around Beverly Center, all I could see were men. Men of every shape, make and size. Men everywhere. *Everywhere.* And at that moment in time, I would've fucked any one of them.

I was so horny, given our last months without sex, and the lack of any passion or love directed toward me in recent times fueled in me an almost uncontrollable urge to fuck anything within sight. Shane loved me—I knew that, but in those short months as I morphed from partner to caregiver, that shift had almost imperceptibly altered our relationship. There was no longing. There was no passion. I was there to serve Shane as nurse. As friend. As lover? At some point, the lines had been blurred.

Here we were, at Beverly Center. My lover had just died hours before, and all I could think about was sex. I wanted to be held, loved, and recognized as more than just one thing. I wanted to shake that caregiver mantle off, at almost any cost.

My friends and I finally found the perfect scrapbooks at

Papyrus, and I would then spend the next several days reading over each journal entry, reviewing each photograph, and recalling each and every moment we had captured during that trip: a coffee-stained napkin from Paris' famous Les Deux Magot café, a Pope John Paul II bottle opener from the Vatican, and a twig of wildflowers from the fields of Provence. And over each, I cried, and cried, and cried. Sex may have been what I thought I wanted, but what I desired most had been ripped from me: that ability to wholeheartedly, unreservedly give myself over to another. That transformative melding of mind/spirit/dick was gone.

Until I reconnected with Eyes.

But that too can wait.

The day of Shane's service, held in Hollywood at a friend's house, was beautiful. As people entered, they were greeted by my trip scrapbooks and framed photos, and a memory book, in which to write their thoughts of Shane. Beer margaritas (beer, tequila, and limeade) were served, a party staple of Shane's circle of friends, as a way of honoring their shared years.

The day wasn't to be a day of mourning as much as a celebration. We wanted people to exchange stories and memories, to laugh about good times and cry about sad times. Our service was a sharing of stories. Funny, biting, sentimental, sad—all were forthrightly told and honored. Then it turned to me.

Standing in front of the crowd, I could see my family, seated to the left of me. For whatever reason, my mother had opted to wear a bright red outfit. I doubt she would've selected the same for the passing of a beloved friend or family member, but at that particular moment, I wasn't up for debate.

Last to address those assembled, I'd prepared my remarks, reading off my memories, highlighting the friends who'd been there on the journey, and ending my moment with a recitation of my love for Shane.

Before closing my remarks, I noted that—weeks prior to being unable to communicate—Shane had made a comment to me as we were driving in my car, as we'd just listened to Andrea Marcovicci's rendition of the classic song, "These Foolish Things." Shane had looked at me and said, "It would be great if you would sing that at my memorial."

I wasn't entirely clear if he were serious or joking, but there was nothing about his delivery which indicated he was being humorous. Was he setting me up, to embarrass myself in front of family and friends, or did he really mean for that song to be a cathartic moment, freeing me, somehow, from him and the past?

Regardless, I took his request seriously and, before those assembled, sang the song acapella. Several times, I stumbled, both on words and pitch, as flashes of our brief years together pierced through me. It was all I could do to finish the last stanza.

Shane had requested that his service end with two songs, the first of which was Pavarotti's "Ave Maria." As that recording began playing, I was still standing, weeping uncontrollably, in the front of the room, all eyes on me, when a movement registered among those gathered. I sensed a woman in red, moving from my left, enveloping me.

It was my mother. It was Dottie. Fully fucking deformed Dottie, wrapping me into her in embrace. And yet I melted, letting myself fold into her. It was in that moment that I realized what Shane had felt, in his last days, calling out for his mother.

These women were our flesh and blood. They had borne us. Our very beings were a direct product of their DNA. They had mothered us, however imperfectly. And yet here they were, in their own way, shepherding us home.

As the service ended and the final song played, Bette Midler's classic "Friends," I was still entwined in my mother's arms. If it had been anyone else, I would've pushed them away. I hadn't thought I needed comforting, or saving, but at that exact moment, I needed both, and Dottie was the only person on the planet who could've given me that.

Finally extracting myself, dabbing my eyes with a Kleenex, I circulated, only to walk smack into one of Shane's friends, a talent agent. "Don't quit your day job!" he joked without nuance, before moving off. I raged inside. *"Don't quit my day job? My day job has been injecting Shane's ass with vitamin B and testosterone shots, shoveling food into his mouth, wiping his ass—and you're critiquing my singing ability?"* It was all I could do not to smack him.

Later in the afternoon, my best friend of many years, JP, suddenly appeared at my side, having been absent the entire ceremony. In fact, I hadn't seen him for weeks, but here he was. He'd begun visiting less and less as Shane had become more ill, stopping altogether when Shane went into the hospital. His excuse? "I don't like hospitals." As if anyone does. Still, service over, Shane's ashes all but scattered, and there JP was asking, "Hey—want to go with me to a club tonight?"

I simply stared. I had been through the wringer and knew I'd been transformed, even if I didn't yet know exactly how. But having felt the depths at which I was capable of going, I knew I didn't need shallow people in my life anymore. I wanted and craved substance. I still do.

Two weeks later, we held another memorial for Shane's family and friends in upstate New York. Much was the same, though this time in a rented tent: Pavarotti, Midler, remembrances... Shane had loved his sister's quaint farmhouse, and it was fitting that this service took place in her backyard, fields stretched out far beyond.

I knew Shane would've loved the location and service, save for the embarrassing remembrance given by an old girlfriend.

Over twenty years prior, at the age of 16, Shane had starred as Hero in the Wappingers Falls' County Players production of *A Funny Thing Happened on the Way to the Forum*. His high school girlfriend at the time, who was also in *Forum*, showed up at his memorial only to get up and proclaim, "Shane and I... We were *LOVERS!*", as if that twenty-year-old nugget were both recent and pertinent. The moment was both hysterically funny and tragically sad, but was quickly followed up and ultimately buried by her singing a key song from *Forum*, entitled "Lovely", to which she had changed the words to reflect Shane: "In the end he couldn't read, write, or even say his name, but he's happy, happy up in Heaven..."

Later, she came up to me and said, "Let's always be close." I never heard from her again.

April 3, 1995:

"Buried Shane today. It was strangely weird. I felt as if I should be broken-hearted, but I could not draw the association between Shane and the box of ash that I put in the ground... It was mentioned that I would be welcome in the plot, if I wanted it."

April 8, 1995:

"Spent the day starting to organize Shane's things— paperwork, etc.—a huge project. I found an essay Shane wrote a few months ago to these people who were giving away a house. It was beautiful."

If you've ever seen the movie *Spitfire Grill*, you're already familiar with the concept of house raffles. In Yankee Magazine, which Shane loved, every so often there would be an ad for a house raffle. For a variety of reasons, people would ask for a small entry fee, along with an essay on why you wanted their house and award the home to some lucky winner. Shane became fixated on one such house, and wrote the following essay intro, which gives a better sense of who he is than I could ever communicate.

"I'd imagine that this essay may be one of the more unusual essays you receive. I'm quite sure most people who have entered this contest are looking for a place to live. A fair number may simply be looking to win the property in the hopes of making a killing by selling it right away. I, too, am looking for a place to live as well as hoping to increase my net worth by winning your beautiful home, but the reality is, I may also be securing a place to die."

EVERY DAY A LITTLE DEATH

In the months following Shane's death, I attempted to bring his circle of friends together—for dinners, game nights, spa pampering parties—but inevitably each bid failed. Soon after Shane's death, his dear friend David fell ill to AIDS as well, and Greg Solem and I hurried to his side. I vividly recall a day at David's mountain cabin retreat, where we three sat out on the deck amidst the evergreens, listening as Bette Midler's new *Bette of Roses* CD blast out into the pines. Thoughts were shared, fears bared, and it wouldn't be long before David was dead.

This circle of friends, once impenetrable, quickly withered. Shane had been its glue, it seemed, and nothing I could do would ever mend that break. It was awful, to have felt such a part of something good, even if for a brief while, only to see friendships as solid and steadfast as theirs fall away, never to be mended.

The months following were a blur. Going through Shane's belongings, figuring out which were rightly his family's and which were mine. Shopping for groceries at Ralph's, only to find myself crying in the produce aisle. Continually cleaning our already-spotless apartment, as if trying to scrub out any reminder of Shane's existence. Then, conversely, playing our *Falsettos'* CDs, to provoke an immediate emotional response in me: yes, Shane and I had loved; yes, we had that profound, solid connection; and, yes, he was gone.

Prior to his death, Shane and I had taken my parents to see the touring production of *Falsettos* in Hollywood. I had wanted my folks to see an example of how our lives were really just like everyone else's, and how—in just a short time—they too would be experiencing, through me, the death of a loved one. It was a test, I guess, although I hadn't really thought that at the time. And when the play was over, and we gathered in the lobby, all had been silent.

That explained the innumerable days, vacuuming our apartment in my underwear, like Melanie Griffith in *Working Girl*, when I'd inexplicably break into tears.

I fielded calls from people, unaware that Shane was gone, and sent certified copies of his death certificate to creditors, who probably couldn't care less.

I resumed work, though by then the work meant little aside from a paycheck, and it was certainly difficult to get up in front of a crowd and preach HIV prevention, when all I really wanted to do was lay down and cry. I put those thoughts into several articles I wrote for SexVibe—and was gratified that people actually took the time to respond, sharing their own pain, appreciative that I'd put such thoughts into words.

April 18, 1995:

"Am I just now realizing that, not only did AIDS take my boyfriend, but my best friend? I haven't ever felt as close to anyone in my life, like I did Shane. Who will I do things with? Who will I talk to—really talk to? I'm busy puttering about, but I'm used to having Shane around for that, too. Just going to the mall alone is strange. My chest is so tight. How does one get through loneliness—without adding people to their life? The answer is not in replacement—I know that."

May 1, 1995:
"Shane was on my mind quite a bit today. I was wondering why he didn't cry the last few days of his life. Could he not understand us? Could he not physically respond? Was he not full of emotion as well? I don't see how he couldn't be—and his eyes focused on whomever was talking—until they couldn't. And yet—no tears.

I guess I started thinking about this in relation to how he and I spoke little of his impending death, except logistically. Maybe we thought that to do so would break the tender line of hope. Regardless, I wish we had spoken. We had no closure—I did, but he didn't. Perhaps he wanted it that way? I guess it bothers me that he did not have more to say to me. I take what pieces I can from letters he wrote to others, or essays he wrote. I wish I'd stumble across some letter he'd written to me. Last words. But that would've happened by now."

Shortly after writing that, I found this, which Shane had written on a random page in his Day Runner:
"I love Kergan more than I've ever loved anyone or anything. He saved my life.
I love Chopin's Polonaise.
I love autumn best, though all seasons have their charms."

In December, nine months after Shane died, a new combination of drugs was introduced, known as the AIDS

Cocktail, which, when taken together, showed promise in slowing down HIV. Shortly following that news, one of my most difficult and perpetually cranky volunteers, HIV-positive himself, plopped himself down opposite me and said, "It's too bad Shane wasn't strong enough to hold on for this."

I was shocked. As if physical strength or a desire to live was all that was needed to stop oneself from falling victim to such a heinous disease.

Years later, this very same combative volunteer finally succumbed to HIV, having become resistant to the life-saving drugs he had once claimed could've saved Shane, if only Shane had been "strong enough." Losing anyone to AIDS is awful, but in this particular person's case, I'm sorry to say, I didn't shed a single tear.

LIFE LESSON #15

Should you go in to receive your HIV test results, only to be told that the truck carrying your samples has mysteriously disappeared and they'll need to redraw your blood, don't panic. That only means that a truck loaded with hundreds of vials of potentially infected blood is roaming recklessly untethered through the streets of Los Angeles. What could possibly go wrong?

I JUST CALLED TO SAY I LOVE YOU

Having spent several months grappling with the loss of Shane and trying to get my own life back on track, I was surprised—and more than a bit befuddled—when I got an unexpected call from Eyes, just after Christmas in December 1995. It had been over two years since we'd last spoken, with Eyes having no idea that in those years I'd both met and lost Shane. He had no idea of the love and connection I'd had or the grieving I'd endured. His rationale for calling? "I was just cleaning out my Day Runner." But all that he then said, his lengthy remembrances of our prior connection, made his call feel anything other than happenstance.

In truth, at that point, I barely remembered who Eyes was. I remembered our prior connection, how I'd then felt about him, but the particulars—any doubts that I'd then surfaced—none were near the forefront of my mind. During that phone call, when he expressed a desire to meet, I couldn't even fully recall what he looked like. All I could remember was that I had thought he had been perfect and was shocked to consider that he might still desire me, years later.

Having been through such a horrific loss with Shane, a message emanated through me: "You deserve this. Eyes is a blessing, given to you as reward for all that you've endured. Don't doubt yourself—you are, in fact, worthy of this type of love. You are deserving."

Eyes and I went on our first official date in January 1996; he'd had asked me to meet him at his home in Orange County, a cute ranch house with hardwood floors. I wore my tightest pair of white Levi jeans and a plaid flannel shirt, with work boots, as was then my custom. I remember knocking on his door, nervously, and Eyes quickly opening it. He was even more handsome than I'd remembered: sparkling eyes, dazzling smile—all the more impressive on his tall frame. The look he gave me—so intense, so resolutely meant for me—I knew that we were destined to be together.

That moment was temporarily interrupted by the appearance of someone darting past us into another room.

"Who is that?" I asked.

"Oh, you know—" Eyes offered. I didn't know. "That's V."

"And he is—?"

"He's just grabbing something out of my room." Eyes lowered his voice. "He's living in the guestroom now."

Later, V gone, I was given a tour of their home and it was explained that the two had recently broken up, and that V was living in the guestroom until he found another place. While it certainly didn't look like anyone was living in the guestroom, I pushed that thought aside. I had no reason to suspect Eyes was lying. Eyes was offering me a way forward, out from the gloom, into the world of the living. Thus, despite that brief appearance of V, I took hold of that chance. I took Eyes at his word. That decision would impact my life for years to come.

DOMESTIC BLISS

We'd only dated a few months when Eyes asked me to move in with him, and I swiftly agreed. Our time together had been idyllic, and for the first time in a very long time, I felt as if I were fully valued in a relationship. I was more than a caregiver and nursemaid. Eyes was loving, attentive, interested in me as a person, and encouraged my personal growth. In hindsight, while I should've certainly applied the brakes and not moved so swiftly, our prior connection made it feel as if simply having known Eyes for a period of years translated into knowing him thoroughly. But I didn't. It turns out, I didn't know Eyes at all.

After Eyes and I broke up, his ex V and I met for lunch, compared notes, and quickly became friends. V shared with me that on that first date at Eyes' house, when I saw V go into the master bedroom, they were indeed still together and V had thought their relationship to be on solid ground. V was shocked, some weeks later, when Eyes suddenly told him to pack up and move out. V was understandably angry at me, thinking their break was all my doing—that I was a homewrecker. But neither of us was told the truth by Eyes, and instead were supremely played against the other.

Prior to living together, Eyes insisted that our finances be combined and that we treat our relationship just as other straight couple would. While we couldn't legally marry in the U.S., Eyes insisted that someday we would have a civil union ceremony, and thus act as married, even if not then allowed to do so under the law.

Just after moving in, Eyes presented me with a Letter of Intent, spelling out for me the commitment we were making and our shared agreements on how our relationship would now evolve. Amidst his declarations of love, he wrote:

"Little needs to be said about the issue of monogamy. Since opening up myself sexually to my partner is much more than the physical act... It can become a window into the soul and therefore a very emotional and spiritual experience. That is something I wouldn't want to share with anyone else except my partner."

As I would be entering his home, I insisted that we repaint and reimagine the space, so that it felt like *ours* rather than his. We painted the living room the warm straw color that Shane and I had so loved, combining our shared furniture, transforming it quickly into a home for both of us. A home to raise children in. A home to grow old in. *A forever home.*

THE EYES HAVE IT

Only a week or so after moving in, I'd arrived home from work, prepared to cook dinner. After setting down my grocery bags, I turned to see Eyes walking toward me, and it was apparent that he'd been crying. Not having a clue as to what was wrong, I rushed to him, pulling him into my arms.

"What's wrong, baby?"

"I—. I can't—" he muttered, burying his head on my shoulder, tears flowing.

"Shh—" I whispered. "It's okay. Whatever it is, it'll be okay."

After a few moments, he pulled back. "I just found out I'm positive."

"What?!?" I was shocked. Not that being HIV positive would be a factor in my love for him, but this was entirely unexpected. "You didn't tell me that you were getting tested... Or even that you had a doctor's appointment today."

"I didn't want to worry you," he murmured, folding back into my arms.

"It's okay," I insisted, kissing his neck. "It'll be okay. This doesn't matter to me one bit. You're going to be fine."

That day was not, however, when Eyes actually discovered his HIV status. After our breakup I would learn that he'd known that fact for some time, but had chosen to lie to me until I was living in his home. Why would he make that choice? Why would he lie, knowing that being with someone HIV-positive wasn't an issue for me? I knew full well how to protect myself and, having gone through the experience of losing Shane, felt strong enough to tackle almost anything. He could've told me the truth on day one, and it wouldn't have changed a single thing. But he chose to lie. And lie. And lie. And the absolute strength I'd found within myself through caring for Shane would eventually come in very handy in dealing with Eyes and his lies.

THE ROAD LESS TRAVELED

In just our first year together, Eyes and I explored locally in California, taking road trips to Julian, Idyllwild, Palm Springs, San Diego, Solvang, San Luis Obispo, and Cambria, among others, with flights to San Francisco and Napa, St. George, UT (to meet his family), Boston, Maine, New York (to see plays and Bobby Short perform at the Café Carlyle), and to my family reunion in Waycross, Georgia. In fact, we made a commitment to take two big trips each year, to Europe or other destinations abroad—and we kept that promise for our six years together.

To have gone from a life focused on AIDS, in both my job at APLA and in being caregiver to Shane, to a life of seemingly endless exploration felt like the difference between life and death. What Eyes and I were now doing was *living*, and it felt so good, so right and so deserved.

I quickly introduced Eyes to my family and friends, and all came to love him. He was inquisitive, seemed to care about the lives of the people I cherished, and it wasn't long before he was well-integrated into my life, and I to his.

After just two months of dating, on my 31st birthday, I threw a party for myself at my friend Greg Solem's café, The Heights, in West Hollywood. My family and friends gathered, enjoying appetizers, and I made my own cakes, which were so good, Greg asked if I wanted to begin supplying his café with desserts. To be celebrating my birthday with my new love, exactly a year after checking Shane into the hospital, was entirely surreal. Seeing those assembled, I was so grateful for their support and love, and acknowledged so in my speech. Sadly, almost none of them are active in my life today.

For Eyes' birthday, I surprised him with a romantic dinner in our living room. I built a large tent frame with PVC pipe, spray painted the piping metallic gold, and covered it with a sheer white fabric which was placed in the middle of the room. Within it, a candlelit dinner for two, with Bobby Short CDs playing softly in the background. It was magical—even more so when Eyes looked at me, inching slowly forward, to show me in words and actions just how much he appreciated it—and me.

THE FAIRY TALE CASTLE

During our first year together, we took a two-week trip to Spain and Portugal—the first of our planned twice-annual trips abroad. As we began planning, it occurred to me that this trip would be the ideal time to propose to Eyes. Initially, I'd envisioned doing it next to some picturesque ruins, but after scouring countless travel books I selected the Alcázar of Segovia, a medieval castle perched high on a hill, as it looked incredibly romantic.

For the flight, we'd gotten buddy passes from Eye's friend, Eddie, who was a flight attendant for TWA. I was so happy to be getting the flights cheaply that I didn't really think much more about our travel. Thus, I was more than a little surprised to find that Eddie was actually working our flight from New York to Madrid. He kept bringing us glasses of Dom Pérignon, drinking two or three glasses to each of our one, and was entirely plastered before we ever landed. Even more surprising, upon arrival, was Eddie's revelation that he'd booked a hotel for us.

Eddie insisted on negotiating with the taxi driver, telling us that he knew Madrid well and could get a good rate, but I'm pretty certain we overpaid the driver. Disembarking from the taxi, we looked around, but there was no hotel to be found. Eddie then gave us a hotel name, which he swore was close by, and we spread out in search of it, bags dragging behind, but found nothing. Eddie then went out solo, swearing that he'd find it. He came back, apparently successful, and we followed him to a hotel many blocks away, which had a different name than what he had said and which did not have a reservation for us. Clearly, Eddie hadn't told us the truth, but at that point, we were happy just to have a hotel. That changed when, entering our room, I saw that it had three single beds. Apparently, Eddie was rooming with us. That was not what I'd envisioned when planning this romantic trip.

Eyes and I pushed two of the beds together, and I could feel Eddie's eyes narrow. He knew that Eyes and I were together—there had been no secret of that. What made him uncomfortable? Had he hoped for a three-way, or did he have a secret crush on one of us? He seemed upset, though I never found out why.

That night, Eddie led us to find his "favorite restaurant in Madrid," which proved to be another wild goose chase, ending with us selecting a spot at random, which actually proved quite good.

Together, the three of us toured the city and took in the sights, until it was time for Eddie's working flight back to the U.S. As Eyes and I would be staying at the hotel a few more days, I asked Eddie if the hotel took credit cards.

"Of course," he said. "I just paid for my portion with one."

It would turn out, that too was a lie. Upon our departure, we learned the hotel only took cash.

I was disappointed, upon first entering Segovia on our bus, with how boringly pedestrian it appeared. Aside from the castle, which looked beautiful from any angle, the city itself didn't seem very special, until we passed the aqueduct, where streets began to narrow, buildings got older, a charming farmer's market materialized, and beautiful reminders of old Europe popped up left and right.

We journeyed to the castle, taking the tour, and the view from the top was magnificent.

"Should I ask him now?" I wondered, wanting the moment to be perfect. With so many tourists about, I decided to wait for a more secluded spot.

We left the castle, wandering down the hill beneath it, where a gentle river wound through a forest of trees. I'd begun to feel sick, my stomach churning and pressure building, which I first chalked it up to nerves, knowing the moment to propose was swiftly approaching, but it became apparent very quickly that "the moment" was not all that was approaching.

I darted behind some trees, lowering my pants just in time.

Finally adjusted, I came out, entirely embarrassed, only to be greeted with a warm smile by Eyes. There was such love in his eyes. Apparently, there was nothing I could do that would make him stop loving me—even shitting amongst the trees. And it was thus that I proposed.

He asked me if I felt as if I were compromising, somehow, with him, and I immediately said no. He was all I wanted. All I'd hoped for.

With Eyes, I wasn't settling at all. I was getting more than I'd dreamed.

A few days later, Eyes and I journeyed by bus into Lisbon, Portugal. The dank hovel of those in desperation was entirely unexpected as we witnessed shabby tent cities and hundreds of homeless from our bus window. *Europe is supposed to be pretty, damn it!* Portugal was a juxtaposition of opulent moments and beautiful sights, surrounded by abject despair; an endless eyeline of hookers and beggars.

One day, we took a train to Sintra, of which it has been said, "Beware, those who visit want to stay forever"—on which I call bullshit.

There was an odd moment immediately after the train ride, which didn't register to me at the time, but which has repeatedly come into my thoughts in the years since. Upon our arrival in Sintra, desperate to pee, Eyes and I went into the train station men's room, which had a long trough urinal. We stepped to opposite ends of it and began to piss, only to have another traveler from the train, whom I had not noticed, step between us at the trough, unzipping, only to pull out a huge, fully erect penis, and begin confidently stroking it.

I was shocked, and quickly finished, leaving the rest room, with Eyes right behind. We joked about it as we explored the town, but later, I wondered: why would a total stranger be that brazen, feel bold enough, to present himself like that? Sure, he could've just been doing it for the kicks, but looking back on it, with the knowledge I now have, I wonder if Eyes had in fact been eyeing him, encouraging his flirtation on the train, all without my knowledge... I might be wrong, but it seems a distinct possibility.

On another, less-lusty train, we journeyed to the seaside town of Cascais. Just like Lisbon, this town literally crawled with all manner of beggars, some missing limbs and some faking it. Up and down the walkways, these sad souls would contort and drag themselves about, desperate for a handout.

Eyes and I had previously discussed that, whenever we were ready, we would each propose to the other. While non-traditional, we wanted to make sure that we were both equals in our partnership, and having us both make the ask seemed a nice way to do that. In his journal that day, Eyes wrote: "Today, I asked Kergan to marry me. A first for me, and I have every intention of making it my last. He said, 'Yes!'"

I did say yes. I meant it, with every fiber of my being. Eyes was perfection. Physically beautiful, nurturing, caring— he had it all. And despite having it all, he could somehow love fully-flawed me??? That was amazing. That kind of love was worth marrying.

GOING TO THE CHAPEL – THE FIRST TIME

Upon our return from Portugal, Eyes and I launched into wedding-planning mode. We decided on a January wedding, as that would mark roughly a year since we'd formally begun our relationship. It would take place in our backyard, and I set about arranging a caterer, etc.

Eyes invited his four siblings to attend the nuptials. All but his half-sister declined, with more than one noting that being gay was a sin and that their presence would mean that they somehow approved of our "sin." Years later, Eyes would become estranged from his accepting half-sister, who has no knowledge as to why he rejected her, while fully embracing the very siblings who had once rejected him.

Eyes and I wanted our wedding to be traditional, yet encapsulate who we were, both as individuals and as a couple. In lieu of the traditional place-setting of pastel butter mints wrapped in netting, we selected Hot Tamales candy wrapped in netting, tied off with a Red Vine. We put together our own playlist of songs that we loved, strung together on a cassette tape. In addition to our wedding cakes, we had the caterers bring out trays of Dairy Queen Blizzards.

The ceremony was conducted by a dear friend of Eyes', Richard Sneed, the definitive Renaissance man. A renowned expert in the Dead Sea Scrolls, Richard had been chancellor of a college, an avid art collector, lover of books, movies, and culture... He could talk to anyone about anything, with a caring and nurturing manner. He was the closest person to a priest that Eyes or I knew and was perfect to officiate. Instead of vows, Eyes and I wrote each other letters, which we exchanged before the assembled and read aloud.

Years later, following my eventual breakup with Eyes, Richard stayed resolutely by my side. He abhorred that Eyes had cheated, and hated even more that, in the months following our split, he and Eyes had met many times, with Eyes repeatedly maintaining to Richard that he'd done nothing wrong, defending his "innocence." Being lied to was something that Richard could never forgive.

In addition to throwing Mason a baby shower, once I became a single dad, Richard would surprise me with occasional checks to help pay for Mason's education. When my first book came out, Richard loved it so much that he bought copies to distribute to his friends. He told me that it reminded him of James Joyce, which is the ultimate compliment.

In December 2017, I received a call from his husband, Tad, telling me that Richard had died. While he had been in failing health for several years, his loss was a brutal blow. In addition to Alzheimer's, Richard had been battling cancer, among other assorted ailments. But because of Alzheimer's, whenever Tad would take him to the doctor, Richard would have no memory of why he was there... He would repeatedly ask, "Tad, do I have cancer?" and Tad would have to explain it all to him, reliving each moment himself, again and again and again.

Prior to reading our wedding vow letters, our respective parents stood and spoke to each of us. My dad said, in part, of me:

"Your arrival in our family was a blessing from God that still endures. I have a storehouse of wonderful memories of your years with us that will warm my heart all of my life... May you live with love and serenity and with the knowledge that I will always be there for you. I love you."

Dottie's speech touted my accomplishments, from pre-school on up, mentioning awards I'd won, as if needing to sell the audience on my worthiness to Eyes as a partner. It was almost as if she couldn't allow herself to get personal, but finally did, ending on an unexpected note, given her strong religious beliefs:

"So, to you two precious people whom I love, and to each of you wonderful people here today, may God's richest blessings be with each of you, now and always."

Portions of my letter to Eyes:

"As I begin writing this affirmation of my love for you, I'm staring at the photograph of you on the train back from Cascais, shortly after you asked me to marry you. My eyes focus on yours, so clear, warm, and knowing, and I am awed by your beauty.

I stand before you today the happiest man in the world. For not only is a long-held dream coming true, but I am offered the opportunity to share my feelings with our closest friends and family. What an amazing experience it is for us to join together with our beloved in honor of our union. A bond that is strong, simple and lasting.

I've never once doubted the power of our love, but I'm

constantly astounded by its depth and fluidity. Just when I think I could not possibly love you more, you glance at me, and I'm taken to a new, astonishing, higher plane."

It is hard for me to read the letter Eyes wrote to me, even all of these years later. Like mine, his is loving, thoughtful, and empowering. It's hard to reconcile it with the events that would soon follow. One paragraph, though, does still ring true. Eyes writes:

"As I learned more than five years ago, you're a man of character and principle and you don't allow others to violate your rights as a human being, not even me."

He was right. I don't allow people to violate my rights, not even him. I won't be stepped on, stepped over, or treated with disrespect. I also won't tolerate deceit, betrayal, or disloyalty. That trait has come in handy as a parent, and that ferocity fueled me to do anything necessary in the coming years to protect our son. It's one quality that I'm sure Eyes later wished I didn't possess... Let's put it this way: You don't want to fuck with me.

A FIVE-YEAR HONEYMOON

Following our wedding, Eyes and I embarked on a honeymoon to Paris, and for the years following, it felt as if our honeymoon would live on forever. We fell into blissful domesticity. We cooked meals at home, sometimes with friends. We puttered at Target, Home Depot and Trader Joe's. We continued to explore the world, taking Dottie on her only trip to Europe, where we introduced her to Paris and Italy. Eyes and I loved being together. It seemed that ours was a universe of two; no one else was really required.

We were a couple, focused on our future. We soon began talking more seriously about opening our family up by adopting children. We would start with one, but we wouldn't stop there. One, two, three...? The number was never defined, but the plan was. I would quit work, become at stay-at-home dad, and indulge in all of my loves: cooking, kids, creating...

It was not a perfect relationship. What relationship is? But any issues that arose, we tackled them together, keeping the lines of communication open. Or so I thought.

For an entire five-year period, our relationship seemed solid and on track. In fact, I'm loathe to admit that I'd compare us to other couples and actually gloat to myself, *"Oh, our relationship is so much stronger than theirs! We are so close. So happy. So perfectly in love. And those poor people—? They'll never have what we have. Our love is superior. So it is, and so it shall be—forever!"*

GREEN EGGS AND HAM

I'd been searching for a temporary job closer to home, one which I would immediately quit the moment our baby was born. I had been working in Los Angeles at the Little Froggy Television Network, known for teen programming, such as *Polyamorous Party of Four, Three Pretty Magical Sisters,* and *The College Girl with the Hair,* but I had come to hate my job. The commute to Burbank from Orange County could be two hours each way, but that wasn't the primary reason I was dissatisfied. I worked for the Co-Presidents of Marketing; one of which was Good Cop and one of which was more than Bad, and they made my life awful.

Each day with Bad would consist of a screaming rant and at least 150 expletives. These two Co-Presidents would barricade themselves in their office all day long, rarely emerging, except to call their promo producers into their sanctum to explain just why the fuck they thought their commercials were stellar, when they were clearly shit. During these review sessions, raised voices would punctuate the air, and Bad's voice would be heard, shouting above the rest, as if he alone knew how to craft TV promo gold.

They'd then call another producer who, upon arrival, would be told to sit on the lobby couch until summoned. That person might sit for an hour, or two, or even three years, before being allowed entrance to Good/Bad's lair. Good Cop and Bad treated their staff dismissively, with even Good Cop having a higher sense of self than warranted. Their egos were out of control, especially considering that the teen audience of the Little Froggy Network would've watched the network's shows regardless of prompting. It was an easy sell.

On one eventful night, all 60 Little Froggy "stars" were brought together on the studio backlot to spend an evening shooting promotional spots. Each show's group of actors would look into camera and say, *"Teenage Beach Party Ninjas,* Tuesdays at 8 on KGIG!" and repeat the same, switching out KGIG for the laundry list of Little Froggy's regional channels. The talent was impossibly gorgeous, with attitude abounding. You could sense their acting rivalries as they shot dirty glances at each other between takes.

During this particular shoot, in addition to the regional promotions, we were filming an anti-drug public service announcement (PSA), which was perfect for our targeted teen viewing audience. In it, each star would read the entire PSA script directly into camera via teleprompter, and we would then edit the footage so that the dialogue would jump between each of our bone-worthy celebrities. Our most popular show, *Down by the Sex Creek,* starred four "teens," but one of them, the show's bad girl, would play that same role during this particular promo shoot.

She and her publicist pulled me and my boss aside. "N'chell doesn't feel comfortable, reading these lines," the publicist noted, shoving the script at my boss, who had written it.

"Is there a problem? A line you'd like changed?" he queried.

N'chell spoke up. "It's not the script, it's the concept."

"Um," my boss stuttered, "you are against teaching kids not to use drugs or alcohol?"

"I just—" she paused dramatically. "That's not my passion. Who am I to tell kids what to do or not do?"

"Well," my boss offered, "we have an opportunity to use this platform, and the success of your show, to teach kids that drugs and alcohol are not the best choice. I understand it may not be your particular passion, but it would be great if you could say a line or two into the camera, given how popular your character is..."

N'chell and her publicist conferred, in hushed tones, then returned to us.

"N'chell is happy to do a PSA for you about illiteracy. Getting kids to read is something she can get behind."

My boss and I exchanged glances, knowing that we did not have a stack of extra PSA scripts lying about, waiting to be filmed.

He smiled, "Well, thank you, N'chell. We appreciate your consideration, but you can go on to station 4, where we are shooting Christmas greetings." As we turned away, he muttered under his breath, "Sure hope you're not Jewish."

While we couldn't force N'chell to film this particular anti-drug PSA, her future husband would tragically die from just such an overdose. What events might have been altered if N'chell had actually filmed that PSA? Given his youth, the actor might have actually seen it. It could have changed his life. That one little PSA, which would've taken all of five minutes to film, could have made a difference.

But today, out of all of the Little Froggy stars, it is N'chell who has had the most successful career. Maybe being a bitch was entirely worth it.

One early morning I was at my desk when I heard my bosses, Good Cop and Bad, coming down the hall. Bad was shouting as normal:

"God damn motherfucker! Who the fuck does he think he is? Like he tells us what the fuck to do? Jesus fucking Christ!"

As they entered, Good Cop nodded a greeting to me. Bad just continued yelling: "That fucking prick—Jesus Christ!"

"Bad," Good interrupted, "Aren't you going to say hello to Kergan?"

"What—? Ain't I fucking talking to him?!?"

I knew then that I needed to find another job, STAT.

I searched and searched before getting a call from a group closer to home, Green Eggs and Ham Marketing. They specialized in hiring boring, bland people who would be willing to put on a polo shirt bearing, for example, the logo of Canon, to be trained on Canon products, and then to walk into a Best Buy and haunt the aisles, hoping they could rope some unsuspecting consumer into buying a Canon printer.

When people think of marketing and advertising, they usually think "creative," as if every day were opportunities to display to the client exciting new projects, with beautiful, enticing art and messaging. Not this. It was a numbers game. Canon wants to sell 3 million Canon printers in the United States this Christmas. How many fake Canon employees can you quickly train and churn out into those Best Buy stores, in order to meet your goal?

After the Little Froggy Television Network, this was not glamorous. Not by a longshot. But it was precisely my former title that enticed the GE & H company to reach out to me, as they felt that the CEO would lap up my celebrity-by-proxy credentials.

As the Director of Human Resources explained to me, the CEO of the company, Mrs. Green Eggs, was—to put it nicely—a handful. No assistant could ever make her happy, and many prospects had run from the building, screaming, in tears. The HR Director, whom I would later learn had his female assistants photograph him shirtless for his online dating profile, asked if I'd ever worked for anyone "challenging" before. I could only laugh and soon had an interview.

GE & H was a non-descript office building, perfectly suiting this non-descript marketing firm, in non-descript Orange County, the land where everything looks exactly the same. As far as you can see, non-descript offices dot the never-ending horizon. One gigantic field of nothingness: no personality, no bright colors; a dust bin for the uninspired. And it was where I would work for the next ten years.

Upon meeting Mrs. Green Eggs, I knew I could handle her. She had been a single mother and raised several young boys, working as a waitress. Through sheer grit and determination, she had pulled herself to the top, becoming CEO of Green Eggs & Ham long before there were many female CEO's. Could she be a pain? Yes. But I totally understood where she was coming from. She was often looked upon as a hurdle. Every time she'd open her mouth, I could see others shrink at the very motion. You knew that whatever she said, it would upset the apple cart. And everyone likes their apple carts nice and tidy.

But when the original owner of GE & H, Mr. Ham, had run the company into the ground thanks to reckless spending, it was Mrs. Green Eggs who stepped in to drag the company out from the quickly-circling drain. Did the employees appreciate her cost-saving measures? Doubtful. But anyone knows that a single mom raising young boys fully understands how to scrimp and save, tighten the belt and find a way forward, with no help from the men.

I "got" her. And I liked her. Which was good, as soon after I was hired, another assistant leaned into me and said, "I'm so glad you took this job. I could never do it—She always leaves me in tears." But not me. No, Mrs. Green Eggs liked me, and liked having someone who had been at the right hand of the Co-Presidents of the Little Froggy Network as her right hand. She felt entitled. And that worked well for me.

LIFE LESSON #16

Never underestimate the impact that walking into a gym shower, only to witness a former boss shaving his balls, can have.

SPAY THE BITCH

Isabella and Sophia, our beagles, were named for Rossellini and Loren, respectively. My original names for them were to be Madame Armfeldt and Countess Malcolm, after two characters in Stephen Sondheim's *A Little Night Music*, as I thought it would be fun to call out for "Countess" or "Madame," but Eyes had overruled me. Thus, we settled on my second choices. That these daffy, dwarfy beagles didn't remotely resemble their statuesque namesakes was immaterial.

We'd gotten them after moving into our new home, the one in which we'd soon raise a baby. Isabella was the quirkier of the two. "Neurotic" would be her most kind description. She could never be tamed and was a tangle of neuroses, always sniffing about as if she were scouring the floor of a crack house for leftovers. Sophia was the more demur and glamourous of the pair. Her tan and white colorings made her a bit more majestic, sharing the coloring of famed Lassie, and her height—a bit taller than most beagles—rendered her more becoming, in my eyes.

The sisters doted on each other, but never on us. Unlike most dogs, they only paid attention to us when they wanted food. Still, on the day they were spayed, I was concerned as to how they were doing and drove home at lunch to check on them. I would never normally leave work in the middle of the day, but knowing that Eyes would have a full day at the office, I wanted to make sure all of their stiches were in place.

Driving up our street, I spotted a dumpy car in our drive. It wasn't our house cleaner's, as she'd come a few days earlier. *"Who could that be,"* I wondered, *"to have parked so familiarly in our driveway?"* Instead of pulling alongside it and entering through our garage as I normally would, which would make excessive noise, I instead parked in the street and crossed silently to our front door, opening it as quietly as I could. Once inside, I loudly called out, "Hello?"

I heard a scurry on the upper floor, then Eyes called back, "Hey! Be right there!" I had no idea what was going on, why Eyes was home, or whose car he'd been in, but he then appeared at the top of the stairs, running down to greet me in his dress socks. He gave me a quick peck on the cheek. "Hey, sweetie! I'm just giving Jorge a tour of the new house. He loves it."

I immediately relaxed. Jorge had worked for Eyes for years in a maintenance role. Two years prior, when the guest toilet at our home malfunctioned just hours before our annual Christmas party, Jorge promptly arrived to fix it, saving the day. He wasn't worthy of suspicion.

"Great," I smiled. "I just came home to check on the dogs."

"We've got to get back to work anyway," Eyes replied. "Just gotta use the bathroom," he said, making his way back upstairs.

I went to find the dogs in the backyard and was relieved to see them looking well. As I sat there, giving them some attention, I began to replay what had just occurred. If Eyes and Jorge had come simply for a quick tour of the house, why had Eyes removed his shoes? Why hadn't Jorge yet appeared? And why had I heard scurrying noises just before Eyes yelled out to me?

None of it made any sense.

Still, I told myself, we had a baby coming, in just a few months. We were happy together. We'd just moved into this beautiful house and spent a small fortune refurbishing it. We'd begun furnishing the nursery, turning over what little savings we had to Babies n' More.

What possible reason could Eyes have to cheat—and if he had, would the straight Mexican subordinate at work be the optimal choice? All of this irrational thought must be in my head, right?

Jorge came out to the patio to greet me. "You have a beautiful home," he smiled, offering his hand, which I shook.

"Thank you. How is your family?" I inquired. One of Jorge's kids had suffered a horrific auto accident a few years prior, and Eyes had helped raise money for her care. As a gesture of kindness, Jorge and his wife had asked Eyes to be her godfather.

"They're doing well. Kids are growing like weeds!"

I nodded, knowing that soon Eyes and I would experience children of our own.

A few minutes later, Eyes and Jorge were gone, headed back to work. I sat in the sun with Sophia and Isabella for a bit, but moments about the exchange kept jumping out at me. I couldn't shake the feeling that something was fundamentally wrong.

"I know," I thought, *"I'll take a look around. If I find a sign,*

even one tell-tale sign, I'll call Eyes out. But if everything's fine, I'll let it go. I'm sure it's all in my head."

And with that, I headed upstairs, carefully examining our bedroom and master bath—all looked normal. Nothing under the bed, nothing odd in drawers, no soiled linen in the hamper, I checked trashcans—and then I went into the guest bath to do the same. Nothing.

Entering the guest bedroom, all seemed okay, until I walked in closer and saw a bottle of lube on the bedside table.

I was completely livid, raging inside. *How could I have been so stupid???* I felt such desperate pain at having been betrayed and immediately called Eyes.

"Tell me the truth," I demanded, with no introduction.

"About what?" he asked, as if clueless.

"I *found* it," I said, louder than warranted.

"You found what? What are you talking about?" he queried innocently. "Sweetie, I have no clue—"

"I found it! I found the lube!" I yelled into the phone.

"The—? Oh, honey—that's not what you think!" he laughed. "Seriously—I know it's not funny—but you've got this all wrong. You think me and Jorge—? He's just a friend. Not even that, really—basically a co-worker. You know that!"

"Then what about the lube?" I demanded.

"It's just—last night, I couldn't sleep, and you were already snoring away. And I was horny. I went into the guestroom to get myself off and must've left the lube in there."

"So, you're giving tours of the house, with lube sitting out?"

Eyes continued to pacify me, until I was sufficiently calmed. "Listen—this was nothing. You know me. I can see why you think it but come on. Jorge? Really?"

Given that Eyes had claimed he wasn't sexually attracted to people of color, I did see his point.

"We'll talk more about this when I come home, but I sure hope you believe me. I love you. We have an amazing life together—and it's only going to get better," he insisted. "Do you believe me?"

I wanted to. I wanted to believe him so badly... "Yes. Yes, I believe you."

"I love you," he cooed.

"I love you, too."

The dial tone sounded and our call was complete.

I did love him. That part was true. I loved him more than I had ever loved anyone. But *believe?* That required a larger leap of faith.

I called my therapist of many years for an emergency phone consult. After explaining the situation, she said, "Has Eyes ever misled you before?"

Though my mind led me to a few tidbits, I could think of nothing concrete. "Not that I know of, for certain. Nothing that I could prove."

"And you have a baby coming..." she reminded.

This was true. Why would Eyes jeopardize our that?

With the help of her gentle prodding, I allowed myself to believe Eyes. Not because my therapist wanted me to, but because I really did love him and the life we were creating. I loved our soon-to-be-child. I loved our family unit.

And had I listened to my gut, no matter how accurate that doubt might have been, Eyes and I wouldn't have had our eventual son, Mason, whom Russ and I live for today.

LIFE LESSON #17

Should your parents learn that your soon-to-be-born son will be African American and treat your child's arrival differently than your sister's children, get thee to therapy.

AND BABY MAKES THREE

We'd begun the adoption process some months prior to Mason's arrival by connecting with a facilitator and crafting our "adoption profile book," a pictorial with promotional copy, advertising us as the best possible adoptive parents for some lady's future kid. After a few calls, we connected with the perfect birth mom.

She wasn't young—29—which in adoption terms is a good thing, as younger women typically get skittish, changing their minds at the last minute. I won't go into all the specifications about why she had decided to place her child for adoption, but they were understandable. We enjoyed our phone conversations with her but it would only be the morning of Mason's birth that we would meet in person.

Eyes and I had flown to her state the night prior to participate in his delivery. We knew that she'd kept her pregnancy a secret from her family, with whom she lived, but it was only in her hospital room, upon greeting her—so impossibly petite—that we realized just how successful she'd been. Her bump was small, leading her to tell her family that she had "female troubles" and was going into the hospital to have a cyst removed. And they believed her.

Eyes and I were a basket of nerves, even more so as the hour approached when she drew closer to delivery. We were with her in the delivery room, and—having never been in one prior—I was astounded at the sensory overload that hit me as I held her hand, encouraging her to push, and all of the subsequent things that happened at my urging. When Mason came out, face impossibly squished and whiter than I am—the whitest white man on the planet—I was shocked. It was here. The moment of which I'd long dreamt, having a child of my own... it was finally happening.

Eyes and I took turns holding Mason in the side room while the other sat with birth mom, who had no one else with her. While that decision to have one of us with her at all times was partly calculated, to ensure there were no opportunities for her to change her mind, I really wanted her to know just how exceptional I thought she was and to confirm that, as hard as it may have been, she'd ultimately made the best decision for her son.

Eyes and I stayed in town for 11 days, until the necessary paperwork was signed by a judge, allowing us to leave the state. With that accomplished, I took Mason home on a flight separately from Eyes. To be alone with my child, independent, jetting home to start a new life was amazing.

On the flight, I almost punched a woman, so irritated was I that she assumed I knew nothing about babies and how to comfort them. *I read the fucking book, ma'am. I babysat my infant nephew for months, changing countless diapers, picking up umpteen binkies, quieting who-knows-how-many-hissy-fits—I know how to calm my son.*

While I understand why people select surrogacy, for me, there was never any option other than adoption. I didn't care remotely that this child be blood-related to me. I wanted to take in a child who otherwise wouldn't have a home. I wanted to help nourish a child needing protection. And I hoped to do that with Mason.

I'll never understand why Eyes went forward with the adoption. As I later learned, he'd been cheating on me for years, long before Mason's birth and long after. Why had he made that implicit promise, made when bringing a child into this life, to do best by it, when he led a secret life? To me, it was unfathomable. Yet, again, without that choice, we would have never met Mason, who brings us endless joy to this day.

LIFE LESSON #18

When you're asked what you want for your birthday, be more specific than necessary.

Mason was two-and-a-half months old, and I'd slept little during that entire time as it was my job to nurse him at night and take care of him through the day. I had quit my job at Green Eggs & Ham to become a full-time dad. Our plan was that I'd never have to work again, as Eyes and I planned to have more children.

On the day I turned 30, I'd admitted Shane to the hospital. On the day I turned 31, I'd thrown myself a party, at which I introduced Eyes to my friends. On this date, I was turning 35.

When Eyes asked me what I wanted for my birthday, the answer came quickly and simply: a day off. "It would be great if you could take care of everything, just for the day. Let me sleep in, lounge about..." Eyes agreed, and I looked forward to having a single day of luxury.

On that birthday morning, I rose, only to find that Sophia and Isabella had thoroughly destroyed their new dog bed, leaving balls of fluff littering the laundry room floor. I mentioned it to Eyes, who nodded, but made no move. I cleaned up the entire mess.

Soon after, it became clear that Mason needed a diaper change. Again, I mentioned it to Eyes, who nodded, but continued to dole out various pharmaceuticals into his weekly pill case. Sighing, I put Mason onto the changing table. Given the early morning chill of March, I had a space heater warming us nearby.

As I changed Mason, projectile poop shot out of his ass, landed on the space heater, and burst into flames.

Eyes just sat there.

LIFE LESSON #19

The first time your husband exposes you to crabs and tells you he likely got them from stretching on the carpet at the gym, take him at his word and believe him.

The second time your husband exposes you to crabs and tells you he likely got them from stretching on the carpet at the gym, don't.

I did believe Eyes, both times, though I should've known better. But it wouldn't be too much longer before I knew all too well who he was and of what he was capable.

THE BEGINNING OF THE END

The first year of Mason's birth was magical. I loved being a full-time dad. My bonding time with him is something I will always treasure, and I have Eyes to thank for that. I loved to hear Mason giggle, to watch his eyes absorb new things, and to push himself—to lift up on his arms, to roll over, to crawl, to walk. I was there for every moment. Eyes was rarely around and missed most of those. Too bad for him.

I spent what little spare time I had writing, needing someplace to channel my creative energy, but I was most happy just being daddy: shopping at Trader Joe's, taking Mason to Target to overspend in their brilliantly merchandised store, crafting homecooked meals, and taking my black son to Orange County Mommy & Me classes, just to thoroughly confuse the local, conservative straight white women.

In August of that year, I surprised Eyes with a birthday party. It was so much a surprise that Eyes almost didn't attend. I'd invited several people from out-of-state, including his parents and his long-estranged brother—a Mormon bishop who'd refused to attend our wedding, as well as his best friend Paula and local friends. Eyes had promised to be home at an agreed-upon time that day and, when he didn't show, I called his cell, leaving several messages, until he finally responded. Eyes was so upset that

I'd demanded he come home that very moment, I never thought to ask where he had been or what he'd been doing—an oversight on my part, and an awkward moment I'd later question. Still, when he did finally arrive to the party, taking in those he cherished, Eyes seemed happy at my efforts, and he was quickly drowned in love by all who'd gathered.

In November of 2000, Eyes' adoption of Mason was finally complete. In those days, California law required that gay couples adopt differently than straight. As Eyes was the bread-winner, and I would be playing the role of mom, Eyes would first adopt Mason, and I would later complete a "second parent" adoption. The process was onerous and the cost substantial, but for gay couples it was the only option. Still, in Mason's birth state, gay couples couldn't even be on the birth certificate together, so we were grateful for this small step forward. Mason was ours and there would be no turning back.

It was a joyful first step in our adoption process. Future steps would be not necessarily be joyful or as perfunctory. In fact, future steps in ensuring my rights to Mason would prove particularly perilous and largely the reason I drink far too much Chardonnay.

At the age of 11 months, we took Mason to Paris and Italy, intent on keeping our "two trips to Europe each year" promise, infant in tow. I fully realized Mason would never remember such trips, but I also believed that exposing him to new sights, sounds, flavors and experiences would help create nuances within, and an appetite for new things.

Soon after Mason turned one, Eyes and I took him to Vermont, to look at bed and breakfast properties. Eyes was becoming more and more insistent that this was to be our future; getting out of crazy-making-California and settling down into familial-bliss, running a B&B.

While in Vermont, we stumbled upon a marathon in Burlington. Watching the participants run/limp across the finish line, I became acutely aware of how many times I'd stood in similar spots, cheering for Eyes as he crossed a finish line, only to think, "I could never do that." Standing there in Burlington, eyes on that line, I thought to myself, *"Why do I always say 'I could never do that'? Why don't I believe in myself?"* Thus, I made a pledge, then and there, to return that very next year and run that race myself.

In my mind, I envisioned Eyes holding Mason up at the finish line, cheering me on. That particular part of the vision would not occur, but I would cross that finish line as pledged, and the year of training it would require would see me through all manner of hardship.

As he'd long been looking for a new job, it came as no surprise when Eyes announced that he had an important interview coming up. I was thrilled, knowing he needed something that would keep him and us moving forward. We went to bed the night prior to his interview excited about what the future might hold.

Despite having ushered Mason through his nightly feedings, I woke up in the pre-dawn hours, around 4:00 a.m., to find Eyes missing—his spot on our bed suspiciously cold. His cell phone and car were gone as well, and no number of voicemails would prompt him to respond.

The next day, just before noon, Eyes finally returned my call. He explained that he'd been so anxious about the job interview that he couldn't sleep. Tossing and turning, he finally bolted out of bed and headed to the beach, where he slept in his car and only woke after sunrise. I expressed how worried I had been. How concerned I was that I had no idea where he'd been or if he was alright. He apologized, promising that should he ever do something similar he would leave a note.

His story didn't add up. It seemed erratic and out of character. The bottom line was that I didn't believe him, but decided to file that moment, making note of it in my journal, should I ever need it.

In the ensuing weeks, Eyes began to act demonstrably different, as if I'd somehow failed him. He was distant, disdainful, and uninterested in me, Mason, or anything to do with our household. He inquired where I'd put his books on philosophy, which indicated a crisis of faith or belief, and I steered him to them. He seemed aloof and unpredictable, not always coming home on time, or with vague excuses as to why he'd been detained. It was as if he'd been replaced by a double, who knew nothing about our life.

I asked Eyes repeatedly if I'd done something wrong, and he said no. I asked if he was having an affair, and he said no. I asked him repeatedly what was going on, but received no concrete information. The closest I got was, *"This has nothing to do with you. I'm going through something. Dealing with my past. My parents..."*

As his mother had abandoned the family while Eyes was quite young, leaving her children with their alcoholic father—that he might be dealing with trauma years later was understandable. I just couldn't imagine why he couldn't— or wouldn't—share such information with me.

Throughout his dilemma, I strove to be supportive, loving, understanding, and helpful, whenever possible. Although I'd already been overseeing Mason almost entirely, I took on even more time, as Eyes felt he had to explore his past and present, in search of answers to questions of which only Eyes knew the motives.

One weekend, as I desperately needed some rest and relaxation, Eyes agreed to keep Mason, and I headed to my parents' condo in Palm Desert for some "me" time. Eyes and Mason were to be spending the weekend at home, prompting confusion on my end when I called our house at 9:00 that evening, only to have the call go unanswered and my message dumped into voicemail. The next morning, I called again, only to leave another message—but I was getting worried. Where could they possibly be?

Later that morning, I again called, this time using my password to retrieve our messages. In addition to the voicemails I myself had left, there was a curious garbled call, left at one in the morning. Who would've called our house at that hour? And why hadn't Eyes heard the phone?

Hours later, I finally got ahold of Eyes. When questioned, Eyes simply stated that he'd been really sleepy the night prior and hadn't heard the many calls, as he'd taken melatonin to ensure he slept well. But that didn't make any sense, given that he was supposed to be caring for an infant. Again, I chose not to engage, but wrote it down, should I ever need it.

Throughout his months of odd behavior, I kept telling myself, *"He loves you. You've been together for five years yet have known each other even longer. You're married, for God's sake! This is but a blip. He wouldn't have adopted a child with you if something was going on. You're imagining this. Give him space."*

This train of thought was further buttressed by Eyes himself. "You're imagining things. I would never... I love you. You know my commitment to you—and Mason." Every question of where he'd been or who he'd seen, was met with quick response. Often, he would say, "Remember, I told you I was going to the store?" when he hadn't. Or, "You're confused. I mentioned that after work I had yoga," when he hadn't. It was gaslighting at its finest.

I had truly turned into Ingrid Bergman, and Eyes was Charles Boyer, shifting things about in our attic with the sole goal being to drive me insane. The only piece missing was *Gaslight's* devious maid.

I so desperately wanted to believe Eyes. I wanted to believe that I had not been wrong. That I, who prides myself on being a shrewd judge of character, couldn't have been fundamentally mistaken about this man whose ring I wore.

Early one summer evening, Eyes came home to announce that a friend of his, the same person who had previously hired hit men, had offered Eyes a house in Newport Beach in which to stay, until Eyes was able to sort out his issues. Eyes stated that he thought some structured time to himself, to contemplate, might help him on his quest. I couldn't believe it. The man I loved wanted to separate. I wanted to be understanding. I wanted to be compassionate, but this seemed more serious than I'd imagined. I asked him to write down the address and phone number, which he said he would.

"So, you're moving out...?" I asked, trying not to appear incredulous.

"Yes."

"When? When are you moving?"

"Tonight," he replied. And with that, Eyes packed a bag and was gone.

With Eyes staying at his friend's beach house twenty-four seven, my life became a living hell. I barely slept, trying to keep the house in order, Mason on track, and attempting to make sense of Eyes and his odd behavior. It was all I could do to keep it together.

Sometime after Eyes moved out, Mason had a full-blown health emergency in the middle of the night. He had a raging fever of 105 degrees, swollen lymph nodes, and a rash all over his body. I gathered him up and rushed to the emergency room, where I called Eyes, dialing both cell and beach house numbers, but received no response. Mason was quickly admitted, and I stayed with him, hitting redial, leaving countless voicemails on Eyes' cell, as well as calling the beach house number, where a phone would ring and ring, endlessly. It was as if I'd married a cipher. I thought that I had known this person inside and out, only to find myself trying to contact a stranger. A total stranger with whom I'd adopted a child.

Later, finger exhausted from dialing, I finally gave up. As the lights in Mason's ER room dimmed, I laid down beside him in bed, holding him in my arms throughout the long night.

THAT'S SOME BEACH HOUSE

One weekend, Eyes and I exchanged cars, as he would be taking Mason to the beach house to give me a much-needed break. My Expedition was safer for a child than Eyes' rough and tumble Jeep Wrangler, so it made sense for us to switch.

Hoping to create a positive moment for us, trying to entice him back, I decided to clean Eyes' Jeep inside and out, as it hadn't been washed in some time. While detailing the inside, I found a baggie with some pills in it, which didn't look familiar. I knew Eyes' HIV meds, and these weren't them.

Was Eyes on drugs? It certainly was a possibility. It would explain some of his inconsistent actions, but didn't seem like something he would do. To my knowledge, he wasn't a druggie, smoked pot only sporadically, and indulged in an occasional beer or margarita. But if the past months had taught me anything, it was that I didn't know Eyes at all. And so it was that I tucked the pill bag into the center console of the Jeep and promptly forgot about it.

That weekend seemed to stretch on forever, and it was killing me to be away from Mason. Needing to see my son, I decided to visit Mason and Eyes at the beach house.

I drove into Newport and pulled up to the address Eyes had provided. It was a triplex. Confused, I pulled out my cell and called the number Eyes had given me as the landline, waiting to hear it ring from one of the flats, but all in the neighborhood was silent. I rang again; same thing.

I then called Eyes on his cell. When he answered, I asked, "Where are you and Mason?"

"At the beach house."

I paused. "The beach house on ___ Street? Number ___? You're at *that* beach house?"

"Yes."

"Eyes, I'm standing right outside."

He hung up.

Unbelieving, I walked up to the triplex, knocking on all three doors. None of those I spoke with knew Eyes as an inhabitant of the house, even when he was described in detail. Hard to miss a tall hunk of man, you know what I'm sayin'?

I asked if they knew the hit man-hiring landlord, whom Eyes had said offered him "the beach house." It turned out that while he did own the property, there wasn't a unit occupied by Eyes. I'd been given a real address, but not a real phone. Who knows where that landline was located, endlessly ringing, never to be answered...

I called Eyes again. "So, you're at the beach house?"

"Yes. Sorry about that bad connection earlier."

"Well, as I said, I'm at the beach house."

"Yeah."

"So, is it a house? Like, as in one house?"

"Yes."

"No, it's not. It is a triplex. I knocked on all three doors, and no one here has ever heard of you."

Again, he hung up.

I was apoplectic, immediately hitting redial. When he answered, I ripped him a new one—

"We need to meet, now. I want Mason back this instant. I don't know where the hell you are or what's going on, but I want Mason."

"I can explain."

"Right now, I just want my son. Where can we meet?"

He named a park we'd been to before. It was neither near our house or "the beach house."

"I'll explain when I see you."

He set a meeting time much later in the day. "Where could he be," I wondered, "that he'd need that much time to handle a simple switch?"

Meeting me, Eyes acted as if everything were normal.

"Wow—thanks for washing my car!" he smiled. He began searching it—opening compartments, looking under seats—almost desperately.

"What are you looking for?"

"Oh, uh—some pills."

"What kind of pills?"

"Quaaludes. I've been having trouble sleeping, so my friend gave them to me."

"Given all of your issues, I don't think Quaaludes will help make the situation any better. And given your emotional state, I don't want Mason with you when you're doing drugs."

"Where are they?"

"I put them in your center console. I didn't even know what they were."

Eyes ducked into the Jeep and found them.

The biggest issue, however, we had yet to discuss. I waited for him to say something, but he just stood there, smiling, acting as if everything were as it should be.

"And the beach house...?" I prompted. "Which you said your friend had lent you?"

"You asked for an address, I needed to give you one."

"The correct one would've been helpful."

"I do have access to one of those apartments. But I've been staying with my friend, Margie. I knew you'd be upset, since you don't really like her, so I just thought it would be easier to let you think I was living at the beach house."

"So, you lied."

"I was trying not to hurt you."

"And who gave you the Quaaludes?"

"My hit man-loving friend. They're just to help me relax, okay? I'm under a lot of stress," he pleaded. "I didn't want you to get mad—me being at Margie's. I knew you wouldn't approve."

I didn't like his friend Margie, that much was true. But I knew I was being played. Thus, I didn't respond. I instead gave Eyes my car keys, and he took mine, and I took Mason home, where he should've been all along.

On the morning of September 11, 2001, I was at a bed and breakfast in Vermont, learning how to be an innkeeper. Odd, I know, as that particular occupation had never been part of some long-held vision for myself, but was, rather, a more recent detour.

Eyes and I had talked of moving to New England eventually, but—for reasons of which I was not yet aware—moving to Vermont suddenly became a priority to him and owning an inn didn't seem like such a bad way to do it. Our plan was that he would continue to work full-time, we'd live and raise our kids in our inn, and share inn operations.

That cool morning in Vermont, as I sat stock-still with my fellow classmates in front of the TV, watching in horror as the second plane hit, I had no idea that the towers were not the only structures in my world that were crumbling.

Immediately, I ran to my room, trying repeatedly to get a phone call through to Eyes on the west coast, but he didn't pick up.

How is it possible, I wondered, that he and Mason would not be home so early in the morning, given it was just after 6:00 his time? Where could he possibly have taken Mason?

All I knew during those first few frightful hours was that I wanted to be with my family. That was all that mattered. Family came first.

Gratefully, the inn-keeping class was brought to an abrupt close, and I found myself on the long drive to Burlington, hoping against hope for a flight out to California. Listening to the studied calm of NPR, I was grateful for their measured approach, and allowed myself to focus only on the factual. *"As awful as this tragedy is,"* I thought, irrationally, *"at least I don't know anyone involved."*

After checking-in to a nondescript Motel 6 and getting situated, I found my way online and saw an email which took my breath away. Our friends Ron Gamboa, Dan

Brandhorst, and their young son, David, had been returning home, having just vacationed on Cape Cod, and were on United Airlines Flight 175, the second plane to hit the World Trade Center. They were in the plane I'd seen fly into that tower. Ron, Dan, David... We'd been part of the same gay dads' group. We'd had them over to our house. And they were gone. Again, I called Eyes, because family comes first, and he finally responded. I was so grateful to connect, I completely forgot to ask where he'd been all morning with our child, completely inaccessible. Or maybe I didn't ask, because I didn't want to face what that answer might entail.

Once back home, it was easily apparent that nothing in our relationship had changed. Eyes was still remote and elusive, despite my continual peppering: *"What have I done?"* *"What is going on?"* *"How can I help?"*

Receiving no substantive responses, I simply continued onward as normal, keeping our home afloat with home-cooked recipes, ensuring Mason's development, and doing everything possible to get Eyes back on board. After several weeks in the abyss, I suggested that we might go see Eye's therapist for some assistance, as he'd been seeing him for the past few months. I was pleasantly encouraged when Eyes agreed and promised to set up an appointment. *"Who knows?"* I thought. *"Maybe we can get our relationship back-on-track, after all."*

YOU'VE GOT MAIL

Two weeks prior to our appointment with his therapist, during one of his quick visits home, Eyes asked to use my laptop in order to check his email. As he'd used my laptop before for a similar request, I had a feeling he was up to something. I pulled up his email sign in screen, entered his user name, put a check mark in the "Remember Me" box, and waited.

I really didn't like snooping. We'd taken vows to trust and respect each other. We'd adopted a child together. But I knew I wasn't being told the truth, and, in my view, the truth outweighed any snooping.

After he'd checked his email and gone, I quickly went to work, pulling up his emails:

A friend I didn't know asked, "How are the wedding plans coming?"

To which Eyes replied, "My relationship is growing stronger and stronger and I should be moving in about two weeks. I already spend every night there. He really is a great guy, and is SO good with Mason."

I felt as if I'd been punched in the gut. Eyes was having an affair, confirming all suspicions, even for the blind, and had actually introduced this person to Mason, our innocent baby boy. I was repulsed, but kept reading:

In another email, a different man asked, "The spouse

you're divorced from and had the child with, was it a guy?...
The first moment I saw you I was immediately attracted to
you. I liked all your body hair."

Yet another man wrote, "How's tricks? Done anymore
lately?" To which Eyes responded, "I have been thinking
about you and want to see you again."

His female former boss emailed, "When does your
radiation treatment start? I'm glad to hear you've been good
about your treatment. After that, your hair will be back to
normal in no time at all. If you are worried about your
looks, please don't. You are very good looking, with or
without hair, and apparently quite a few women think that,
too! What is really a concern: what message does that send
to your ex-wife? She might question your hair loss and
suspect the cause. Are you going to have the nanny pick up
Mason, so there is no visual contact with your ex?"

And to his best friend, Paula, he wrote, "I have seriously
questioned whether I'm gay or not."

Eyes may not have considered himself to be gay but
based on all that I had just read, he was at least an
exceptional actor, going above and beyond in the name of
his craft.

Now, *let's unpack*, shall we?

Eyes was not only cheating on me with his new partner,
whom he'd soon be moving in with, but he'd had other
affairs as well. Check.

Eyes had questioned his sexuality, but only to his best
friend, who had a crush on him. Was that a ploy—giving
her false hope—or was his sexual identity truly a struggle?

He sure was sucking a lot of dicks to be straight. (Maybe to help burn calories?)

Eyes had told his former boss that he was straight, and that he and his ex-wife shared Mason, who was taken care of by a nanny. I guess I was both ex-wife and nanny. Got it.

Eyes also told his former boss that he had cancer and was undergoing both chemo and radiation, which was untrue, but certainly explained why one day Eyes surprised me by showing up with a completely shaved head. I asked him why he'd done it and he replied, "Oh, I've always wanted to." Odd, in our five-plus years together, that this was the first I'd ever heard of that particular desire.

But shaving off one's hair to convince others of a cancer diagnosis? How fucked up is *that?*

It was a lot to learn in one sitting. I was married to a psychopath. That much was clear. I'd expected to find an affair. Maybe two. Or three. But the reality of what he'd done was much worse than my wildest imaginings. Pretending he'd been married to a woman. Pretending to have cancer. Introducing Mason to his lover. It was too much to even take in. It was too overwhelming. And there would be much more to learn in the days that followed.

DON'T NOBODY BRING ME NO BAD NEWS

I made an appointment with an attorney as soon as I was able. I wanted out of this toxic relationship but needed to ensure I would maintain my status as Mason's primary parent. On that, there was extremely bad news.

Given the laws in the state in which Mason was born, gay couples were not permitted to adopt together, so Eyes had adopted Mason as a "single" parent, and I was to adopt later in California as a "second parent." However, the lawyer informed me, until my adoption was finalized by the court, I had no legal right to Mason whatsoever. Whether I had any relationship with Mason at all could now be entirely in Eyes' hands.

I was advised not to confront Eyes about all I'd discovered and instead act as if nothing was wrong, until my second parent adoption was complete. Given that my hearing wouldn't occur for some months, that seemed impossible to attempt. Keep quiet for six months or longer? Just pretend as if nothing had happened?

I wanted vengeance. I wanted Eyes to pay. I wanted to kick the sick motherfucker to the curb. But instead, I stayed silent. I would do whatever necessary to keep Mason from harm and in my life.

WHERE KERGAN BECOMES A SPY

My days became a routine: take care of Mason, keep up house and appearances, and track down every possible clue and puzzle piece. How did this scenario occur? What lead to it? Who was involved? What didn't I know?

I read through every page of Eyes' old diaries, piecing together clues as to what might have led to his subsequent actions.

On his every visit to our house, I would secretly comb through his wallet, examining receipts and writing down the phone numbers found on torn pieces of paper and business cards.

I went through years of credit card statements, noting any irregularities or odd purchases.

I browsed boxes of old photos, finding some of Eyes, a guy named Mark, and Mark's two children—taken during my relationship with Eyes. The photos clearly depicted a blissfully happy family. Eyes would later admit that Mark had broken up their relationship once discovering he wasn't Eyes' only one. Good for him.

I found letters and cards from other lovers.

As I knew Eyes' voicemail password, I would call his cell when I knew he wouldn't be able to answer and listen to the messages left by other men.

One night, a woman left a message on Eyes' voicemail. It was the voice of a woman scorned. Not a friend, family member, or co-worker. This woman had been betrayed, screaming and crying a blue streak, saying she wanted nothing more to do with Eyes ever again. Who was this woman? Was Eyes telling the truth about questioning his sexuality? Did he have an affair with her? To this day, I have no idea who she was. But the rage and torment in her voice stays with me.

This long, unending list of unsuspecting victims... Eyes had played us, and continued to, with no regard for emotional toll. I knew all of this when Eyes and I went to see his therapist.

YOUR HOUR IS UP

The therapist had an office in a nondescript building, where I met Eyes in the hallway. It was awkward to be facing him, knowing everything I knew, unable to say a word. Instead, sitting in the doctor's office, I listened as both Eyes and his therapist insisted that it was my doubts about Eyes—*my insecurities*, to be precise—which had caused Eyes to become remote.

I was told that I needed to have faith. That Eyes was on a journey of discovery, healing old wounds. I was told by the therapist that it was my lack of self-esteem that had caused any problems in our relationship. That I needed to trust Eyes, in order for us to get through this as a couple. I was, apparently, just making things worse.

This went on for a full hour. As we closed, the therapist leaned in with a smile and said, "You know, Eyes is one of the most moral and ethical clients I've ever had. You need to give him some breathing space to continue on his journey."

As the office door closed and I hightailed it to my car, it hit me. Eyes had been seeing this therapist for three entire months and hadn't begun to tell the truth.

SEAFOOD, AGAIN?!?

Eyes surprised me one evening, stopping by unannounced to see Mason, when he suddenly asked to spend the night. Dubious, I agreed, sticking to my plan to be supportive at all cost. Still, having him sleep beside me led to an extremely poor night's sleep.

The next morning, Eyes remarked that the sheets on our bed must've had too much soap in them, because he'd been scratching all night. Later that day, I found a bottle of crab shampoo in his gym bag, which meant that he'd told the "too much soap" story so that I would rewash the sheets.

This time, the third time Eyes had crabs (to my knowledge), I knew better than to believe him, and instead took date-stamped photos of the shampoo bottle, jotted down the incident in my journal of Eyes' activities, and then sent the processed photos to my friends, Bob and Karen, for safe-keeping.

Spay the bitch, indeed.

THE PRESCRIPTIONS IN EYES' MEDICINE CABINET - 2001

Celexa (20mg) 1 per day — Used to treat depression.
Prinivil (20mg) 1 per day — Used to treat high blood pressure.
Klonopin (5mg) 1-3 at bedtime — Also known as *Clonazepam*, it is used to alleviate panic attacks and relieve stress. It can also be addictive.
Viramune (200mg) 2 per day — An antiviral medicine that prevents human immunodeficiency virus (HIV) from multiplying in one's body.
Zerit (40mg) 2 per day — Another antiviral, used in conjunction with *Viramune*, to fight HIV.
Epivir (150mg) 2 per day — Used in combination with the others, for treating HIV.
Viagra (100mg) ½ to 1 as needed — Used for Eyes' favorite pastime.

AN UNEXPECTED RECONCILIATION

Two days before Halloween, in 2001, Eyes announced he would be moving back home. It wasn't a conversation. It was a statement. The house was in both of our names, so he had a legal right to be there. Plus, I figured it would be easier to track his whereabouts if he was stationed at our home instead of "Margie's" or the "beach house." Still, I knew that this move on his part was not any sign of interest in getting back together with me. More likely, it signaled that there was trouble in Eyes' paradise.

This was made clear when I asked when he'd be moving back in, and he stated that he'd return in the next two or three weeks. But he was back, instead, the very next day.

PUT A RING ON IT

A week after he'd returned "home," searching Eyes' Jeep, I found a silver ring. Our wedding rings were gold. I took the ring and gave it to a friend for safekeeping.

The next day, Eyes asked me, "Did you happen to find a ring in my car?"

"What kind of ring?" I asked, as sincerely as I could

"Oh, just—a ring. I found it in one of our buildings at work. It was just lying on the floor."

"So, you kept it?"

"I put out the word. Told folks I'd found it. I was just hanging onto it until somebody claimed it."

As it would turn out, that silver ring was actually the ring that Eyes and his lover-of-one-year, Mr. OC, had blessed by a Catholic priest in a ring ceremony. Thus, Eyes would come home to me, put the silver ring in the Jeep's ashtray, and switch to our wedding ring, reversing course as he went back to Mr. OC.

The same night that Eyes had asked if I'd found the ring, I would also discover two new phone numbers tucked away in his wallet. The man never stopped.

To explain that ring's sudden absence, Eyes went on to

steal Mr. OC's ring from the nightstand and wear it, telling Mr. OC that he must've misplaced his own.

I still have that ring to this day.

DO YOU KNOW THE WAY TO SAN JOSE?

The day after I found the silver ring, there was a voicemail on Eyes' cell from Jose, yet another lover of one-year:

"I really understand what you're going through and am glad you shared it with me. You're my guy. If you need me to fly out, to come to L.A. tonight, or whenever, I'll be there. I hope the CAT scan will be fine. Call me."

I would later learn that Jose believed that Eyes was in the process of selling our home, so that Eyes could move up to Northern California permanently in order to live with Jose. But apparently, Eyes needed to remain local for his ongoing chemotherapy treatments. Poor thing.

MORE GASLIGHTING

While all too aware of the truth, I was going crazy, trying to juggle the facts, jotting everything down, and always trying to appear the dutifully patient spouse. We were steamrolling toward Thanksgiving, and it seemed like all I had to do was cough and another lover would appear, like a genie out of a bottle. And yet Eyes would say that the myriad of genies was only in my head.

For example, he would tell him he'd been home all day, watching Mason, when I knew this to be a lie, as I'd called multiple times, to no reply.

Or Eyes might say he was going to yoga, but not come home until very late. The next day, I'd discover a message on his cell from a guy saying, "I had a great time last night. You really put a smile on my face. I love you and am very happy about the way things are going."

Even when Eyes would take Sophia and Isabella out for a walk, I knew that he was also making secret calls to people unseen, who I was told didn't exist.

And this entire time, I had to keep my fucking mouth shut.

EVEN A GOOD EGG CAN CRACK

It had been over two months since all was uncovered, and I was going out of my mind. I'd chosen to share Eyes' secrets with my best friends, Bob and Karen, as well as another friend, removed from Eyes. Ironically, Bob and Karen had first been friends with Eyes and V, long before I'd ever come into the picture. Once Eyes had booted V from the house, Bob and Karen maintained their friendship with Eyes, thinking Eyes to be blameless, which pained V greatly.

In my five years with Eyes, we spent much time with Bob and Karen. We dined together regularly, traveled together, and just generally enjoyed each other. Bob and Karen are the most down-to-earth people I know, always up to talk about sex, love, politics, religion—no subject is off limits. The four of us were in-sync, as couples and as individuals, and our many provocative and lively discussions created a sense of knowing, of being fully attuned to each other.

Once I shared what I had discovered about Eyes, Bob and Karen were horrified to have been so wrong about someone, and it would be to them that I would turn, forwarding all emails for safe-keeping and alerting them to my latest discovery. They helped me navigate every twist and turn. It was clear that none of us had ever really *known* Eyes, despite what we'd believed, and their feelings of betrayal easily matched my own.

Despite their ongoing support, I knew I could not go much longer without confronting Eyes. The daily barrage of lies, attempting to make me feel as it were my own issues which were fueling Eyes' actions, was tearing me up. To compound this, my second parent adoption—and all other second parent adoptions in California—were suddenly put on hold, indefinitely.

A lower court ruling called into question the legitimacy of second parent adoptions, prompting the California Supreme Court to jump in to settle the matter. This meant that my adoption of Mason—the only reason I was remaining silent—would remain in limbo until said matter was resolved. I'd been silent for almost two months. I was going insane, and that part—holding it all in—had to stop.

I hatched a plan. Over Thanksgiving, Eyes and I flew with Mason to visit Eyes' family, staying at his Mormon brother's mountain cabin. In between snowmobiling excursions, I finally confronted Eyes—but I chose to confront him about only about one specific incident. I encouraged him to tell the truth and noted, should he do so, I promised that all would be forgiven.

He admitted to that one specific incident and affirmed that there had been no other indiscretions. That this specific instance was the only time he'd strayed.

I then casually brought up another incident, which he also confirmed, only to swear that had absolutely been *it*. There were no more than these two indiscretions, he promised. I let him think I believed him, and suggested that his "honesty" meant that there might be a path forward for us. Perhaps we might somehow find a way to repair our relationship, now that the "truth" was finally out...

This was clearly a lie on my part. However, "supportive husband" was a role I could easily play until my adoption of Mason was final, whenever that might happen. And, on some level, I wanted to believe that reconciliation was possible. I wanted to believe that Eyes could change and that redemption was achievable.

Even knowing all that I knew, I hoped that there would be a path forward. There must be some way, I thought, to forgive Eyes and salvage our fragile family unit, allowing it to remain intact as originally intended. The alternative would be that we would break up, I would return to work as a single parent, and that Mason would end up in daycare, shuttling between two houses—none of which had been my intention. In adopting him, Eyes and I had made an unspoken promise that we were welcoming our child into a better life. I was doing everything in my power to ensure we gave Mason just that.

After Eyes confessed to these two indiscretions, I told Eyes that in order to consider staying in the relationship, I would need the following from him:

1. Total and absolute honesty, including a full inventory and accounting of all that he'd done and lied about, so that I could fully understand his actions, and—

2. I needed to make sure that he loved me, as he had once claimed. I needed some assurance that love for me was included in our reparations.

Neither of which was Eyes able to do.

AN AMERICAN ORGASM IN LONDON
(OR, WHERE KERGAN BECOMES A WHORE)

While we hadn't yet booked our tickets, the trip had been months in the planning. It was to be a pre-Christmas jaunt to London; our twice-yearly trip abroad, to a city I was eager to visit, as I'd never been. As Mason would be staying with my family, this would be a chance for some one-on-one time, during which Eyes and I might heal and move forward. Or not.

Despite the copious proof of Eyes' transgressions, his continued inability to be honest or show any remote sign of love for me, and despite a lack of remorse for any pain he'd caused, I decided to go ahead with our planned visit to London. Even knowing everything, I wanted Eyes back.

At first, it seemed that might be a possibility. As we began going over the details of our trip, talking over sights, recommended restaurants and plays, a spark was reignited. For a brief moment, Eyes and I were just like any other married couple, planning an adventure, and that planning made us seem more united than we actually were.

Once in London, everything changed. In the back of my mind, I assessed and reassessed every situation. Something as simple as a selection of restaurant or a museum seemed rife with consequence. I needed to ensure that whatever path we took forward, Mason and I would be together at the end, regardless.

Throughout our trip, I'd sneak moments away from Eyes in order to check his voicemail, of which I still had access. During one such check, I wasn't altogether surprised to learn that Mr. OC believed that Eyes was in Haiti building an orphanage for the less-fortunate, rather than in London, with me. There was a small germ of truth in his assumption (or in what he was told by Eyes): Such an orphanage was being built in Haiti, but not by Eyes. It was being built by Eyes' brother, the gay-hating Mormon bishop. Eyes was currently in London, sharing a small hotel bed with me, with each of us dancing around our collective and singular futures.

At this point, we'd been in London several days, coming to the end of our "fun-filled" vacation. Each and every time that Eyes got up early, dressed, and departed our hotel for a "walk," I knew that he did so in order to secretly call Mr. OC. That Mr. OC believed Eyes to be in Haiti was a minor detail—one I was willing to ignore.

At this particular juncture, my bottom line was that in our six years together, I'd never had sex with anyone else. I'd had thoughts and desires, of course, but had put them aside, given my commitment to Eyes and our child. But now it was clear that not only had Eyes *not* kept those same commitments, but that he'd plunged off the monogamous diving board into the pool of free love. And, to some degree, I was jealous.

Throughout our years together, I'd been the one begging for more and varied sexual experiences, and yet Eyes had been the one secretly indulging. I wanted to cry out, *"What about me, you motherfucker? You think I haven't been bored? I've asked you for more times a week, more positions, more variety, and suddenly you're a fucking circus act? I begged, and you ignored. I pleaded, and you said no..."*

That last night in London, at the end of our trip, I so wanted to feel valued, even if by someone insane. Looking back, I'm not sure what time of night it was or what prompted it, but my actions were selfish, entirely so.

It was late and we were in bed.

I lay next to Eyes in the darkness and started to stroke myself. Reaching over to him, I grabbed his hand, putting his hand on my chest. Eyes' hand lay there limply, as if wounded in war.

I continued to stroke myself, wanting to feel connected to Eyes, or desired by Eyes, or wanted by Eyes—or anyone. A simple touch would have been enough.

I moved Eyes' hand down to my cock, hoping he'd finish me off, but he just left his hand lie there for a few moments, dormant, before finally removing it.

"Am I that horrid," I wondered, *"that you, who've had anyone and everyone, can't abide me?"*

Eyes rolled over, his back to me, as I tried to finish what I had started. I continued to jack off, with my other hand tracing all over my body: my chest, my abs, my ass. But I couldn't cum. I simply couldn't finish the task at hand.

I was lying in a bed with another, yet totally alone, in one of the most intoxicating cities in the world. Millions within my reach, if I'd really wanted it. But as Eyes began to snore, the truth was made abundantly clear: Eyes didn't want me, and no one else would either.

THE MORE YOU KNOW

Upon our return to the states, the Truth Train began to roll, wrecking everything in its path. As I continued to dive deeper into Eyes' past, reading his journals and talking to his oldest friends, more facts emerged. In his younger days, Eyes had been arrested for shoplifting twice (once for stealing "temple cards" from his Mormon church.) While both such incidents were expunged from his record, he wrote about them in a diary.

Through reading his journal entries, I also learned that at a prior job, he would leave work in the middle of the day to cruise for guys in parks, steam rooms, and more. His sexuality then so filled Eyes with shame that he would often have to drink in order to get up the nerve to approach someone. Long before I entered the picture, that excessive drinking would have devastating effects, as Eyes suffered a motorcycle accident on the way home from a cruise park, driving drunk. He broke his back and was arrested on a DUI but was somehow able to get that dropped from his record as well.

Eyes' best friend, Paula, had been the victim of a violent rape several years prior. As a result, she understandably had trust issues with men, leaving her father and Eyes as the only two men she still trusted. Eyes had never told Paula he was HIV positive, a fact he'd kept hidden from most others as well.

Upon learning the truth, Paula felt a deep sense of betrayal. She and Eyes had been "best friends," and yet he'd kept the real truths from her, just as he had me. She shared that Eyes had secretly told her that he would father a child with her, if she desired, as she was then single and questioning if she'd ever find the "right man." The sudden revelation of his HIV status meant that she would not only go on to mourn the child she would never have, but to also ponder, had she and Eyes gone through with it, whether she and the baby would've become infected. These questions would forever alter Paula's approach to life and men.

As more Truth Train facts were revealed, Eyes began to suffer a breakdown. Mr. OC confronted Eyes about who *I* was, and Eyes finally revealed that truth, leading to their break up—but not without repeated emotional pleas by Eyes for a reconciliation.

With Mr. OC finally knowing the truth, Mr. OC then contacted Jose in San Jose, informing him of Eyes' indiscretions, but Eyes somehow channeled Houdini and was able to do damage control; his relationship with Jose would continue for an unknown duration.

In an awkward face-to-face meeting at his home, Mr. OC and I compared stories, and the lies told to each of us were plentiful. Despite Eyes telling me that Mary Chapin Carpenter was his favorite singer, as she was also mine, Eyes had told Mr. OC that he hated the music I listened to. Despite our years together watching all manner of indie films, from documentaries to queer dramas, Eyes told Mr. OC that he much preferred big Hollywood movies. It was as if Eyes engineered himself to be whoever the person with whom he was interfacing wanted him to be. From food, to entertainment, to sexual proclivities, what he had told me and Mr. OC about his preferences rarely aligned. He was the very definition of well-hung chameleon.

During my exchange with Mr. OC, it became clear that Eyes' biggest lie was in leading Mr. OC to believe that Eyes was actually HIV-negative, when he most certainly was not. To keep his secret, Eyes would hide his HIV medications in the hollow compartment beneath the CD holder in his Jeep, out of eyesight. For an entire year, Eyes and Mr. OC repeatedly engaged in reciprocal anal sex, ejaculating inside of each other, never once using protection. Understandably, Mr. OC was shocked to learn he had been so deceived and feared that he'd been infected. Luckily, he would later test negative for the virus.

You may be wondering if Eyes was aware that his purposeful exposure of HIV to another person was a crime; of that, he most definitely was informed. At that time in California, intentionally exposing a partner to HIV was a felony and we had discussed several news stories of such exposure, with Eyes expressing revulsion at anyone committing such an act.

Eyes may not have been an actual murderer, but he certainly didn't mind exposing others to a potentially fatal virus. He was fully aware of what he was doing.

LIFE LESSON #20

If you had been lingering in bed one bright and sunny weekend morning, only to receive a call from Eyes, shocking you awake with a relentless screaming rant, please know, dearest Karen, that while you are many things, you are certainly *not* a "fucking cunt."

LIFE LESSON #21

Should you combine finances with your beloved and decide to sell your house, please know that on the day the funds are deposited into your joint account, said beloved may go to the bank, withdraw all funds except those he believes are due you, and take the rest for himself.

While upon our coupling Eyes had insisted that we treat our relationship like any other married couple, when push came to shove, I would get none of "our" retirement, none of "our" savings and none of "our" home equity. I would be left with half of the actual cash made on the sale of our house. He would take the rest. And there was nothing I could do about it.

FIX IT OR FLIP IT

As our relationship was unable to be fixed, Eyes and I finally sold the house in which we'd intended to raise Mason and our future children, and go our separate ways. However, to ensure I became Mason's legal parent, I continued to dangle the future possibility that Eyes and I might somehow be able to patch things up.

I found a cute 1928 Tudor bungalow rental in a sketchy part of Santa Ana, and Eyes moved into an apartment a few miles away. On the day of my move, as I was unpacking in my new kitchen, preparing for life as a single parent, a S.W.A.T. team surrounded a vehicle in front of our house, and I ducked until it was over. Things had certainly changed.

Eyes and I attempted to co-parent as best we could, but it was awful. I hated being away from Mason all day, now that I had returned to work, and didn't remotely trust the time that Eyes spent with him. Mason was becoming more and more verbal, and the number of "uncles" he had through Eyes was astounding. All were men that Eyes had met during his adventures outside our home—I knew none personally—and it greatly disturbed me to hear Mason repeat their names, so uncertain was I as to what role they played in Mason's life.

Still, Eyes and I tried to be amicable, for Mason's sake. We went to a mediator to help us establish a parenting agreement in order to avoid a court battle. Once that parenting agreement was in motion, having been able to return to my previous job back at Green Eggs and Ham, we were sharing Mason almost equally, which had never been the case prior. I had always been the primary parent, handling Mason's needs, and it was a huge adjustment to not to be with Mason as much, especially knowing that Eyes' judgment was questionable, at best.

One of the stranger provisions of our parenting agreement was that while I got to have Mason on all major holidays, to give stability and consistency with traditions, Eyes was "welcome" to join us. This created a situation in which multiple times each year, my entire family was forced to make small talk with the same man who'd decimated our family unit. All knew of his misdeeds, yet had to pretend nothing unpleasant had ever occurred.

As time went on, Eyes became increasingly more competitive with me. One winter, he asked what I was getting Mason for his big Christmas gift, and I told him a bike, so Eyes got him a bike as well. On another occasion, I bought me and Mason annual passes to Disneyland, so Eyes did the same—taking him almost weekly, making my purchase pointless. After Russ and I got together, Russ bought a mountain cabin as a weekend retreat. Soon after, Eyes did the same. His aggressive rivalry was unrelenting.

In April 2002, Eyes did one of the few selfless things he'd done in his entire life: he let my adoption of Mason become final. After many months in purgatory, the courts had begun processing second parent adoptions and a date was set. Still, even as I entered the courtroom, I doubted that

Eyes would allow my adoption to occur. Throughout our tangles, Eyes knew he had the upper hand, and had repeatedly threatened that this adoption might not happen, if I didn't acquiesce to his particular desire of the day.

But there we were in the courtroom, Eyes standing next to me, when the judge finalized the adoption and Mason was legally mine. I was both mindful of all that Mason and I had endured to get to that point and grateful to Eyes for letting it go through. After we'd posed for pictures with the judge, Eyes handed me a card to note the occasion, in which he called me the best dad ever. I believe that, despite everything, Eyes knew he wasn't cut out to be a dad, even if he would go on to fight for that designation for years to come. Parenting wasn't his strong suit. It was a role he played, one he could put on and take off, as one would a jacket. It wasn't *who he is*, unlike me, who had prepared for fatherhood since my earliest recollections.

Still, as I carried Mason out, with Eyes directly behind, I vowed to never again become beholden to him. I had kept him dangling for my own selfish purposes, but now my sole focus would be on Mason. There would be no more begging or twisting of arms. Eyes and I were finally on equal legal footing, and I would challenge him repeatedly in the years ahead, with Mason always at the forefront of my mind.

Soon after my adoption was finalized, Mason began suffering from night terrors, which are similar to nightmares but occur when a person is fully awake. Mason would wake, screaming, trying to brush imaginary spiders off himself, and it could last for 10 minutes or more, taking forever to calm him. I began giving him spray bottles to sleep with, containing water, with a label reading "Monsters Away." Those helped somewhat, but Mason then began biting his fingernails and shredding the surrounding tissue—a nervous habit which continues to this day.

I finally got Eyes to agree to let me take Mason to counseling, as our parenting agreement forbade me from doing so without his consent, and the therapist noted that Mason was indeed suffering from ongoing stress. To me, that meant that either the back and forth of his young life— no longer having me as his constant—was the cause, or the stresses Mason was being exposed to by Eyes were to blame for his anxiety.

These factors would lead to our first court battle, with me insisting on a return to more time with Mason. It would be a costly battle, one which I would eventually win.

Another battle would be over Eyes' income, as I knew he wasn't paying his proper share of child support. His previous support had been based solely on salary, but I eventually realized that he had many other sources of revenue, none of which had been factored into the equation. For example, Eyes had bought a home and had a roommate. His support payment didn't take into account the few thousand dollars his roommate paid monthly to Eyes, nor did the support consider the income Eyes received from two other properties he owned, a full-time rental and a seasonal cabin rental.

To avoid paying his fair share, Eyes ended up submitting signed statements to the court that his roommate was not simply a roommate, but that they had a relationship of a "close, intimate nature." He then put the roommate's name on the deed to the house, to further make it look like they were lovers, as well as noting the roommate was his "partner" on his court-required profit and loss paperwork.

Eyes further provided documents claiming that not a single one of his investment properties made any income at all, which must've meant that he wasn't a very good landlord. Consequently, Eyes' deceptions meant that he would win this particular battle, burying money which should have gone toward Mason's upbringing under whatever stone he could find.

In a later court battle, Eyes would state under oath that he and his roommate had never had a romantic relationship. I don't think Eyes realized that in that particular instant, he'd perjured himself. Either the two had been romantic as he'd once claimed, or had not as he later stated, but either way, going after him for perjury would've been an endlessly expensive battle. One I wasn't prepared to fight.

LIFE LESSON #22

Should your hubby ever write a letter granting you full custodial rights to your child, with two witness signatures, do not—under any circumstances or misplaced pangs of sympathy or hopes of a never-to-happen reconciliation—give that paper back to him. With each court battle, you will regret it.

REGRETS, I'VE HAD A FEW

I want to be absolutely clear about something. While Eyes had more than his share of poor behavior, both in and out of our relationship, I am not entirely blameless. Lots of mistakes were made as Eyes and I battled it out over the years, particularly when I was in my insane spy mode, rifling through his belongings in search of "the truth," and I fully own up to my part of the craziness.

Eyes once accused me of having a detective stalk him and take covert photos. While untrue, I let Eyes believe it. Better and more tactical for him to think I had that kind of time and money to have his ass watched 24/7 than to deny it.

In another interaction, I had a co-worker of mine call and leave a message on Eyes' voicemail, pretending it was my voicemail and "confirming" my imminent appointment with a new attorney. While I did indeed have a new attorney, I set up this call to give Eyes fair warning that I was coming for him, to put the fear of God into him.

But my biggest regret was that I revealed Eyes' HIV status. Having the impression that he might have purposely exposed yet another individual to HIV, I created a fake email account through which I let that person know Eyes' status, as well as sharing other unseemly details. As it turned out, I was entirely mistaken; that person was only a friend and had understandably felt intimidated and scared by my unwelcome emails.

I fully knew, as an HIV advocate and educator, that sharing such information was wrong. I have no excuse, other than to say, I'll do anything necessary to protect my child. Whatever my "reasons," at the end of the day, I am a grown man. I could have and should have charted a different path. In conducting myself so poorly, I proved only that I am not all that dissimilar from Eyes, even if at the time I felt my actions were justified.

Still, this revelation, telling someone else's truth, is what I most regret.

LIFE LESSON #23

Should you be at your gay doctor's, being checked for gonorrhea, and he admiringly remarks that the head of your penis is rather large, find another doctor.

(BTW, I didn't have it.)

LIFE LESSON #24

Following your first marathon, bone tired and desperately in need of a massage, it is best to speak up upon discovering that the therapist has exited to let you change out of your clothes, but not left a sheet under which to lie.

Otherwise, upon the therapist's return, seeing your bare ass right up in the air might be enough to get you permanently banned from the establishment.

LIFE LESSON #25

Should you be on Match.com and connect with a guy with the user name SnugMan3000, please be aware that despite his ultra-butch photographs, you will soon discover that the living room of his apartment is filled with glass curio cabinets containing porcelain kitty cats and that the arms of his furniture are draped in handmade lace doilies. You're welcome.

A MATCH.COM SUCCESS STORY

Newly single and ready to mingle, I wasn't a huge fan of gay bars and didn't really know where to meet prospective dates, especially given my responsibilities with Mason. After a friend suggested Match.com, I decided to give it a whirl.

I met some very nice people on it, with whom I'd likely have become friends if we weren't all on there with such single-minded "match" focus. I dated a few guys and finally had sex again. (Here's a mini-life lesson for you: Pulling a lubed dildo, whose ball base has become severed, out of someone's ass isn't as easy as it might seem.)

And then I met Russ on Match. His photos were gorgeous—compact frame, terrific smile, and coiffed blond hair so perfect, it mirrored that of my youth—and our initial phone calls were promising, as we talked for hours. Our first date, however, was completely unmemorable. In fact, we were both a bit underwhelmed. Still, we decided to meet again, more casually, and it was during that seaside lunch that things began to gel.

Russ never had major aspirations of being a father, and his hesitation in committing to a relationship with me, who already had one kid and wanted another, led to some initial back and forth. Russ had come out later in life, at 38, and could then be primarily found dancing shirtless on a box at a club, experiencing his delayed gay youth. Being a father would mean a complete change of pace, and I could tell that most of his friends, who only knew Russ as the "guy on the box," were incredibly puzzled by our dating. They didn't know that, prior to coming out, Russ had assumed he'd one day marry a woman and have children, even if "kids" wasn't something he particularly desired. After all, in East Tennessee, where Russ was from, marriage and children was the expectation, one he would dutifully follow. Upon coming out, however, Russ figured, "I'm never going to be a dad now," and readjusted accordingly, enjoying his new life and dancing his ass off.

A friend helped create his Match.com profile, as Russ had recently ended a relationship, and was encouraged to get right back up on that horse. And so it was that I saw Russ' beautiful photos and messaged him.

I would've never guessed that Russ would eventually be the one to give me so much pleasure in life. That this creative and challenging genius would be the one to offer loving support and constructive advice. That we would become best friends, leaning on each other through all manner of hardship. That this visionary, often underutilized and undervalued, would prove to be a brilliant artist, capable of picking up a brush after 30 years of not painting, only to create a work of art in just two days that is so staggering, it draws gasps when people see it displayed above our fireplace. I could've never foreseen that this crazy-sexy man, once on a box, would climb down from the life he had been living, to embrace a life with little old me, and dive so fully into the choppy waters of the parenting pool. And yet dive he did.

I had strict rules about waiting to introduce any date to Mason until I was sure there would be some longevity. On the night Russ finally came to dinner with me and Mason, and knocked on the front door, he was certainly shocked by the teetering bow-legged boy who opened up the door, growling, "Hiya, Russ!"

At our first restaurant dinner, I left Russ and Mason momentarily, to use the restroom, only to return to find Russ pinning Mason into his highchair, as Mason was determined to come find me.

Before Eyes and I officially split, knowing that I would need to return to work in order to pay rent in a new place, I'd given Green Eggs and Ham Marketing a call, which turned out to be perfect timing. Apparently, the man who had replaced me as Executive Assistant to the CEO had somehow embezzled several hundred thousand dollars from the company and was presently in jail.

Mrs. Green Eggs was close to retiring, which Mr. Ham was encouraging with as much motivation as possible, but she simply dug in her well-honed heels.

On one occasion, when Eyes and I were still together, I had asked Mrs. Green Eggs for time off for a vacation, to which this sixty-something rich lady replied with a long sigh, "I've always wanted to go to Europe." She'd spent her life scraping her way up the corporate ladder, focused on making a living for her sons, and had never made time for her own dreams. Her husband was then an invalid, and I knew her later years would be spent feeding him soup. She would never go to Europe. Her one big dream would never happen.

It is certainly not the end of the world to never go to Europe, or the far east, or South America, or wherever one dreams of going. But to have the means, and to sublimate that deep-seated desire and longing for exploration, seems a sadly missed opportunity.

Given my flair for event planning, Mrs. Green Eggs tasked me with organizing the company's annual holiday party, which was always a huge extravaganza. One year, she was very particular: as entertainment, she wanted an old-time trained dog act and a troop of elderly women tap dancers from the local retirement village. However, the highlight of the evening was Russ, dirty dancing with Mrs. Green Eggs. I'm sure she didn't know what hit her.

For Mason's third birthday, we had a Blue's Clues-themed party, with blue macaroni and cheese, blue Jello fingers, blue juice, blue jelly beans, and a blue cake of Blue. As you can imagine, we all had blue poop for days.

For Mason's fourth birthday, we had a Spiderman-themed birthday, the highlight of which was Russ, dressed as Spiderman, perched perilously on our pitched roof, shooting silly string out over the crowd. Following, as he circulated silently greeting the kids, Mason remarked, "He has the same shoes as Russ."

And my friend Karen, knowing of Russ' debilitating fear of heights, remarked with an assured grin, "He's a keeper."

Russ and I had been together for many months, and were on the road, taking Mason on a day trip to one of my favorite California towns, Julian. I can't remember exactly what Eyes had recently done to prompt this particular exchange, but it was Russ' response which resonated.

"Whenever Eyes does something awful, you get upset. And I get it. He burned you, and exposed Mason to God-knows-what. But you need to extinguish the power he has over you. You need to treat him like an ant at the picnic. Irritating, yes, but get rid of him with a simple flick of your finger. Allowing yourself to be emotionally manipulated each time he does something means that he wins. Don't let him win. Don't let him define you."

And Russ was right. In that very exchange, my entire relationship to and interactions with Eyes changed, all for the better. There would still be battles ahead, but Eyes would never have quite the same power over me again.

LIFE LESSON #26

Please be fully warned that your parents have it within themselves to supremely piss you off, no matter how old you may be.

My parents knew I wanted to adopt another child, and that Russ and I were settling in nicely together. Thus, it came as a surprise when they called out of the blue one night to share that they had been thinking about me and my career, and had decided that I would make a good realtor. This, despite any lack of interest in doing so on my part.

They further inquired if I'd really tried hard enough to be straight. Perhaps I might marry a woman?

I tried my best to explain to them that:

1. I had no sexual interest in women, and never have.

2. I reminded them that I had a five-year-old black son, currently sleeping. Thus, any woman I picked would need to be comfortable with having a black son and a gay husband. And—

3. That by encouraging me to enter into a loveless relationship, my parents were putting their own happiness ahead of my own personal satisfaction.

Oh, and I reminded them that there would be another black child coming into my life, just as soon as I could arrange it.

LITTLE CABIN IN THE WOODS

During our first years together, Russ maintained his house in Aliso Viejo to be able to work in his home office during the day, then come to our house most evenings for dinner and spend the night. While we acted like a family, we were more on our way to *becoming* a family, which would all come together spectacularly in 2004, in some unexpected ways.

Russ had always dreamed of owning a mountain cabin, and we found the perfect one in Idyllwild, CA—a cute artsy village located high above the Palm Springs desert. It was a traditional log cabin, complete with stone fireplace and a moose head above it. When Russ was done with the exquisite décor, it looked like a place Ralph Lauren would've lived. Soon after the sale closed and we'd begun a two-week stay to get the cabin in order, I got what I'd always wanted.

The call was entirely unexpected. I'd recently completed the foster-adoption process, finishing the necessary courses, home visits, and paperwork in order to become a licensed foster parent, to be able to then adopt another child. Still, I was told that the process would be quite lengthy, and not to expect anything for some time. But here was the foster-adopt coordinator on the phone, just the same, telling me about a potential child, Marcus.

When I first met Marcus, he was two and a half years-old. His social worker and I drove out to his foster home. Upon spotting me—a total stranger—he immediately ran up and gave me a hug. *"Surely,"* I thought, *"this is a sign that our adoption of him is meant to be."* The next time I saw him, I took him to a park by myself, and he cried for an hour straight, until he finally fell asleep in my arms. I chose not to view that as a sign.

After meeting Marcus three times, once with Mason, I got another call. Would we like to have Marcus for an overnight visit? Having just begun our stay at the new cabin, I said, "Sure!" and drove down the hill to pick him up.

Our first night went well, and so I checked in with the coordinator the next day. After she inquired about our time together, I asked when he needed to be returned, and she said, "If all is going well, why don't you just come pick up his clothes?" And with that, Marcus was ours.

Marcus did not have the easiest start in life. He was born with club feet, but as his birth mom had issues of her own, she could not make it a priority to get his feet straightened. Instead she took him to a crack house, which was then raided, resulting in Marcus being placed with child services. Once in foster care, his feet were corrected, but due to his delayed muscle development, when he first came to us, Marcus was very clumsy. The way that kid fell—up, down, up, down—Russ and I sometimes felt as if we were watching a Keystone Cop movie. But the important thing was that Marcus kept getting back up.

In addition to his various physical challenges, due to the neglect he'd experienced, Marcus was also initially a bit remote, and it took a while for him to really engage and learn to communicate with us. Lucky for him, Mason was a terrific big brother, showing Marcus how to do things, helping him when he fell, and engaging in all manner of play, all with a patience that Russ and I sometimes found hard to muster.

I loved to watch the two, dressed as cowboys, galivanting in our forest and playing in their teepee. I loved their first Halloween together, with both dressed as Indians, and Mason tucking his arm protectively around Marcus' shoulders. And I'll always recall Marcus' first school performance, when as another group was centerstage performing a choreographed number to Kool and the Gang's "Celebration," Marcus suddenly appeared behind them, doing his own inspired dance and blowing the roof off the place in the process.

These two might not have been related by blood, but their brotherly bond was solid, and my hope is that they'll continue to nurture it into old age.

NEVER MEET YOUR IDOLS: MISTAKE #2

With the boys staying with my parents, for my 40th birthday, Russ surprised me with a trip to New York for an amazing weekend. We saw one of my idols, Jessica Lange, in *The Glass Menagerie*, and another idol, Betty Broadway, in concert at a small café. Both were phenomenal.

During Betty's show, we were seated directly in front of her, and she laughed and flirted with us, pointing out to the audience how spiffy we looked in our suits, ties and pocket squares.

Following the show, Betty lingered in the back of the café, being greeted by well-wishers. I excused myself from Russ and went to wait in line, not only to tell Betty how divine she had been, but also that we had a friend in common, who used to be Betty's assistant. When I finally made it up to Betty and after I'd gushed about her performance, I mentioned the woman's name. Like Jekyll and Hyde, Betty instantly turned into a monster, insisting that she didn't know my friend, and that this woman must obviously be CRAZY.

I gently tried to extract myself, murmuring pleasantries, but Betty went on, becoming infuriated and kind of psychotic, insisting that "I don't know this person! She's crazy—*Crazy* I tell you!!!" I was mortified and left as graciously as I could manage. Russ, thinking that we'd later be partying with Betty given the accolades he knew I would give, was substantially thrown as well.

I had heard from others that Betty Broadway was a bit insane, but her reaction was so extreme, it made me wonder if what my friend, who had claimed to have once been Betty's assistant, had told me were actually true. She'd said that while Betty didn't identify as lesbian, she and Betty actually had a brief affair—testing the waters, so to speak.

A sane person, when confronted with an "assistant" she hadn't met would've simply said, "I'm sorry, but you're mistaken. She was never my assistant." Instead, Betty Broadway chose to explode at little old me, making me think that where there is smoke, there is most definitely fire. That kind of eruption made sense when factoring in that Betty, afraid that I knew about that old affair, might turn on me and hope that her rage might keep me quiet.

But that didn't work out so well for her, did it?

As Russ likes to say, "It is a good thing we didn't run into Jessica! Who knows what kind of mask might've been pulled away there?"

LIFE LESSON #27

People can change.

At least, my parents proved they were capable.

Despite any initial misgivings and missteps, Dottie and Fred fully embraced their roles as grandparents to our two boys. During their retirement years at their Palm Desert country club, Dottie and Fred unabashedly assumed their grandparental duties, taking the kids out for spins in the golf cart, to swim in the club pool, and introducing the boys to their friends at the club's restaurant. There were never any issues, and my parents took great delight in our sons, and continue to do so. For that, I'm endlessly grateful.

TURN ON YOUR FLESHLIGHT, LET IT SHINE
WHEREVER YOU GO

As much as we loved our mountain cabin, after three years together, the time finally came for us all to live under one roof. Within a span of days, Russ sold his place in Aliso Viejo, I gave notice at my rental, we sold our mountain cabin, and we all moved into our one home in Orange, California. Our family unit of four was finally complete.

Soon after we moved in, the boys were out one day, exploring the palatial front yard. I was in the kitchen when Marcus sauntered in, swinging around what appeared to be a black flashlight. Oddly, though, there was a piece of plastic—a lid—covering where the light should've been.

"What's that?" I asked.

"Flashlight," he nonchalantly replied.

"Where'd you get it?"

"It was buried in the yard."

Knowing something was up, I borrowed the light from him and took it into another room, where I quickly found, upon unscrewing the lid, a rubber replica vagina staring me in the face.

Screwing the lid back on, as tightly as I could, I tucked the "light" away where it wouldn't be found, then went out to join the boys, still exploring the yard.

"Marcus, honey—?"

"Hmm?"

Personality Type, making it the most rare type of all. And that percentage is even lower among men.

For too many years, I had felt alone, blaming myself for some perceived flaw, only to discover that there was a fully rational factor that, indeed, made me different. Changing this from a fault to a gift allowed a fundamental shift to occur in how I viewed both myself and others.

Today, I'm still a freak. But at least now I know that I'm a freak of *nature*.

LIFE LESSON #28

Words matter.

In my youth, I used them to keep people away. Today, I use them to draw people close.

AIDS. REMEMBER ME?

Written in March, 2012.

On the morning of my thirtieth birthday, I checked my then-partner, Shane Sawick, into the hospital. He would not come out alive. Shane died just two weeks later, suffering from Progressive Multifocal Leukoencephalopathy (PML); one disease, among many, battled in his long war against AIDS. Once in the hospital, the illness quickly progressed, and in just a matter of days, he could no longer speak, blink, nor respond in any way. Through it all, though, his mind still raced, and processed, and thought.

Long before that ill-fated sojourn, I remember lying next to Shane one night, reading, when he suddenly grasped my hand. "Will you remember me?" he asked. I smiled and nodded benignly, "Of course," as if this were a given. He more firmly squeezed, focusing his eyes on mine. "No," he insisted, "I want to be remembered."

At the time, the notion that knowledge of him would remain when so many others before had died, largely forgotten, seemed almost lofty. And yet I instinctively knew that I needed to find some way to pay tribute, for I too had felt that same desire: to have walked the earth and for it to have mattered.

Since then, my life has changed dramatically. My partner of nine years and I are the proud fathers of two amazing boys.

My days have gone from being filled with parsing out pills and leading safer sex workshops, to ones focused almost exclusively on the kids' schooling and sports, where the most traumatic of incidents can often be cured with a simple kiss. And yet I am also fully aware that my ability to be both parent and partner is directly formed through my experience as caregiver for Shane and my friends. Were it not for them and that tumultuous time, I would not be the writer, father, lover, or person I am, and I owe a debt of gratitude to those lost during those tragic years.

More often than not, that period is often spoken of as if it were a purely historical event, a footnote in our collective history. There seems to be an unwillingness to delve more fully into that experience, to examine it, and discover its inherent value. Indeed, something about the reticence of the LGBT community to fully explore the AIDS epidemic reminds me of Shane's catatonic state. Just like him, there are emotions and thoughts coursing throughout, just under the surface, even if unacknowledged.

I understand the need to move on and fully realize that not all may be willing or able to return to that era in any manner. Many have found other causes to adopt. Some have attempted to lose themselves in parties and clubs. And others are still exhausted, trying to recover from the toll AIDS has taken, both in numbers lost and in our own emotional health.

Other communities, however, have also experienced horrible atrocities, but have found paths forward, and it is essential that we do the same.

Imagine the Jewish community without any mention of the Holocaust, or African American community without any discussion of slavery or the fight for civil rights. More recently, imagine the United States without any mention of 9/11. It has been my experience that in the LGBT community, AIDS seems to be most often spoken of in whispers, further compounding the notion that who we are, what we do, and the issues we face are somehow illicit. How can we adequately pay tribute and honor when even the mere mention of those years is met with uncomfortable silence?

In 2006, there was an article in the L.A. Times which I still find haunting—perhaps because I so identify with it. The story was about the NAMES Project AIDS Memorial Quilt and how it now lays largely in a warehouse in Atlanta, gathering dust. And yet there is a woman there who tends the quilt, who has been there since that first day in San Francisco with Cleve Jones. She works endlessly, patching and mending panels as they are returned from exhibits. She plays dance music to "her boys" as she works, often alone late at night, and wonders why people have forgotten.

Everyone has their own way of honoring. There is no one correct way of doing so. While for that woman, honoring took the form of the quilt, I chose to write.

Over 12 years ago, a single line popped into my head, which I immediately wrote down. At the time, I didn't know who was speaking it, what that line meant, or what it would become. But as I continued to write, it became clear that the voice in my head was Shane's, and that simple sentence would eventually become the opening line of my novel, *Songs for the New Depression*, which attempts to honor those we've lost.

Each person will have their own manner of paying tribute. It is not so important how we choose to remember, but that we remember and honor at all.

So write a story. Sing a song. Beat a drum. Create a work of art. Read a book. Talk with friends. March in the streets. Whatever you do, find a way to honor our fallen, lost to AIDS. Together, we can break through the sorrow of those tragic days, but we first must dare speak its name.

SONGS FOR THE NEW DEPRESSION

Twelve years writing a novel is a long time. Of course, that was done in fits and starts, in between children, life, and three husbands. I started soon after Shane's death, worked through Eyes, and finished with Russ, who was the impetus to finally completing it. I'd talked about the book repeatedly with him, but had actually written only a third of it in its entirety. As Russ' 50th birthday was then approaching, I knew that the moment had come. Finally, it was time to shit or get off the pot. I used that deadline to launch myself into action, knocking out the rest of the book, and presented him with the first bound copy at his party.

While inspired by Shane, the lead character, Gabe, isn't really Shane and isn't me, either. Gabe is a dramatically enhanced version of Shane's occasional cynicism, mixed with my power of the poisoned pen. Through this character, who hates himself, I was able to say all manner of nasty things, creating a character who is witty, damaged and tough to love.

Having banged on many doors, trying to sell the book, only to find all shut, I finally got a lovely rejection letter from the agent of Pulitzer Prize-winning author Michael Cunningham, acknowledging that despite how much she liked it, finding the writing "fresh and contemporary," she had no idea how to sell it. Having gotten a similar rejection letter from a well-respected small imprint, I decided to take matters into my own hands, creating my own publishing company and doing the rest on my own.

It was a huge learning curve, at 45-years-old, to be figuring out how to build a website, how to edit promo videos, how to distribute the book to reviewers, and how to negotiate publishing agreements. But I did it. And I was pleased at the reaction, as the book received awards and unexpected accolades. Never say never, indeed.

WRITE ON

Once I'd fully committed to writing, I never stopped, writing for my assorted day jobs, as money from my novel was barely enough to buy ice cream—even a single scoop at Thrifty's, which now sells for $1.99. I wrote blog posts, contributed to The Huffington Post website, conducted oral and written interviews to promote my book, and captured moments of our family's life in Facebook posts. My posts were a mix of endearing moments with our kids, self-serving book promotion, and endless political rants against the Republican ass-hat of the day.

One morning, with the 2012 election looming, and Republican Presidential candidate Mitt Romney voicing support for the Defense of Marriage Act (DOMA), which would directly and negatively impact our family, I woke early, unable to sleep, and decided to put into words some random thoughts that had been stirring inside of me throughout the election cycle.

I vomited forth a Facebook post entitled "Please De-Friend Me" and within a matter of hours, that post had been liked and shared several thousand times, with that traction going into overdrive when it appeared on The Huffington Post, with over 150,000 reactions. It inspired similar posts and articles, and even counter-articles, showing the power of the written word.

The point of the post was this: I am a person of value. I deserve every protection under the law, and so does everyone else. We may not agree on every issue, but if you're voting for a person or party platform that explicitly is against equality, fuck off. If you're in favor of people who articulate positions not in favor of the planet, animals or people, I want nothing to do with you. If you're in favor of defunding the arts, culture or education, goodbye. To be in my life, you need to be a decent and caring person, about both people and planet. Greed and ignorance are unattractive qualities.

We don't all need to be cookie-cutter-the-same, but be a compassionate person, and we'll get along just fine.

And now, some fun anecdotes about our kids.

SH*T MY KIDS SAY

Taken from my Facebook posts.

Marcus (singing): "I hate you, you hate me, let's get together and kill Barney..."
Me: "What did Barney ever do to you?"
Marcus: "He stabs people. He's friends with Chucky."
Me: "What?!?"
Marcus: "It's true. I heard it on the news."

Marcus: "If you have a wife, you mostly have to listen to her. Girls are bossy, right?"

Me (in Cockney accent): "It's time to get ye to school, Harry Potter!"
Marcus: "Dad, he doesn't speak French..."

Me, scoffing, to our 11-year-old: "Mason, you don't want to be popular..."
Mason: "Yes, I do. I'm on that trajectory."

Marcus, trying to hurry me along: "Babies are cryin'—Get a move on, Mama!"

Me: "Your fortune cookie says, 'You will be fortunate in all you put your hands on.'"

Marcus: "So, it could be a girl?"

While at Subway Sandwiches...
Me: "Marcus, don't play with your privates."
Marcus: "But they're jiggily!"

Marcus: "You've just gotta let me stay up until 10! There is an important new show on tonight!"
Me: "What is it?"
Marcus: "*My Babysitter is a Vampire!*"

Me: "How did that pinecone get into our garage?"
Mason: "Trust me, Dad, there are *lots* of ways."

Marcus: "Okay, people—who is lookin' for a boyfriend, cuz I am available."

I bought Marcus a cool hoodie tonight, but he was very upset that the arms were a bit long. A little while later...
Marcus: "Daddy, do sleeves grow???"

Mason: "Marcus, you are seriously off-topic."

Marcus: "Daddy, you know when I say I hate you that I really love you—Right?"

Marcus: "I'm a sidekick."

FAMILY LIFE: IT'S WHAT'S FOR BREAKFAST

Even before Eyes, I'd longed to be a dad. I can't really explain why, but I instinctively knew that I'd be good at it. While in elementary school, over the summer break I organized "summer vacation camps", during which I'd shepherd younger neighbor children through crafts and activities in the side yard of our house. In both primary school and college, I fell into directing, giving guidance and helping others, usually younger, flourish. Shortly after Shane died, I went to an LGBT parenting conference, to explore all possibilities as a single parent, only to find I was the only single person there.

And so, once I had kids, I fully embraced the opportunity to parent. For many years, I was the "Room Mom" at Mason's elementary, until one year, Eyes, trying to one-up me, ran quickly ahead of me to the signup table. (It should be noted that his year wasn't nearly as well-received as any of my previous.)

Another year, despite little knowledge of the sport, I coached Mason's soccer team, as no one had stepped up to volunteer, and we ended up winning the league championship. (I still vividly recall our final regional game, which we were going to lose, where in the final quarter I told the kids to forget their positions and just go out and try to score. Havoc ensued, and we lost, but fun was had by all.)

One summer, Russ and I took the boys to Italy for an amazing adventure. Our first hotel, Villa Vignamaggio in Tuscany, was the birthplace of the woman who inspired the Mona Lisa, as well as the stunning location Kenneth Branagh (who never should've left Emma Thompson) selected as the filming location for his movie, *Much Ado About Nothing*. Just wandering about the estates' gardens at sunrise, you could feel the weight and beauty of the villa. It was there that both boys had their first glass of wine, many years before they'd be able to do so legally in the U.S.

It was also at Vignamaggio that Marcus lost a tooth. In order to save his tooth for the tooth fairy, Russ hid it in our suite's only bathroom. Later that night, Russ woke me to explain that Marcus, anxious to find his tooth, was now trapped in the bathroom, as the skeleton keys on both sides of the door had fallen and he was unable to get out. I fixed it.

That same trip in Tuscany, staying near one of my favorite towns, San Gimignano, our hotel was built on the site of an old windmill, the turret of which was our suite. It was a quaint auberge, run by Germans, catering to fellow Germans, and we found ourselves the only American family, and certainly the only family within many miles with two white gay dads and two black kids.

On occasional nights, the auberge would serve dinner, and we thus booked a meal in advance. It was fancy dress, so we all wore suits. Inevitably, as occurs in Europe, the wait between meal and dessert stretched on, so our bored boys joined some other guests' kids playing outside. Just as the dessert course was to be served, Mason walked into the dining room, with Marcus directly behind in his suit, dripping wet from head to toe. Aghast, Russ and I asked, "What happened?"

"Marcus fell into the pool," Mason answered.

All eyes in the restaurant fell upon us, as Russ quickly ushered Marcus upstairs to change.

Later that night, the German tourists had assembled on the patio below our turret for their evening smokes, when I heard Marcus, out on our balcony, clad only in his underwear, singing out to the crowd *"I like to move it, move it!"*, complete with choreographed pelvic thrusts. All I can recall is Russ' hand, coming out from behind Marcus through the drapes, and pulling him back inside to safety. That auberge would never be the same.

That same summer, our family journeyed to Waycross for my mother's family reunion, and Russ was terrified. He knew Dottie and feared facing an entire infantry of mini-Dottie's, each rigid and angry, with him in their crosshairs. He would prove to be incorrect. The rest of my mother's family was warm, welcoming, and kind. But there were two particularly memorable episodes on this trip.

In one, Mason ate an entire plate of fried alligator, only to barf it up at the entry to our room at the Holiday Inn, necessitating a full cleansing of the walkway outside. And, two—

One morning, Mason and I awoke early in our shared two-queen room, with Russ and Marcus still fast asleep, only to hear Marcus singing in the darkness, "Ah, ah, ah, ah, stayin' alive, stayin' alive. Ah, ah, ah, ah, stayin' alive—." Mason and I stifled our giggles, as Marcus continued his deep-sleep Bee Gees tribute act.

SH*T MY KIDS SAY, PART II

Me: "Marcus, it is 6:00 a.m. What are you doing up, trying to get into that ice cream?!?"
Marcus: "I need energy."

Marcus: "Do babies have balls when they're born?"
Me: "Well, boy babies do."
Marcus: "Yeah, I know... Girls have cracks."

Me: "I sure hope I'm there to see you when you find someone you love and maybe have kids."
Marcus: "But if you're not, I'll do the funeral and dig and put you in there."

Mason: "You know that woman with the voice? On *The Nanny?*... It's an old-time show."

Me: "The thing Mason feels most passionately about is football."
Marcus: "And sagging his jeans."

Marcus: "My hair has *lots* of great qualities. It is *soft,* and *curly,* and, uh..." Deep sigh. "Maybe that's it."

Chaperoning a 6th grade field trip to Disneyland, on the Pirates of the Caribbean ride, going through the bayou swamp...

Me: "I can't imagine any place I would like to live less than a swamp."
Mason: "I'd even live in New York."

Marcus, accompanying me on a run: "Keep going, Daddy! Don't give up! If you don't stop running, you'll get a big kissy from me when we get home!" #BestCoachEver

Mason: "Girls have smellier farts than guys."
Me: "What makes you think so?"
Mason: "Cuz they hold 'em in for the longest time..."

Me, weeks before Christmas: "Guess what I just did? Wrapped presents for you two. They're under the tree."
Marcus: "If it was a puppy, it would die, right?"

Mason: "Are you Santa?"
Me: "What makes you ask?"
Mason: "I just want to know."
Me: "Santa has many helpers."
Mason: "I always thought Santa was African-American."
Me: "Why do you say that?"
Mason: "He's so jolly, with the big belly and all. Maybe I can be him next Halloween."
Me: "All I know is, people who believe in Santa get presents. The rest don't."
Mason: "So, can you get me an iPad?"

Me: "You smell like chocolate."
Marcus: "That's cuz I'm brown."

Note from Mason:
"Dear Dad, Thank you for showing me that life isn't boring and being my dad. I wish there was no such thing as dying so you could be with me forever. You are a very nice dad and I love you. Thank you for encouraging me in doing big things. You are a cool dad. I wish you could make Marcus the same as you. Love you, Mason. P.S. Don't show this to Marcus."

Marcus: "I had a very sad dream last night. Want to hear it?"
Me: "Sure."
Marcus: "We were Ninjas, well–good Ninjas, fighting the bad Ninjas. And we had penguins. But they wandered away from us, and me and Mason couldn't find them, so we were sad."

Me: "Mason, I want to ask you something—"
Mason: "No, Dad! *NOT* 'the talk'. Not again..."

Marcus, watching perfect physical specimens Darren Criss and Matthew Bomer sing a duet of "Somebody That I Used to Know" on *Glee*: "They probably fart, right—in real life?"

Me: "Do you know what a syllable is?"
Marcus: "Yes... Butt" (clap) "Hole!" (clap)

And, lastly, in my favorite Facebook post of 2013, I wrote: "So tonight, for Russ' birthday dinner, Marcus made a sign which he put on the table, directing 'Praisetents here!' My first reaction was to correct him, to 'presents,' but the more I thought about it, with the emphasis on 'praise,' the more I liked it. From now on, whenever I give a gift, I'm really giving a praisetent."

PRAISETENTS NOT YET GIVEN

I'd really hoped to make a living as a writer. With my novel and a follow-up collection of short stories, *Gifts Not Yet Given*, I invested money into promoting both, which left me with little besides enormous credit card debt. It was a gamble I had been willing to take, but one from which would take me years to recover. Still, investing in myself and my talent felt like the right move. How else would I move up the ladder from a "job" to a career if I wasn't prepared to take chances?

During the Great Recession, our family was treading water financially. We were newly entrenched in our beautiful home, bought just before the bubble burst, only to soon find ourselves literally living month-to-month. Russ, a brand strategist for luxury clients, felt the burn first, as high-end brands immediately stopped spending money. Following over 10 years at Green Eggs & Ham Marketing, in their third round of staff layoffs, I was let go, as was the entire administrative team. The male executives then brought in their wives to answer calls and help as needed.

To be out of a job at that time was unnerving. And yet while that stress was untenable, having been freed from a job at which I'd been tethered for too long also allowed me to dream about the future and what I might do next. It provided me time to write and create, and to be there for our kids, shepherding them to sports and school activities, and to be more a part of their lives, which is what I'd always wanted.

Still, after a year of being laid off, when a fulltime job finally landed in my lap, I jumped. I should have known the headaches in store for me, having once before worked at a nonprofit, but at that point, I was happy just to have a job.

Plastic Surgeons Anonymous (PSA) was a group of plastic surgeons who thought of themselves as the best of the best— an exclusive organization that one had to be asked to join. These surgeons' egos were often larger than their female patients' breast implants. While undoubtably some of these surgeons were likely responsible for such horrific mishaps as Meg Ryan's lips, Jennifer Grey's nose, Tara Reid's belly, and Jocelyn "The Catwoman" Wildenstein's—well, everything— at PSA, there would be no discussion of such "missteps." Our organization's focus was on continuing clinical education to produce the most natural-looking results possible, with a hacksaw and a couple of staples.

My job was to get these surgeons to attend our annual educational convention, as well as smaller symposia throughout the year, and to purchase our products, for which I oversaw the creation and marketing. In theory, this job should've allowed me to flourish creatively, coming up with inventive ways to get people to spend their money.

If I'd been allowed to simply do my job, it would have been terrific. However, said job also meant interacting with other company employees, who were at best a mixed bag. To get hired at PSA, you either needed to be a relative—no matter how distant—of the Executive Director, of which there were millions, or an expectant mother with no discernable skill set yet desiring a paycheck for just barely showing up—and supervisors endlessly understanding when you didn't. There really were no other qualifications for getting a job at PSA. And, as an added bonus, if you could not fulfill basic duties, such as reading and responding to email, you'd quickly receive a promotion, raise, and tenure. It was a dream job, for some.

The rest of us, the doers, received no such raises or promotions, even when begged for. We might occasionally receive a crumb—a slight bump in salary to keep us on the hook—but even that was less than a basic cost of living increase, which PSA had ceased giving.

Besides myself, about the only other person who did not meet PSA's strict hiring requirements was the grumpy, misogynistic old man employed as Senior Staff Curmudgeon, whose sole job was to be contrary and complain about everything. He looked down on women who had plastic surgery, viewing them as bimbos, which is a problematic when one's job is educating the public about the benefits of cosmetic procedures. A liberal Archie Bunker, he threw a wrench into almost everything I did, but I took pleasure one day, walking into his office, to catch him cruising men on Mister. I hope his husband knew...

Each year we put on a massive educational convention, which bounced to different towns, with a great deal of work falling on my shoulders. I shot promotional videos, set up email blasts, and oversaw creation of the show look, all marketing collateral, signage, and booth design, to name but a few. During the convention itself, for an entire week I would run myself ragged, up at 5:00 a.m., bed at midnight, sprinting across the convention center to attend to all manner of details. It was exhausting, and made all the more so once I realized that out of 30-odd staff, there were only a handful of others with similar work loads, and a whole lot of folks who were dead weight. If any one of us "doers" were to be struck dead, the entire convention would've screeched to a halt. Conversely, at one such convention, two senior staffers were allowed to leave and no one even missed them. I had endless conversations with our Executive Director about my concerns, but never got more than a sympathetic nod. There would never be any improvements leading to a more effective organization. The dead weights were allowed to continue doing little, and we doers were left to twist in the wind.

For more than eight long years, everything I did made money for the company, and yet—despite repeated requests—I was making roughly the same as I had as an Executive Assistant for Green Eggs & Ham. PSA was the very definition of Dysfunction Junction. Simply being a nice person shouldn't be the sole qualification for getting a job, and to reward someone repeatedly for their inadequacies was unfathomable.

But I did occasionally get free Botox, so I'm grateful for that.

CAN WE GET A MULTIPLE COURT BATTLE DISCOUNT?

In the fall of 2013, out of the blue, I got an email from Eyes, requesting that we reduce his child support from roughly $1500 each month to a new amount he proposed, $150 per month.

His rationale? He had been laid off.

"When?" I asked in an email. "I wasn't aware you'd had any job change," which our court-ordered agreement noted we were both to do, the minute either of our situations should be modified.

He replied: "In April of last year."

For a year and a half, Eyes had pretended that he had a job. He would get "dressed for work," talk about "work," and "come home from work," lying to his son that entire time. One and a half year of dressing up, pretending and lying to Mason. Let that sink in.

GOING TO THE CHAPEL – THE SECOND TIME

One morning in 2013, upon hearing that marriage equality was finally legal in California, Marcus came bounding into our room, jumping up and down on our bed. "What're you waiting for, people? Let's go get married!"

Soon after, Russ and I would do just that; the first time getting married in secret. As I needed to have spinal surgery and was concerned about potential pesky complications, such as death, I wanted to ensure that Russ' legal status with our sons was solid. Thus, all of us dressed in suits, we took our boys to the Orange County courthouse and they served as witnesses to our union. It was quick, perfunctory, completely unemotional and entirely legal. The four of us celebrated at Morton's Steakhouse, but didn't share word of our union any further. We wanted the time and place for the "real thing" to be right.

That would come in 2014, when we got married in a French-themed wedding at our home, surrounded by our dearest family and friends. Mason and Marcus played key roles, writing their own "vows", which they shared with the assembled. Russ and I wrote our vows as well, and I followed mine up by serenading Russ with a rocky but heartfelt rendition of "La Vie en Rose," singing the intro in pidgin French.

The highlight of the ceremony came when those assembled walked to where we four stood, with each participant placing a single flower into a large vase, eventually creating an enormous beautiful bouquet. During this, one of my favorite singers, Angela Carole Brown, joined us and sang Bob Dylan's poignant "Forever Young." That moment symbolized the importance of community support, joining together in love and encouragement, and allowed each of the wedding party to fully acknowledge and connect with those assembled. It was only sullied by the nasty fake smile of the wife of one of those gathered, a bitchy Annie Potts, who had never thought that I was a good enough match for Russ.

Following, we celebrated with an amazing array of French delicacies (served by a very unpleasant caterer), a drooping Arc du Triomphe wedding cake (which I was *not* happy with—despite having provided the baker with photos of a similar cake, done correctly), and toasts by cherished friends.

The pièce de résistance, however, was our very-French photo booth, set up by our pool. From a local prop house, Russ and I had rented a metallic 15 foot tall silver replica of the Eiffel Tower, which was placed over our jacuzzi, and a gold-gilded ornate sofa, which served as the photo booth, on which we placed an impeccably dressed mannequin, the supermodel Colette, complete with sunglasses and French beret, who perched on the edge of the couch and graciously obliged our guests with photos.

Here's the thing about marriage that I didn't anticipate: it changes you. As Russ and I had been together for so many years, I never thought that a formal celebration would mean so much to me emotionally, but it did. As gay people, taught from a young age that our very basic desires of love and acceptance are an illness and, in some places, punishable by death—that can be a hard foundation from which to grow. I fully understand the lost gay men I've seen, drowning in pain and sorrow, day drinking and hooking up in bars. How can one ever hope to create a healthy life and future when the message you receive from others is that you are physically sick, evil, and morally reprehensible?

On our formal wedding day, we had over a hundred people surrounding and lifting us up with love. It was an emotional day, unexpectedly so. I had thought that the experience would be a formality, but I was on the verge of tears a good portion of the day. To be loved by our community. To be loved by our children. For me to be loved by my brilliant partner and best friend. And to be celebrated by all around us—that was impactful. It helped shore up my sometimes-shaky foundation. It helped move me forward as a human. And it gave me better understanding into how important it is to simply show one another love.

If you have an LGBT friend, co-worker, or family member you value, please tell them. Express to them just how much their presence in your life means. That very simple acknowledgement can be a gift—and might actually save a life.

ROCKY MOUNTAIN HIGH

Our years in Orange County were both extremely blessed, having great friends, my family living close by, and a beautiful home in which to live, as well as extremely trying, given the Great Recession's financial stress, unnecessary drama with Eyes, and a beautiful and expensive home in which to live. Bought at the peak of the market, that house in Orange increasingly became unsustainable. Not only was it challenging to pay the mortgage each month, but the upkeep costs were insane. With monthly water bills alone of over $200, it was not a situation we could win.

As we'd been our happiest in our mountain cabin, and having the luxury of working remotely, Russ and I discussed a potential move with our boys. While, as teens, neither exactly relished the idea of leaving their friends, both were excited about potentially living in the mountains, and Mason, in particular, reaffirmed his desire to live with us, should something in our custody situation go wrong. Thus, we cast our location net wide: we wanted to be near a big city, but not in a big city; we wanted good schools; we wanted seasons, but not East coast winters; we wanted to be near both a ski area and an easily-accessible airport. While we researched and considered many places, we kept coming back to a mountain town just outside Denver: the perfectly named, Evergreen.

LIFE LESSON #29

Never become friends with realtors. No matter how many wonderful occasions you might spend together, if you don't let them sell your house, they'll drop you faster than a soiled condom.

BUYER AND SELLER

It's easy to be flippant, but the truth is that the loss of our realtor friends still hurts deeply, all these years later. We first met Buyer and Seller at our progressive church and immediately felt a kinship.

Buyer cared passionately about many of the causes that we did, and—unlike others—put his money where his mouth is. He spent time engaged in trying to create change in the world, whether that meant volunteering on the board of a school for those less fortunate, learning about environmentally friendly urban gardening, or standing up against inequality, wherever he saw it.

Seller was exquisitely beautiful, reminding me of a famous TV actress, with a lovely laugh and a twinkle in her eye. While Buyer dealt largely in short sales, Seller was the couple's bread winner, working in a retirement market, which resulted in an endless life/death sales-cycle. She was often exhausted from her duties, but always found time to connect with friends and her two doting children. While just as caring as Buyer about "the world," Seller put her efforts into her relationships with others, including us.

From the moment we met, I knew we'd be forever friends. The four of us connected in a fully caring and supportive bond, and we had many nights of deep conversations and raucous laughter, usually with another close couple, Wife and Wife. We'd crack open bottles of wine and enjoy appetizers while catching up on each other's lives, current events, and causes about which we were passionate. No topic was off limits. These were the kind of people you hope to meet your entire life, who care about you and support you, offering a hand when you're down.

One Sunday afternoon at brunch with Buyer and Seller, an acquaintance of theirs came to our table, mistakenly assuming that Russ and I were their sons, despite us being only 10 years younger than Buyer/Seller. We laughed, and this singular moment led to an ongoing joke. We sent Seller Mother's Day cards and gave Buyer a nose hair trimmer on his birthday. We were their "sons," and took awkward photographs of ourselves, mimicking terrible high school photos, and sent them with love.

We sat through one of their son's sales pitch for Cutco knives and ended up spending over $300 on the knives, just to show support for him. (Carving a pumpkin with one of them, Russ later ended up in the ER with five stitches as a result.)

The other son of theirs took a job with Russ' company, as he wanted to learn more about marketing. I warned Russ against hiring him, as I knew what might later come, but Russ wanted to help. Once in the position, however, it became apparent this son wasn't the go-getter Russ' team thought they were hiring, as his sole focus was a recent breakup with his girlfriend. After being given many chances to improve, he was finally fired by Russ' company. Did that factor contribute to our breakup with these friends? Well, it certainly didn't help.

Still, Buyer and Seller spoke at our wedding. We spent New Year's Eve with them, sharing our plans to soon sell our house and make a huge move, leaving our friends and family in California, to make a new life in Colorado, and they were entirely supportive.

In February, I called Buyer to tell him that our house was finally being listed, knowing that he'd soon see it on MLS. His comment? "You know we're realtors, right?"

Of course, we did. Russ and I agonized over our choice of realtors, as ours was considered a luxury home, valued at over a million dollars. Even as things stood, we would be taking a considerable loss, given the economic crash the country had endured, and it was essential we get as much for it as we could. We needed an expert in the luxury market, not someone specializing in short sales. We also didn't want to mix business with pleasure, having experienced similar situations in the past. While we knew Buyer might be hurt, this was our investment—the biggest asset in our portfolio—and we needed to maximize it for all we could manage. We hoped time might help ease his unhappiness.

In March, we called, emailed, and texted both Buyer and Seller, trying to arrange my usual birthday celebration. Aside from a cryptic text from Seller ("We love you!"), there was radio silence. No response was given as to dates they might be free. We waited and waited, hoping for some sign from them that all was forgiven. We're still waiting.

How can such a friendship turn out to be purely transactional? Were we simply a commodity? How could we have been so blind not to see that the relationship we'd cherished was actually paper thin?

There is a reason that I've named them here as Buyer and

Seller. At some point, we ceased being people to them, and became only property. Our years of friendship were seemingly based solely on the idea that one day, we might let them sell our house.

I still find it hard to believe that people we knew so well could turn out to be so awful. But it had happened with Eyes and it happened with them.

That June, we moved from California to Colorado. While I'm glad to be gone, I can't help but feel that we left part of our hearts behind.

ROBERT MICHAEL MORRIS

If you've ever seen the hysterical TV show, *The Comeback*, you know Michael. He played the daffy, dishy hairdresser, Mickey, to Lisa Kudrow's clueless Valerie Cherish. Russ and I were fortunate enough to meet Michael through our good friend, writer/director Glenn Gaylord. Glenn knew of our love for the first season of *The Comeback*, especially the character Mickey, and had directed Michael in an earlier TV pilot. One night, Glenn brought Michael to dinner at our place, and we quickly became fast friends. We would meet Michael regularly for lunch at Shenandoah at the Arbor restaurant in Los Alamitos, as we loved the food and patio—and as it was central to where we all lived, given that Michael hated to drive—especially at night.

Michael was smart, sassy, and funny—but not entirely as immediately endearing as his role as the beloved Mickey on *The Comeback*. In real life, there were times he could be like an old auntie, scolding when he didn't approve of something. Michael had been a teacher for years, for both high school and college, which perhaps explains his tendency to mother people.

His generosity knew no bounds. When I was gathering items for a silent auction to help those battling HIV/AIDS, Michael promptly showered me with boxes of random trinkets and jewelry he'd collected through the years, as well as several paintings. I doubt that he knew the monetary value of any of them—they'd just struck his fancy—and it is likely he felt that if they were worth something to him, they'd mean something to someone else as well.

Michael was also a prolific writer, with enough plays to fill four anthology volumes. Rumor also has it that, prior to his death, he was at work or had completed a memoir. How I'd love to read that!

In the months prior to his death, Michael sent us a beautiful and expensive Lladró porcelain, depicting Shakespeare's Othello and Desdemona, worth over two thousand dollars. He'd intended it to honor Russ and my artistic endeavors, as well as our similarly dark-skinned children; Michael had mentioned more than once that he found our adoption of them somewhat noble. While to us there was nothing noble about these adoptions—we simply wanted healthy children—we were thoroughly appreciative of Michael's unwavering support. Still, when we unpacked the gift, I looked at Russ and said, "Do you think he's preparing for the end?"

We'd known about Michael's cancer for some time, and when Michael found out that they were indeed going to film a second season of *The Comeback*, 10 years after the first, he shared that his illness would be part of the storyline. His performance in season two should have won an Emmy. There are moments throughout between Mickey and Valerie Cherish that are simply magical-breathtaking-emotional-riveting. Their relationship proved to be the show's strongest, allowing each a shoulder on which to rely. Season two marked some of the best television anywhere and was

Michael's finest performance. He also gave memorable appearances on *Running Wilde, How I Met Your Mother*, and *Brothers and Sisters*, to name but a few.

In the end, I'll best remember Michael for his repeated simple kindnesses... The way, when sharing some bit of news particularly delicious, he'd place his hand on yours, giving it a squeeze, showing he trusted your confidence... His hearty laugh, which inevitably made an appearance in every encounter...

Robert Michael Morris was a class act and deserved even more professional recognition than he received. Kind, caring, and witty, Michael lives on in the heart of anyone who ever heard him utter, "Oh, Red..."

QUIT YER WHININ'

Moving to Colorado was a huge step for me. I was a Southern Californian, born and bred, and while I'd never felt entirely "Southern Californian," I had never lived anywhere else, either. When Russ and I made the decision to move, we were most concerned about Marcus. Given his developmental delays and learning disabilities, he'd formed a tight circle of elementary school friends, and we were uncertain as to how he would adjust. However, it was he who, upon our move, immediately had the most friends.

Russ and I met our new friends relatively quickly, through both boys' sports and school activities, and through area mixers we hosted at our house. Fully recognizing the difficulty of establishing new friendships, we hosted "Meet the Street" mixers for those in our neighborhood, local LGBT mixers, and "Evergreen NICE People" mixers (with NICE standing for Nurturing, Inquisitive, Compassionate, and Environmentally Friendly), and we met quite a lot of NICE people as a result.

Mason, however, who had always been the most adaptable of any of us, given his back-and-forth between two households, initially had the hardest time making friends.

Prior to putting our house on the market, Russ and I discussed the potential move with both boys to gather buy-in, to ensure we were doing the right thing for all of us. While hesitant, both boys agreed to our plan. We contacted a realtor and I alerted Eyes, when he suddenly pounced like a panther into action. Despite never having been Mason's primary parent, Eyes took it upon himself to try to deter Mason from moving with us. One day, he asked Mason, already 15, if he really wanted to leave his group of friends, and Mason truthfully replied, "No." Eyes did not, however, follow up with the all-important question, "Well, would you want to live with me?"

Thus, just prior to our move, we were greeted with a 50-page legal missive from Eyes, suing us for full parental rights. We immediately sat down with Mason.

"If this is what you want, sweetie, that is fine. Of course, we'd love for you to be with us, but if you want to stay in California with Eyes, we will make that happen. But if you want to move to Colorado with us, we will fight for that."

Mason once again stated that he wanted to remain with us, thus beginning one of the most tumultuous and draining periods of our lives.

Eyes went after us like an anaconda to a pig, fighting every step of the way. We endured months of legal battles, appointments with court-ordered assessors, with both parties trying to prove they were the more committed parent, doing the right thing for their child.

My attorney advised against going into the entire sordid history of Eyes or his worthiness to be a parent, as that might appear as if we were attempting to slander him to get what we wanted. Eyes' own attorney, however, must not have given his client the same advice, as they tried to take me down at every turn.

We learned that Eyes had requested that Mason's best friend's mother, who was also our friend, come to court to speak against us. *What on earth,* I wondered, *could this person say?* We'd been nothing but kind to them, but I knew that Eyes had likely filled their head with all manner of doubt.

In one of our hearings, Eyes brought scrapbooks of Mason, many of which I had put together myself, to demonstrate their tight, "singular" parental bond. In one particularly memorable moment on the stand, Eyes' attorney asked him how he talked about racial issues with Mason, prompting Eyes to channel Mister Rogers' soft, nurturing voice:

"I put my hand atop his, and I said, 'You see how my skin is white, and yours is black? There really isn't a difference, is there? We are all the same, underneath.'"

When I later mentioned that episode to Mason, he stated unequivocally, "That never happened."

Eyes' attorney asked me, on the witness stand, intimidatingly, if I was writing a book about Eyes. Before I could fully answer, my attorney jumped in, and the judge extinguished further questioning.

I wasn't, truly, writing a book "about Eyes," so much as I was then writing a memoir of my entire life—the very book you are now reading—but afterward Eyes would accuse me of perjury. Given that he himself had given contradictory claims under oath and submitted false paperwork in order to not pay full child support, that is one the few he said/he said battles I would've been happy to fight.

Over the years, many have asked me why Eyes fought so hard for Mason, and to that, like so many of the things Eyes did, I have no answer.

Part of me believes that, as Eyes had no true moral center, he placed that onto Mason. I think he saw what an honorable and upstanding person Mason had become and convinced himself that he was responsible for it. If that goodness were to be taken away, what would be left for Eyes?

If I had done half the things Eyes had done, wronging so many in the process, I would hope that I would have held myself accountable, sought help, and tried to right my wrongs. Eyes did none of that. If anything, he made it his job to fight me at every opportunity. It is my belief that Eyes blamed me for making the truth about him public, "ruining his life" in the process, and therefore made it his ongoing mission to destroy me, rather than simply accepting that the consequences of all that occurred were the result of his actions.

Still, the amount of money spent on our many court battles could've put Mason through college, grad school, and any other schooling he ever desired. Aside from the financial strain these battles caused, the emotional toll Eyes' actions took on our family is one from which we are only now recovering.

This turmoil went on for months. While Russ, Marcus and I moved to Colorado, whether Mason would move as well was a question to which we didn't yet know the answer. We could not technically "move" Mason to Colorado without the court's blessing, so Mason's things were left with my parents, where he occupied their hot, stifling guest room with its bumpy mattress, and Mason would fly back and forth between the two states and "homes," as his schedule allowed, until the situation was finally resolved.

That resolution would not occur until Evergreen High School had already begun their 2015 fall semester. Indeed, the very day prior to their start of school, when Mason should have been attending new student orientation, Mason and I were in court in California, finally winning our case. While Mason remained outside the courthouse with my dad, in the event he should be called, the judge—a younger woman new to the bench—actually teared up, so persuasive were Eyes' magical parenting moments, only to say that she and her staff truly didn't know which of us was the better parent. Luckily, in Mason's private interview off-stand, he had specifically indicated a desire to remain with us, mentioning his bond with Marcus, and it was that statement that allowed us to remain as a family. We immediately made plans to fly "home" the next day.

In the courtyard, my attorney and I encountered Eyes' lawyer, and I complimented him on his dramatic recitation of Eyes' demonstrably false "parenting moments." He merely shrugged and laughed. "Gotta work with what you've got, right?!?"

While Mason and I were at the courthouse, Russ, unable to focus on his work, took Marcus off to Estes Park, at the entrance to the Rocky Mountain National Park, for peace and solitude. But a peaceful heart was impossible for Russ. This man who hadn't necessarily wanted to be a father had so fully embraced our boys as his own that he was torn up inside, so fearful was he that our family might be split. And he was more than conscious of the dramatic toll it had taken on me and Mason.

This long, unnecessary, emotional and protracted court battle meant that Mason wouldn't be there for his first day of school in Evergreen. This unending fight also meant that Mason couldn't fully commit to the Evergreen football team, diminishing him in the eyes of the coaches. This standoff meant that for many months, Mason had no idea where his home would be. And that doubt—that uncertainty—created in Mason a hesitancy in bonding with people. The court battle also created a rift between Mason and Eyes, whether Eyes fully realized it or not. It would take some time before Mason felt secure enough to put down roots. But, upon doing so, fully giving himself over to his new life in Evergreen, Mason would go on to create enduring friendships.

I, however, didn't fair quite as well as Mason. Trying to keep my head above water throughout this ordeal, both figuratively and financially, I started self-medicating with my beloved Chardonnay. I've always liked wine, but many years ago, I was satisfied with simply a glass or two. Upon my breakup with Eyes, that increased to a bottle a night. During our final court battle, that increased to more than a bottle a night.

I gained quite a bit of weight as a result but could never stop imbibing. I'd never wanted to be overweight. My dad had been overweight for years, until he got older and ate like a bird, and I'd always vowed that being fat would never be my fate. In the back of my mind, I recalled a jealous boyfriend of a guy I was dating in my twenties repeatedly calling me "Pudgy," though I was anything but. But recently, I've had to acknowledge the truth about what I have done to myself.

It may have started as a reaction to Eyes, but he was not entirely to blame. I started self-medicating due to the emotional turmoil I faced. There we were, getting ready to leave California for another state, trying to make a better life for ourselves, only to find that we were once-again fighting my arch-nemesis for the son I'd fought almost half my life to protect. Then, to find myself faced with astounding attorney fees, $24,000 in one-month alone, and my future looked incredibly bleak. To pay these attorney fees, I opened every credit card account imaginable, and ended up almost $150,000 in debt. And my measly paycheck from PSA barely covered my monthly credit card payments, let alone allow me to envision any way out of the mess.

I never wanted to be the ultimate sad cliché: a gay overweight alcoholic writer. But it seemed it was to be my fate. There were some really rough nights ahead, drinking too much, my pointed tongue at the ready, but Russ was patient, as were our boys. They seemed to know that the vision in front of them wasn't entirely me. I'm not saying that they didn't have concerns, but their faith helped pull me through.

Russ, throughout all, was a Godsend. He'd always been the breadwinner and had taken on the role of disciplinarian in our family as well. He kept our family on track, come hell or high-water. It killed him to see what this battle was doing emotionally to me and Mason, and he himself was on edge for months.

Compounded financial debt. Emotional duress. The uncertainty of not knowing. Keeping our family intact. Respecting Mason's wishes. Paying our fucking mortgage. All of that took its toll. None would be immune from its damage.

Finally, after three years underwater, we were able to get a home equity line of credit, at a reasonable monthly payment and percentage, enabling me to banish that crushing credit card debt once and for all. To have that burden immediately lifted was like being able to breathe again, after years under water. Getting off the sauce, however, would be a more gradual process.

OH MY GOD

Throughout my life there have been many times when I've called on God to help me out. Especially during my unexpectedly tumultuous adult life. I've asked him to bring me peace, closure, a new bicycle... But I've never fully believed in Him. I've wanted to believe—sometimes desperately—but even that desire felt as if I were buying into something false.

As a child in Sunday school, being taught the wonderful Bible stories with characters on a felt board, I intrinsically knew that what I was hearing were just that—stories. I played the part of dutiful religious boy, learning Bible verses, singing in the choir, and leading summer Vacation Bible School, but I never truly believed. Even with conservative Christian parents like mine, their version of the Gospel seemed more focus on judgment of others than with following the teachings of Christ: helping the poor, being good stewards of the planet, and offering unconditional love to all humankind. It really isn't that hard of a concept to grasp and embrace.

Still, I vividly recall the coffee breaks between Sunday services, where as a child I could circulate without really being seen, eavesdropping on the perfectly coiffed women, dressed to the nines, an exaggerated smile on their lips, dissing everyone under hushed breath.

I think the greatest disservice my parents did was to keep from us just how challenging life can be. They never argued in front of us, which is admirable, but all consequential conversations happened out of view as well. I grew up believing that good things happen to good people. That karma would be the reward for those who were not. Both of which are nice ideas, but patently false. Shitty things happen to good people. Shitty people aren't necessarily punished for their shitty acts. Of this, I'm now certain.

The fact is, life is a game of roulette. Sometimes you're up, and others down, but neither state is determined by how amazing you happen to be.

While we were still in California, Russ and I were members of a wonderful progressive church dedicated to peace and justice, equality, and helping those in need. Many at the church didn't even consider themselves Christians, as traditionally defined. Many didn't believe in a higher power, or that Christ was truly divine, which made prayer in the church a bit odd. Who were we praying to, and why—if no one is up there? These people simply believed that in following Jesus' actions and example, one might find oneself on the path to something divine.

I led the Open & Affirming ministry for several years, scheduling a variety of LGBT and peace-and-justice films nights, booking a speaking panel of transgendered people as a young member of our church was transitioning, and recruiting speakers on an array of social justice and environmental issues to enlighten our congregation. When our church stumbled, I helped rally support. When gay marriage was up for referendum in California, I organized protests. Russ and I opened our house for discussion groups and hosted fundraisers. It was enlightened activism and I was proud to do my part.

I was asked to become a church elder and agreed. Having a pulpit from which to proselytize seemed a great idea, yet when asking people to join me in prayer, I cringed a bit. I was rallying people to the cause of peace and justice, and all of that felt right. But offering a prayer made me feel like a huckster, trying to sell something which didn't exist.

The final straw for me came as we neared the Easter season, and the topics of Ash Wednesday and Maundy Thursday came up. Apparently, elders were supposed to wash feet and to offer ash on people's foreheads in the sign of the cross. *Who am I*, I wondered, *to offer such services?* There is nothing about me that is remotely holy. Holey, yes, but not *holy*. To have done either task would've been the ultimate hypocrisy, which prompted me to quit.

I believe in being a good person. I believe in caring for Mother Earth. I believe in extending kindness. I believe in advocating for the less fortunate. I believe in equality for all and fighting for that right, whenever necessary. I believe in being trying to be a good example. In living your truth. I came up with a mantra some years back, which I often used as my inscription at book signings. "Tell your story. Live authentically. Change the world." And through all my many ups and downs, I've tried to do just that.

Where is the disconnect between what most of us were taught about religion, versus what is most likely accurate? I think most humans want answers. Who is good and who is bad? What is right and what is wrong? When watching a movie, ambiguous endings give us pause. We want closure. When watching *All My Children* all those years ago in my dorm room, I needed certainty. Did Erika get the guy? Did right triumph? Was there a happy ending? The worst thing ever were those Friday cliffhangers, with no resolution until Monday.

It's hard to live with unanswered questions, but with God, I'm okay not knowing. I'm happy if he is there, but also okay if he is not. Why do we feel the need for closure on everything—even that which is outside our control? That desire seems hardwired into our DNA, and yet, we can't know all. Even if there is a God, does he have the capacity to monitor every single one of us flawed beings, like some airplane traffic controller, homing in on our every impulse? Praising or blaming him for each happy or tragic event in the world seems far outside his pay grade.

As much as I don't believe that Jesus physically rose from the dead, I do appreciate the metaphor. Redemption is a wonderful aspiration, and the act of repenting and rising again is something I strive for daily. Imagine what good we could do in the world if we simply treated others and our planet with kindness.

TODAY AND TOMORROW

As I write this, Mason has completed his sophomore year of college. He's on the shorter side, but strong as an ox, benching 335 lbs. Throughout his life, Mason's main focus has been on sports, and seeing him following through on his goal, playing college football and pursuing a degree in Exercise Science, is thrilling for us. He's kind, considerate, and compassionate—exactly the traits I so admire, which will serve him well as he fully enters adulthood.

Marcus will be a senior, working towards his high school graduation, and continues to bring us joy and laughter with his comedic spirit. He's on the verge of adulthood as well, and yet is still capable of endearing affection towards his parents, which we will never turn away. He's not sure what he wants to do as a career, potentially something with animal advocacy, but for now loves playing football and hanging out with his friends.

Russ and I, having finally emerged from our financial hell, have begun to heal. With both kids almost out of the nest, we're considering our future options. Will we stay in Evergreen? Move? Downsize? Travel? I know we both seek greater connection with our friends, and can't wait until our boys are settled, so that we can enjoy whatever families they might create. It's hard to know where we might end up, but we do have a clear picture of what we're looking for, and an idea of how to get there.

I know that Evergreen might not be our permanent home, but for me, it has been a place of respite, providing peace. It's been a place where every elk or deer wandering through our yard sends me scurrying to the window. Where the amazing mountain views provide a sense of calm. Where the mostly cool days have invigorated me, especially when juxtaposed to California, where I rarely wanted to venture into the heat.

Colorado proved to be the perfect place for me to hunker down and heal. I love the peace it brings, and the friends we have found. Who knows what tomorrow may hold, but as I write this today, this entrancing place feels like *home*.

EYES' DEMISE

The end for Eyes came about much like the end of our relationship, all those years ago. He sent a simple email, this time intended for me: "I'm going out on disability tomorrow." I wrote back, asking for more details, but he declined to give them, stating his need for privacy. I thought, "You fucking pretended to have cancer, you bastard—and shaved your head to make people believe it. *Proof is damn well needed!*" But none came.

The first thing Mason said was, "I bet he's lying."

What a sad legacy, to have your child not trust your word. But Mason's reaction was much the same as many others burned by Eyes. *"How can you believe him?"*

It's a fair question. But my initial reaction was exactly that—to believe him—despite our sordid history. I still loved him. Not that I wanted to be with him, or didn't have immense anger for the years of mistreatment, costly court battles, and emotional warfare. But Eyes had been my ideal. I had wanted to marry him, to have children with him, and to grow old with him. I wanted him to repent and make right for all he'd done. To be the person I'd imagined when we first met. I wanted to look into Eyes' eyes and see truth, honor, and compassion. I wanted to discover that I hadn't been wrong after all. But I *was* wrong; fundamentally so.

Eyes' final act of kindness to me was to not pay his share

of Mason's dorm room expenses, saddling me with almost $1,000 in receipts.

Eyes was still the same untruthful, shitty person. He asked for a reduction in child support, given his disability claim. Having known his history, and his ability to charm, it was entirely within the realm of possibility that he'd concocted this scenario as a way to pay even less in support. I asked for proof of his illness but none came. I asked for details on his finances but received only a copy of his initial disability check.

Eyes claimed to be too sick to work but had in fact been fired. Yet he also said that he couldn't afford *not* to work and might return "soon." Mason relayed that Eyes had "stacks" of hundred-dollar bills in his condo. Mason also reported that Eyes had told him that he had "spots on his brain," but nonetheless Eyes drove across four states, solo, to spend time with Mason. Too sick to work, too sick to perform basic tasks, but perfectly fine to drive days to our house, showing up looking normal. Continually declining to give details on his health, but fully expecting our compassion and understanding in return...

During that visit to Colorado, I asked Eyes if Mason was provided for in both his will and life insurance. He replied that his disease was progressive, and that he wouldn't die until after Mason graduated high school, which was over a year away. Odd, to be facing some supposedly terminal disease, to have "spots on the brain," and yet to somehow know that you'd live through his graduation.

I Googled "spots on the brain," which essentially translates into lesions on the brain. I wondered: could it be possible that Eyes had been struck with the same poison arrow that had killed Shane, Progressive Multifocal Leukoencephalopathy? It was a disease endured by others battling AIDS.

There was something so morbidly poetic about that possibility... I've never considered myself a particularly vindictive person, but as Eyes' end finally came into sight, and with few facts upon which to draw another conclusion, I gravitated to this diagnosis.

I pictured Eyes lying in bed, unable to move or respond. I saw a long line of the aggrieved stretching down the long hospital corridor, down the stairs, and out into the street. Not the "grieving" mind you, but the "aggrieved." The line held those abused by Eyes, lied to by Eyes, and the countless many whose lives would never be the same, due to his years of betrayals. With him unmoving, I pictured each person walking up to his inert body, speaking their piece, then moving forward and moving on. It would take many hours, of course, for everyone to reach his bed, but I pictured that cathartic act helping those damaged taking one step closer to closure.

Is there ever "closure," you might ask? Can one ever draw closed the curtain, forever, on such painful episodes? No. Most certainly not.

But I'd like to try.

LIFE LESSON #30

Life is precious.

AN EXPLANATION

I don't mean "life is precious" as in cute or dainty, but life is indeed precious, when viewed as a thin porcelain teacup, held by a tremulous hand. And not the dainty teacup held by Mr. Peacock, showily, as he dissed me on that flight from Boston. Life can be shattered at any moment, as families recovering from accidents, traumatic incidents, or terminal illnesses can easily attest. We all want the easy or quick resolution. We want advance knowledge of our end, in order to set plans in place and ensure that our loved ones are cared for. We want time to attempt to heal old wounds and make peace with our past, before we go.

But life is a teacup. It can suddenly fall, transforming all of one's hopes and dreams into a million pieces... Peace. Pieces. Death doesn't necessarily bring closure.

Eyes learned that lesson the hard way. He died, hopefully with loved ones around him, but did they bring him comfort? What of those hurt by him for years, who either didn't know about his death or simply didn't care? What of them? Does his death bring closure?

It hasn't brought closure for me and it hasn't for Mason. For me, there is most certainly relief. There is peace in knowing that no further unnecessary drama can ever come from Eyes. No more sudden, unexplained emails, intended for me or not. No more lying. No more statements made, asserting that my state of being was to blame for my interpretations of the "truth." No more attempts to spread HIV to unwitting lovers. No more lying to one's child. Just, no more.

A LETTER TO MY SON

In November 2001, unable to break my silence with Eyes and confront him with all I'd discovered, and thoroughly mindful of his friend who'd hired hit men, I began to grow fearful: What would happen if something happened to me? How could I let others know what Mason and I had endured? How could I prompt Eyes to seek the help he so desperately needed?

Given this, I set about writing a series of letters. I wrote a letter to Eyes, detailing what I knew thus far. I wrote a similar letter to Eyes' brother, the Mormon bishop, urging him to get Eyes help. I wrote letters to common friends, letting them know what I'd discovered. I wanted to lay the groundwork, should my body be discovered in less than its normal state, for everyone else to move forward. And I gave all these letters to my dear friends, Bob and Karen, for distribution upon my death.

One of those letters was to Mason, then almost two-years-old:

My most darling son, Mason,

For me to leave you so soon in your young life hurts me deeply but leave I must. Death is not something to be scared of, for it is just another part of life, as natural as the ocean's tide. But as natural as death is, it is important for you to know that I never wanted to leave you, as you are my world. Unfortunately, I had no choice.

Mason, you are the light of my life, and I have absolutely loved being your daddy. You are such a wonderful boy and my only regret is that I will not be able to see you grow into the fine young man that I know you will be.

I can already see such wonderful qualities in you, and these will only continue to flourish as you learn and grow. You are very smart, as seen in your ability to draw connections between words and things you see, saying the words out loud. You are also in great physical shape, eating all kinds of good food and exercising your muscles daily. Take good care of your body, and it will take good care of you!

More importantly, I can see what a great personality you have. You love to laugh and smile and give great pleasure to others when you do. I love your sweet face, and the way you hug me and call me "daddy."

You have such a great spirit, full of joy, which will stay with you always.

I'm not saying that life will be easy for you, because I know that may not be true. Unfortunately, just being an African American in today's world can be tough. People are not always fair, or kind. And since you have two white daddies, you can be fairly certain that at some point, someone will call you a bad name or make fun of you. As hard as it is, you have to let their words roll right off your back, just like a dog shakes off water. Although it is okay to feel sad when someone says such things, it is important that you not believe the bad things they say. You know the truth: you are a wonderful boy, who has brought your two daddies much love and happiness. It is important that you always remember how wonderful you are, and how much we love you, no matter what.

You should never be ashamed of who or what you are. Instead, feel sad for the poor people who don't treat others with respect and kindness. Just keep reminding yourself of how loved you are, and you will get through almost anything.

I have so many wonderful memories of you, and wish I could be there for more, but I cannot. Just remember how much I love you, and how I long to put my arms around you, squeeze you tight, and give you a big, fat, noisy kiss. I hope that you always follow your heart, because it will never steer you wrong. You can do anything you want with your life, but the key is to enjoy whichever path you choose.

I love you more than words can say. Though my heart aches right now, for my active role in your life has come to an end, remember that one thing that will never end is my amazing love for you. I send you tons of hugs and kiss, and kisses and hugs, and hugs and kisses...

I love you,
Daddy

A FINAL CLOSING THOUGHT

I have written that it is essential to tell the truth, and every experience captured herein actually occurred. Every single experience was as accounted, to the very best of my ability. Save one. And that is just a simple gift that I've decided to give myself.

EPILOGUE

This manuscript was completed in January 2020, just prior to our world being thoroughly upended, bringing heretofore unimaginable loss. My heart aches for those beautiful lives no longer with us, depriving us of their joy, knowledge, laughter, and rich experiences. If we have learned nothing else through this pandemic, it should be that experience, intelligence, competence, and empathy matter. We learn from those around us and those we select as our leaders, and owe it to a younger generation to be better.

As I send this off to print, the future of the world is still very much uncertain, with so much out of our control. But let's agree to move forward with grace, determination, and inquisitive natures. Seek out truth. Work on behalf of justice. Lift up those around you. And remember that trading your soul for riches is a devil's bargain which can never be undone.

We should have learned these simple lessons long ago, but now we have been given a tremendous kick in the pants to get our acts together and leave this world better than when we entered it.

To you and yours, I send my best wishes for peace, love and laughter.

Kergan

ACKNOWLEDGEMENTS

First and foremost, much gratitude to my family, Russ Noe, Mason Edwards, Marcus Edwards, and sister, Laurel Provenzano, for their support and feedback on this effort, and their encouragement when writing proved difficult. For her expert gift of copyediting skills, my thanks to Rebecca Johnson. The manuscript was helped immensely through the detailed notes of Ken Harrison. I greatly appreciate the early readings by Frank Adams, Vincent Bennett, Paige Blackburn, Mason Edwards, Karen Jaker Napack, Patrice Johnson, Susan Kiker, Pamela Milam, Bob Napack, Russ Noe, Carey Parrish, Bill Richardson, Lisa Stout, and Jill Michele Talsky-Sawick. To Jeffrey Sapp, thank you for your grace.

It is hard to tell your truth and I thank all who have been a part of my journey. In addition to my beloved family, my deepest appreciation goes up into the heavens to both Shane Michael Sawick and Eyes for our years of partnership and the valuable learnings I gained from each. I've tried to live as authentically as I can, and each and every experience, good, mundane, bad, or downright awful, has helped craft who I am. And, lastly, I thank you, dear reader, for being an important part of my journey as well. Now, let's go out there and change the world.

ABOUT THE AUTHOR

Kergan Edwards-Stout is an award-winning author and social activist. *Never Turn Your Back on the Tide*, his memoir, won a 2020 IndieDiscovery Award for LGBTQ+ nonfiction and was a finalist for the Next Generation Indie Book Awards. His debut novel, *Songs for the New Depression*, won a 2012 Next Generation Indie Book Award, was shortlisted for the Independent Literary Awards, was named one of the Top Books for 2012 by Out in Print, and received a starred review from Library Journal. His collection, *Gifts Not Yet Given*, landed on multiple Best Book lists and was named a finalist in the Next Generation Indie Book Awards. His greatest honor, however, was to have been named one of the Human Rights Campaign's 2011 Fathers of the Year, as his husband and children nominated him.

CPSIA information can be obtained
at www.ICGtesting.com
Printed in the USA
JSHW030023130720
6633JS00004B/17